FORTY WEEKS

A Journey of Healing And Transformation

FOR PRIESTS

With
Dr. Bob Schuchts

Foreword by Archbishop J. Peter Sartain

William M. Watson, SJ

Other Books by William M. Watson, SJ

Sacred Story:
An Ignatian Examen for the Third Millennium

Inviting God into Your Life:
A Practical Guide for Prayer

Reflections and Homilies:
The Gonzaga Collection

Sacred Story Rosary:
An Ignatian Way to Pray the Mysteries

Sacred Story Affirmations

The Whole-Life Confession

My Sacred Story Missal

Understanding the Spiritual World

Forty Weeks: Letters from Prison

Sacred Story Press
1401 E Jefferson St, STE 405
Seattle, WA 98122

Dedicated to Our Lady of the Way

IMPRIMI POTEST
Scott R. Santarosa, S.J.

NIHIL OBSTAT
Rev. David T. Mulholland, JD

IMPRIMATUR
J. Peter Sartain, D.D., S.T.L.
Archbishop of Seattle

Unless otherwise indicated, Scripture quotations are from the Holy Bible, New American Bible, revised edition © 2010, 1991, 1986, 1970 Confraternity of Christian Doctrine, Washington, D.C.

Cover and Book Design: William Watson, SJ

Cover & Interior Art: "The Washing of the Feet" Ghislaine Howard, 2004 (Used with permission of the Methodist Modern Art Collection: https://www.methodist.org.uk/artcollection)

General Editor: Betsy Stokes ~ Copy Editing: Eileen Meinert

Manufactured in the United States of America
ISBN: 9781721778249

Encouragement for Priests

Steeped in the wisdom of St. Ignatius and the insights of Catholic psychology, "Forty Weeks: A Journey of Healing and Transformation for Priests", helps priests draw closer to the heart of God the Father using Fr. Watson's Sacred Story method of prayer. With these powerful tools, priests can build the foundation for lifelong growth in intimacy with the Holy Trinity.

Most Reverend Samuel J. Aquila, S.T.L., Archbishop of Denver.

There are a lot of books out there to help priests build up their parishes, like Divine Renovation and Rebuilt. I'm glad now there's a book to help build us up as priests. I like this one because it is eminently "doable" — in short 15 to 30 minute prayer blocks, convenient for our busy lives.

It is also solid, built on the scripture and the saints, with an eye to the insights of a psychologist who is a practicing Catholic. I highly recommend you give it a try, and then share it with your priest support group. It's helping me.

Michael C. Barber, S.J., Bishop of Oakland

It is a good sign that you have picked up this book. It means that God is moving, inspiring you to "more" in your life. I encourage you to dive in. Make the commitment. There is nothing more essential, nothing more profound and practical for your priesthood than to continually deepen your friendship with Christ. Too often we want instant results. Forty Weeks: A Journey of Healing and Transformation for Priests is not about instant gratification. No this book clearly intends to facilitate what you surrendered to on your day of ordination when your bishop said "understand what you do, imitate the mysteries that you celebrate, and conform your life to the mystery of the cross."

The life of a priest cannot flourish without some intimate "gut check" with Jesus Christ on daily basis. The renewal of our Church needs nothing less than the healing, transformation of every priestly heart; in this case; your heart! I am grateful to Fr. Watson and Dr. Schuchts for providing the wisdom and format of this book. I sense the pathway they lay out, to be followed individually or with a group, will let the astute reader know they are not alone. The spiritual fathers, St. Ignatius of Loyola and St. John Paul II, permeate these reflections with the breath of the Spirit; urging us onward to that utter and complete surrender that nothing less will satisfy our priestly heart.

James F. Checchio, M.B.A., J.C.D., Bishop of Metuchen

In a time when parish priests are increasingly overwhelmed by the growing demands placed upon them by parishioners and superiors and live in a world with many distractions, their spiritual, mental, and physical health are increasingly challenged. As a seasoned pastor, I have experienced this personally and witnessed it in the lives of fellow priests.

This book is an extraordinary resource for priests. It may be used on an individual basis or in a small group setting by priests who are serious about becoming and remaining holy priests after the heart of Jesus Christ. This resource will place them solidly on a path to holiness and provide them with the tools to stay on it in the midst of the complex world of pastoral ministry in the 21st century.

Msgr. Michael Clay, D. Min.
Associate Dean of Graduate Ministerial Studies
The Catholic University of America

Brothers, this book by Fr. Watson and Dr. Schuchts is a straightforward tool for busy priests wanting to deepen their relationship with the Lord.

Fr. Darrin Connall, Vicar General - Diocese of Spokane

Brother priests, over the years I made at least three unsuccessful attempts to solidify the discipline of the Ignatian Examen into my prayer life. Fr. Watson's process of teaching and distilling it in the Forty Weeks worked for me. Since then, the Examen has significantly deepened the quality of my prayer time, and helped me be much more attentive to the Lord Jesus in day-to-day ministry. Also, I regard the ministry of The John Paul II Healing Center to be the most important ministry to us priests currently operating in North America, and so Dr. Schuchts' collaboration and reflections with Fr. Watson in FORTY WEEKS ~ A Journey of Healing and Transformation for Priests makes it an incredibly relevant and important spiritual resource for us priests.

Fr. Brad Hagelin: Pastor – Saint Luke Parish, Seattle

I am a priest of 62 years and have spent most of them trying to share a spirituality of hope with consecrated religious, seminarians and priests. Forty Weeks offers a way to keep the truth of Christ's healing power alive each and every day in the heart of the priestly shepherd of a flock so that he can be a witness of that healing power and an encouragement to those under his care.

Rev. Joseph Henchey, C.S.S., Mundelein Seminary

On several occasions I have posed the following question to groups of priests: "Has there been a particularly powerful encounter with Jesus in your life?" The responses were hard to hear. Deflection, confusion, and a general poverty of articulation moved me to wonder how we share our faith together. Too many brother priests do not remain in touch with their personal and intimate story of God's laboring to love each of us. Fr. Watson has provided a gift for both a new and lived encounter with the Father in the Son through the Holy Spirit, and a new way of learning our brother priests' intimacy with God. In working with seminarians, I urge them to notice that how we relate to one another often says something about how we relate to God, and vice versa.

After reading this text and appreciating its helpful format, clear content, and inviting tone, I am convinced that the compounding gift of receiving the Exercises and sharing their fruits will open new horizons for the "intimate and unceasing union" with God that our spiritual training and priestly brotherhood is meant facilitate.

Fr. Paul C. Hoesing, Dean of Seminarians: Kenrick-Glennon Seminary

This book is invaluable. It teaches diocesan priests the fruitfulness of the Examen Prayer. This 15 minute a day prayer is the primary mechanism, built into us by God, that promotes the daily encounter with Jesus' Spirit. If we exercise the gift of faith by learning to practice this way of listening for and following Jesus' presence in discernment, the reign of God is tasted and seen in the everyday. Sharing in Jesus' trials become occasions to savor real hope and joy!

Rev. John Horn, S.J., Co-Founder of the Institute for Priestly Formation and Professor of Spiritual Theology at St. Vincent de Paul Regional Seminary, Boynton Beach, FL.

Fr. Bill Watson has been a good friend and mentor since my undergraduate days when he was a young priest at Georgetown. I've also benefited from the wisdom gained at Dr. Bob Schuchts' conferences and from his book <u>Be Healed</u>.

Their respective insights into St. Ignatius' Spiritual Exercises and spiritual healing have facilitated my own spiritual and human growth, as well as enhanced my retreat and spiritual direction ministry. As someone now working full-time in a major seminary, I welcome the collaboration of these two wonderful guides, and am excited to share this new resource with seminarians and brother priests.

Fr. Rob Kroll, S.J.: Director of Spiritual Formation – St. Francis de Sales Seminary, WI.

Forty Weeks was a great boost for me just when I was looking for a way to take a step deeper into a life of prayer and conversion. The process of praying the examen led me to a begin and continue through in a deeper and more serious life of prayer. I would definitely encourage my brother priests to consider Forty Weeks ~ A Journey of Healing and Transformation for priests.

Fr. Derek Lappe, Pastor, Star of the Sea, Bremerton

Priesthood is not a theological abstraction, and ministry is no mere idea. It is lived and expressed concretely, in the Church, in often difficult circumstances, amid the trials and stresses of every-day living. Priests, sacramentally conformed to Christ, minister to the Body, yes, but the grace of their vocation has come to them in and through the Body of Christ. Sustainable and fruitful priesthood is nurtured by a constant renewal and deepening of that ecclesial grace. Forty Weeks brings the wisdom of the Ignatian spiritual tradition to bear specifically on the lives of priests, helping them to trace the working of God's grace in the sacred story of their vocation and election, to be renewed in that grace and election, to know themselves as loved sons of the Father. This books is not a program as much as it is a school of prayer. It supports authentic renewal, offering the priest who uses it not novelty, but a profound reminder of perennial truths and the sustaining love of God as the true dynamism of ministry.

Most Rev. Steven J. Lopes
Bishop, Ordinariate of the Chair of Saint Peter

One of the gifts of seminary formation is a structured prayer life. Daily Holy Hours, bi-monthly spiritual direction, and spiritual reading and classes are built into the schedule. After ordination, it is not uncommon for a priest to struggle a bit with the loss of this structure and busyness of parish life. FORTY WEEKS provides an excellent opportunity for any priest to not only add structure and accountability to their daily prayer life but a means to deeper growth in spiritual awareness and our need of the Divine Physician's healing power. A prayerful reading of FORTY WEEKS can move a priest to be motivated to daily prayer by desire rather than obligation and relationship rather than duty.

Fr. James Mason, President-Rector, Kenrick-Glennon Seminary

To my brother priests: You are a priest—which means you are likely tired, probably spread too thin, and certainly under spiritual attack. Only your growing union with Christ will preserve you in a ministry that is faithful and fruitful. The world and the tempter tell you have every reason not to pray. But as your brother priest, I tell you that you have every reason to pray—this book shows you why, and especially, this book shows you how. This book is written for priests who are wounded (all of us) and who must learn and re-learn to give themselves to Christ so Christ can be given to others. Please, read and pray this book!

Father Robert McTeigue, S.J., Ph.D., Host & Producer: "The Catholic Current", TheStationOfTheCross.com

If you want to truly know who you are as a beloved son of the Father and live that identity as God has called you as a priest of Jesus Christ, then Forty Weeks for Priests is for you. You will be taken on a daily and weekly journey to the center of your heart; the place where the Lord Jesus speaks to you most intimately as a son and His priest. These reflections will help shape your personal sacred story and will bear much fruit in your life and in your ministry. God bless you.

Fr. David Mulholland, J.D., Pastor, St. Patrick Parish, Tacoma

My brother priest or bishop, Forty Weeks ~ A Journey of Healing and Transformation was written for us. But if it sits on our shelf, we will never reap the benefits. Pick it up! Pick it up today! Start reading a section right now and begin a journey that will change your life forever.

Most Reverend George V. Murry, SJ, Bishop of Youngstown

The Spiritual Exercises of St. Ignatius proved to be of great benefit for me in my formation and preparation for priestly ministry. As a seminarian I had the opportunity to do the extended 33 day retreat and it became a well from which I continue to drink regularly the gift of God's mercy and love. Fr. Bill Watson's 40 Weeks journey has been a renewal of the experience that I had as a seminarian and has helped me to plumb even further the depth of the well of God's mercy and love as I journeyed through the exercises day by day for forty weeks. It has been a great help in my own continuing discernment of God's will and in giving spiritual direction to my parishioners.

Fr. Watson uses language and examples that resonate in one's heart and illuminate the key concepts of the spiritual life as taught so wonderfully by St. Ignatius.
Fr. Jack Shrum, St. Anthony Parish, Seattle

Forty Weeks can help every priest deepen his own relationship with Christ and find inner healing. Following the process found in the book will help you find more meaning and joy in your priesthood.
Fr. Bryce Sibley, Pastor and Chaplain - Our Lady of Wisdom Church and Catholic Student Center, Lafayette, LA

Brothers: Jesus wants his priests to be healed, healthy and whole. I've recommended both Sacred Story and JP II Healing Center to priests in the past, but now to see Fr. Watson and Dr. Schuchts working together in this one book is an amazing conflagration of grace. I highly recommend this work for the health of the priest and the renewal of the Church.
Fr. Ed White, Pastor at St Stephen The Martyr, Renton, WA

To my brother priests, I invite you to commit to the 40-week journey discussed in this book. Though it explores many dimensions of the spiritual life, inner healing, and the Ignatian tradition, its real focus is on you and the Lord's presence in you. If you commit to at least 15 minutes per day to do the meditations in this book, you will find a whole new dimension of your transcendent self-animated by the Lord which will bring both healing and a new inner light and purpose to your priestly life and ministry.

We live in a world that prizes external accomplishments and performance, but the priestly life is so much more – imitating Jesus as contemplatives in action. This requires concerted attention to our life's story, our inner weaknesses and strengths, and the Lord's healing and transformative love within us. If taken seriously, this book will transform your priestly life.
Fr. Robert Spitzer, S.J., Ph.D.

Fr Watson is a gifted teacher and wise spiritual guide. My hope and prayer is that this "Forty Week" journey that our priests can take for their healing and transformation might lead to the deeper spiritual renewal so needed for our Church too. I encourage all of my brothers to make this spiritual sojourn.

Most Reverend Joseph J. Tyson, Bishop of Yakima

Nearly all priests and bishops lament that we are not praying enough or reading enough. This book helps us to do both at the same time – while assisting us in our personal growth and in our ability to minister to others. Many books on spirituality, though beautiful, are not exactly directed to us priests. Forty Weeks – A Journey of Healing and Transformation for Priests is exactly what we need. It is realistic and easy-to-use, and it puts us in touch with the spirituality of one of our greatest saints and guides, St. Ignatius of Loyola. We all say "I need to pray more". Because of the many demands on our time and energy however, we fall back into believing that "My work is my prayer." The reflections in this book help us to bring our daily work and our very selves TO our prayer, so that we can become the priests and disciples that God calls us to be. Dear brother priests, I invite you to use this book for your own spiritual benefit and for the good of your ministry to others.

Most Reverend William Wack, CSC, Bishop of Pensacola-Tallahassee

Dedication

I have a profound admiration for the vocation of the diocesan parish priest. It has been described as a relentless vocation with constant demands. In the Constitutions of the Society of Jesus, Ignatius writes that "the education of priests, as a work of the highest value, is to be considered one of the chief ministries of the Society." (VII #290)

Yet the wellspring of any priest's successful ministry is a deep, personal, daily relationship with Jesus Christ. It is the deeper spiritual formation that Ignatian Spirituality can so well serve priests in their ongoing formation.

We dedicate this edition of *Forty Weeks* to all diocesan priests who hunger for Jesus' healing and transformative love and mercy in their daily lives. Christ shares both his priesthood and its graces with you, his brothers, as well as a special place in his Sacred Heart.

Dr. Schuchts and I pray that this spiritual resource will give you a way to nourish your soul and so increase the fruitfulness of your ministry of sharing in Jesus' priesthood.

Contents

Preface

This book is a personal guide to a spiritual formation process called *Forty Weeks*. It is written for priests and in collaboration with other priests who participated in a pilot program. Fr. William Watson, SJ, is the main author who invited me to collaborate with him along with about twenty priests who were involved in the pilot project. You will see their reflections throughout the book.

I first heard about Fr. Watson and his *Forty Weeks* program through a mutual friend, Fr. David Mulholland, who at the time was the Vicar of Clergy for the Archdiocese of Seattle. Fr. Mulholland enthusiastically shared with me how much healing and transformation he had been receiving personally by working through Fr. Watson's materials in conjunction with mine.

Fr. David found it amazing that Fr. Bill and I used some of the same concepts and images, but in different and complementary ways that added insights and tools for integrating the pillars of priestly formation. He could see that as a spiritual director and retreat master, Fr. Watson approaches human formation through the lens of spiritual formation. In contrast, as a former therapist and teacher of human relationships and healing, I approach spiritual formation through the lens of human formation.

Fr. Mulholland's enthusiasm motivated him to first send me Fr. Watson's books (*Sacred Story* and *Forty Weeks*) and then later to invite me to lead

1

a priest conference in the Archdiocese of Seattle at the beautiful Palisades retreat center. It is there at the Palisades overlooking the Puget Sound that I met Fr. Watson for the first time. The vision for this book was conceived in that pristine setting.

As Fr. Watson and I began to get to know each other at the end of the conference we discovered among other things a shared love for Jesus, St. Ignatius (the founder of his religious order) and St. John Paul II (the patron of the ministry in which I serve). We also discovered that we share a mutual love for the Church and a calling to serve priests. This shared passion and mission is what motivated us to collaborate in this current work: *Forty Weeks: A Journey of Healing and Transformation for Priests.*

As you can see by its title and size, this is not a book to be read casually. It is a well-designed and inspired process for how to grow in holiness and to become whole in body, soul and spirit (See 1 Th. 5:23). Obviously holiness and wholeness do not happen in a few pages or over a few weeks. They require a serious level of investment to reap the rewards.

If you engage in this process with an open heart and with perseverance, I am confident it will bring about deep and lasting transformation in your life and a renewed vision for your participation in the priesthood of Jesus Christ. Though I am confident this material will have many benefits for your ministry, while equipping you to serve others, I encourage you to work through it first for your own spiritual growth and healing. As you will see in my reflections throughout the *Forty Weeks*, I personally engaged in the process and applied this first in my own life.

Over and over again, I was amazed at the insights I received. I found this material to be a valuable augment to my ongoing spiritual direction and prayer life. Even after completing the Forty Weeks process formally, I continue to reflect on the material and incorporate much of what I discovered in my daily prayer and ongoing discernment.

The discernment principles that Fr. Watson lays out in this book come originally from St. Ignatius' "Rules for the Discernment of Spirits" from *The Spiritual Exercises*. But his approach is quite different from any other book on St. Ignatius "Rules" that I have studied. He does not just talk about the principles of Ignatian Spirituality; he leads the reader/retreatant step by step in how to apply these principles in daily life.

The material from *Forty Weeks* has been tried and tested by many thousands over the years. I know of several parishes in the Seattle Archdiocese who have done this study together, as well as many priests, religious and lay people throughout the country and beyond who have benefitted from this process. In addition Fr. Watson has recently published a *Forty Weeks* for prisoners and is working on one for Married Couples, Men and Wounded Warriors.

I am honored that Fr. Watson invited me to collaborate with him in this project exclusively written for priests. As he knows, the priesthood is at the heart of our mission at the *John Paul II Healing Center*. Though we offer conferences and resources for the whole Church, our mission began as a way to help priests and seminarians integrate human and spiritual formation into their personal lives and ministry.

Ministry to priests and seminarians still remains central to our mission of bringing transformation into the heart of the Church. I am grateful to have this additional resource to offer bishops, priests and seminarians to assist in their formation and transformation.

Pilot Program and Format

This book developed out of a pilot program where Fr. Bill and I invited priests who had participated in one of the *John Paul II Healing Center* conferences to participate in the *Forty Weeks* process. This is an excerpt of the e-mail that we sent to each of the participating priests who expressed a desire to be part of the program. I include it here so you can see how the pilot program developed and also as a way of considering your own approach to the *Forty Weeks*.

Dear Fathers:
I pray that you are each doing well and living more fully from your true identity and authentic desires. I mentioned to you in my previous e-mail that I would be contacting you to propose a follow-up that would build on our time together at the Palisades. That is the purpose of this current e-mail.

Many of you know Fr. Bill Watson, S.J. president and founder of the Sacred Story Institute. For those of you who don't recognize his name, he is the one who spoke on the morning of our last day together. Immediately following the Holy Desire conference, Fr. Bill and I met and discussed how we could work together to help support you in your spiritual walk, and to develop an additional resource that will be of aid to other priests.

I have long desired a way to provide ongoing support for priests after our conferences, and Fr. Bill has developed a great resource for that. He and I also want to collaborate with you to develop a more specific resource for priests integrating our respective charisms of Ignatian spirituality and healing, and drawing on your experiences in walking through this process.

Our first desire is to assist you in your spiritual growth and healing as a follow-up to the Holy Desire Conference. To that end, we want to invite you to participate in Fr. Bill's **Forty Weeks—An Ignatian Path to Christ with Sacred Story Prayer.** This is an excellent resource helping you to continue to grow spiritually and discern the movements of your heart, while continuing to encourage one another in your healing journey.

As you engage in this, we also want to invite you to assist us in developing a resource to help hundreds and thousands of more priests find the journey to deeper healing and transformation in their lives. You can accomplish these objectives by participating in the following process:

You would each commit 15-30 minutes each day walking through the "Forty Weeks" process.

If you decide to make the commitment, you will have the option to do this individually or as part of a group. Fr. David Mulholland and Fr. Ed White have offered to be the facilitators of this process. And Fr. Bill and I will each play a part in the way it unfolds.

This is what your commitment will involve:

1)   You will work through the Forty Week Spiritual growth program. This commitment will involve specific reading and prayer every day (in one or two 15 minute segments).

2) *If you are part of a group with other priests, you will meet weekly, either in person, or by skype.*

3) *The group will provide a safe place for you to share with one another and encourage each other as brothers on the journey.*

4) *Each week you will take a survey and give confidential feedback on your experience of the previous week's exercises.*

5) *Sacred Story Institute will send an email to each participating priest during the entire Forty Week program.*

6) *Fr. Bill will then send the aggregated data from each week to me and I will read the hopes and challenges that you express.*

7) *From that feedback, I will write a 2-3 page spiritual reflection on your comments, offering my insights and counsel related to the issues you raise in the surveys. The purpose is to help you along the journey of healing, prayer, and discernment based on the hopes and challenges you identify as you walk through each of the Forty Weeks.*

8) *My reflections will be sent to each one of you. You will then have an opportunity to give feedback on what Fr. Bill and I have written.*

9) *Fr. Bill and I will take the feedback and do a final version of each week's reflections that will be collated into a book at the project's end.*

We are excited about working collaboratively with you to help yourself and other priests grow spiritually and continue your healing journey. This will not only benefit you, but the whole Church, through you.

Do you desire to grow in this way and to help your brother priests in their holiness and wholeness? Are you willing to make the commitment to participate for the entire forty weeks? If so, send us your "yes" and your preferred email and we will begin preparing for the process. We will coordinate with Fr. David and Fr. Ed, planning when and where the groups will meet. We anticipate a start date around early November. We will be in touch once we have your responses.

Thank you for your holy desires and good will.
In communion,

Bob Schuchts & Fr. Bill Watson, S.J.

As you can see from this correspondence with the priests who participated in the pilot project, the format set the pattern for this book. First there is the *Forty Weeks* material and exercises from Fr. Watson. Next are my reflections, and finally the comments from your brother priests. Each week we chose two to four reflections from the twenty or so priests who participated.

The process was dynamic and interactive because we wanted a resource that would be personally adapted to your life as a priest. We know it is not easy to grow in wholeness and holiness while facing the challenges of daily ministry. It is difficult to add even fifteen minutes into an already overly full day of ministry. But as you know all the time you invest in praying and growing personally benefits everyone you serve.

Your priesthood is a participation in Christ's own priesthood. He is the model and the source of your ministry. Even he needed time to enter into focused prayer. By entering into this process, you will increase your union with him and his life will flow more freely through you to touch many lives.

These words he spoke personally to his first priests apply just as much to you: "I am the vine and you are the branches. Whoever remains in me and I in him will bear much fruit, because without me you can do nothing...You did not choose me, but I chose you, and appointed you to go and bear fruit."

I pray that this resource will assist you first and foremost to grow in ever greater union with the priesthood of Jesus Christ and through that you will bear much fruit. All of creation is waiting for your "yes."

Bob Schuchts
Founder of John Paul II Healing Center

Foreword

My Dear Brother in the Lord,

When St. Bernard entered the Cistercian order, he was quickly recognized for his holiness, wisdom, and leadership ability. At the age of 22, he was sent by his abbot, along with 12 other monks, to found a new monastery at Clairvaux, which eventually became the motherhouse of 68 other abbeys.

Toward the end of his life, Bernard witnessed the coronation of one of his own monks, Bernardo Pignatelli, as Pope Eugene III. As a means of offering support and advice to his former charge, Bernard wrote *Five Books On Consideration*, which offered practical counsel on matters pertaining to the pope's life and ministry – from the importance of prayer to how to recognize passive aggression.

Bernard warns Eugene not to succumb to relentless busyness, to the neglect of prayer and leisure. Of particular concern to Bernard is that Eugene will become so accustomed to a hectic schedule that he will become calloused and unreflective. This way of life, Bernard suggests, leads not to inner peace, but to hardness of heart.

It is not the virtue of patience to permit yourself to be enslaved when you can be free... Are you less a slave because you serve not one but all?... I praise your devotion to humanity, but only if it be complete. Now, how can it be complete when you have excluded yourself? You too are human... You also should drink from the waters of your well... If you are a stranger to yourself, to whom are you not? If a man is no use to himself, to whom is he useful?[1]

The American work ethic is legendary. It is all too easy, however, to fall prey to the kind of busyness which Bernard describes and neglect God, our parishioners, our families, and ourselves. Such neglect is a recipe for disaster, for it can estrange us from those we love, cause feelings of resentment, lull us away from the source of our hope, cause us to fall prey to narcissism, weaken our spiritual guard against sin, and rob us of the simple and necessary joys of rest and leisure.

Bernard recognized these dangers in his own life and that of the pope, but his caveat applies to every person in every occupation, and especially to us priests. It is ironic that the very work we undertake for the good of others can, if we are not careful, be the cause of our neglecting them. Mothers and fathers who get trapped needlessly on the treadmill of their jobs can lose touch with the children they are working to support; priests, deacons and religious who are committed to lives of service in God's name can allow their schedules to become so overcrowded that they neglect prayer and friendship. These are the roads to exhaustion, alienation, anger and disappointment.

Most of us could say that there never seems to be an end to the work on our dockets, but as Bernard warned Pope Eugene, we must be careful not to give in to the illusion that we can get everything done. We must step off the treadmill regularly, deliberately and without guilt. It is crucial that we take time for prayer, for rest, for activities that relax and refresh us, for extended time with family and friends. We must let God fill us up so we will have something to give – to others and to ourselves. If we never

---

[1] Bernard of Clairvaux, *Five Books on Consideration: Advice to a Pope.* Kalamazoo, MI: Cistercian Publications, 1982. Cf. pp. 30-33.

get off the treadmill, the world will pass us by – though we are thinking all along that we are the only ones moving.

Priestly ministry is a participation in God's work of re-creation in Christ, and here is where we must remind ourselves that he is the creator; we are not. Jesus is the Savior, we are not. The Holy Spirit is our advocate and guide, and we are not lone rangers. We cannot get everything done, but God can, in his good time and in his wise way.

Perhaps it seems strange that I would introduce a wonderful book grounded in the *Spiritual Exercises* and the Ignatian method of Examen with advice from a Cistercian! Because the roots of my own seminary formation are deeply Benedictine, Benedict and Bernard have been my teachers for many years. At the same time, their insights sent me to Ignatius Loyola, Catherine of Siena, Teresa of Avila, John of the Cross, Pope St. John Paul II, and Hans Urs von Balthasar.

One insight, one perspective, has elucidated another for me, time after time. Moreover, it goes without saying that the great spiritual masters of the Church were also sound psychologists: like Jesus, they understood the human heart, for as John writes, "Jesus… did not need anyone to testify about human nature. He himself understood it well" (John 2:25). An eminently wise psychologist, Ignatius understood and loved those he guided in the ways of holiness with the Lord's own love and understanding.

Prayer puts us in touch with God's heart, and there he shares with us his knowledge of us. In his classic book on the Eucharist, Louis Bouyer wrote that in prayer, everything

takes on its meaning in our knowledge of God as the one who first knows us. Before we have any consciousness of anything, before we exist, he knows us. He knows us with a knowledge that is love. Once we discover it, all things become resolved in his love.[2]

Whether your spiritual roots are Ignatian, Franciscan, Carmelite, Benedictine, or linked to any of a host of solid doctors of souls, you will find in *Forty Weeks: A Journey of Healing and Transformation for Priests* a sure guide for developing a deeper relationship with Christ in the midst of – and *through* – the many tasks before you each day.

As with all of us diocesan priests, early in priestly ministry I began to struggle with how to cope with the relentless busyness of my life. I feared literally losing myself in my schedule (and not as the Lord intends) as the familiar routine of seminary drifted farther and farther into the past. The many encounters and challenges I met each day also revealed to me those recesses of my heart that needed healing and transformation, the areas of life that I had not yet surrendered to the Lord, and my need to cling unfailingly to Jesus in his mercy. One day it dawned on me that the challenge before me was *depth* and that I did not need to be in a monastery to journey deep within. In other words, I could do so even in the midst of a hectic, unpredictable schedule if I allowed Ignatius and other great doctors of souls to walk with me, step by step, to Jesus.

St. Charles Borromeo reminds us: Are you in charge of a parish? If so, do not neglect the parish of your own soul, do not give yourself to others so completely that you have nothing left for yourself. You have to be mindful of your people without becoming forgetful of yourself.

Fr. William M. Watson, SJ and Dr. Bob Schuchts have drawn on their own love for God and the vocation to holiness, as well as their profound understanding of the human heart and priestly ministry, to offer us the wisdom of Ignatius Loyola in a manner suited marvelously to the lives of diocesan priests. Knowing and understanding us as he does, loving us as he does, God attracts us to himself in a way seamlessly suited to each of

---

[2] Louis Bouyer, *The Eucharist.* South Bend: University of Notre Dame Press, 1989, p. 93.

us; all he asks is that we "show up," that we pray and listen, that we take time to reflect, in a spirit of honest openness and humility, to the abiding presence of the Holy Spirit within.

Some years ago, a Presbyterian minister with whom I enjoyed many spiritual conversations gave me a little book to which I have often Returned, *The Art of Pastoring: Contemplative Reflections.*[3] In a brief chapter titled "Losses," William C. Martin writes:

> Taking care of others will drain a pastor's strength.
> What is lost is compassion for his own soul.
> How can he pretend to love the Spirit,
> when his own receives so little care?
> Every soul within the congregation is blessed
> When he keeps his own alive and well.
>
> A pastor's life is spread so thin.
> What is lost is depth.
> Go deep, not thin.

Go deep, my brother in the Lord, go deep, not thin. There you will find the Lord who called and sustains you, who heals and encourages you, and who loves and understands you more than you can possibly imagine.

Sincerely in Christ,
J. Peter Sartain
Archbishop of Seattle

---

[3] William C. Martin, *The Art of Pastoring: Contemplative Reflections.* Decatur, GA: CTS Press, 1994.

There are very few who realize what God would make of them if they abandoned themselves entirely to His hands, and let themselves be formed by His grace. A thick and shapeless tree trunk would never believe that it could become a statue, admired as a miracle of sculpture...and would never consent to submit itself to the chisel of the sculptor who, as St. Augustine says, sees by his genius what he can make of it. Many people who, we see, now scarcely live as Christians, do not understand that they could become saints, if they would let themselves be formed by the grace of God, if they did not ruin His plans by resisting the work which He wants to do.

St. Ignatius Loyola[1]

Introduction

St. Ignatius became a great spiritual guide by surrendering his heart to Christ under the guidance of the Church. He passed his wisdom along in his *Spiritual Exercises* and the methods of Examen (on which *Forty Weeks* is based), and in his letters and instructions. His spiritual disciplines invite a deep, personal relationship with Christ. It is Christ's forgiving and healing love that burns away the selfishness and hardheartedness of sin's legacy in one's history, transforming it into a sacred story, with fruit that endures to eternity.

Following Ignatius' wisdom, all you need to engage this spiritual journey is a generous heart and a willingness to be transformed by Christ's purifying forgiveness and mercy. It is the narrow path to holiness held out by the Church for millennia and the one followed by every saint in our history. The weekly lessons are not complicated. Pray for a generous heart, and ask Christ for His help every step of the way. Simple enough!

What Do We Mean by "Weeks?"

You may be engaging this prayer journey as an individual or as part of a group. If you are doing this by yourself, you may find it beneficial to discipline yourself to stick to a seven-day week for each chapter of Forty Weeks. St. Ignatius's spiritual wisdom for the four weeks of the Spiritual Exercises was to allow one to move forward based on the fruit being experienced. In this framework, a "week" was measured by the spiritual profit being received, and not by hours and days. Use the time frame of spiritual fruit to measure your weeks if you so desire. Sometimes it may be helpful to repeat a week several times to fully internalize the lesson! Trust your heart.

If you are part of a group doing these spiritual disciplines, my best advice is to discipline yourself to stay together as a group. That is, keep a seven-day week structure for the whole forty weeks. You can mark places and weeks that you may want to revisit for additional reflection and spiritual profit. Great spiritual fruit is also gained by tracking your "weeks" with the community you belong to.

No matter which way you are doing Forty Weeks—solo or with a group—realize that the exercises are incremental, building on each other. Doing them slowly and in order will help you stay better focused and live in the present moment. Trust the structure, and do not read or practice the disciplines out of their natural order.

Listen to your heart, at all times, in the present moment. God is in the present moment. This way, the Sacred Story prayer will, by God's grace and your free submission, lead you to the deepest desires of your heart.

How and When to Engage Forty Weeks

St. Ignatius proposed fifteen minutes as the optimal time for his Examen prayer discipline. Twice daily was the recommendation for Jesuits. The laity who practiced the prayer were encouraged to do it at least once daily. As you begin this prayer journey, make a decision whether you want to pray once or twice daily. You can always adjust your commitment to either of the options, but setting a goal for your practice is important.

Our extensive experience has shown that those who have practiced the Sacred Story Examen method in Forty Weeks have found praying in the morning, at midday, or midafternoon to be the most sustainable over time. Those who set evening hours for their prayer were less faithful to the discipline. Use your judgment. Ignatius advised it be done at midday and after the evening meal. Everyone has different schedules and life rhythms.

You will receive further guidance on the structure and use of these fifteen-minute times of quiet as the lessons progress. For now, it is sufficient to choose the time(s) you intend to pray daily. You would do well also to select a primary location for your fifteen-minute prayer times. Let it be a place apart—a technology-free zone. If you are incarcerated, you might have difficulty finding quiet and a place apart. Fear not. Ask God for the best place to be and you will find it.

Ask God to strengthen your resolve and desire for entering these times of reflection. Your fidelity to Sacred Story depends less on you, and more on your decision to continually ask God to be faithful.

Many of the instructions are written in the personal "I." For example, "I am invited; I will now...". This wording is intended to affirm your role in opening to Christ. It also helps emphasize the relational dimension of faith and prayer.

Additional Resources for Your Spiritual Journey

Know that there are lots of resources provided free online at sacredstory.net that you can download and print out and send to those you are helping along the way. There is a weekly series of supplemental resources we call "Encouragements and Wisdom" or "E&W." The E&W are important aids for deepening your understanding of the prayer materials. They are available when you register (at no cost) as a member at sacredstory.net. Many of the additional questions you and they have are likely to be contained in this very helpful supplemental prayer resource.

A simple journal exercise is a discipline linked to the Forty Weeks Sacred Story prayer. Purchase a small spiral notebook at the commissary or have a friend mail you one for this purpose. Have it with you when you do your structured fifteen-minute prayer periods. There is a blank page at the end of each week and eight more at the back of the book for your notes. Feel free to use this book as your notebook if you so desire. A free logbook can also downloaded from the Members section of sacredstory.net.

If You Hit a Wall

If you reach a point in the forty-week prayer process where you think you can't continue, here is my advice: Jump to the last chapter, "Abide in Me," and read it. I placed this chapter at the end to encourage people to commit to a lifelong process of Sacred Story prayer. But sometimes, that encouragement is necessary to simply complete the process that will carry you for life. Just keep trying, and "Be not afraid!"

Use Forty Weeks for Your Priest Fraternity Group

Forty Weeks has to be done on an individual basis but we strongly suggest that seminarians, priests or bishops who do the program to use it as the basis for a weekly or monthly faith support group. You will be amazed at how much deeper your sharing and conversation will be as a result of this process

Fr. Bill Watson, S.J.
Feast of St. Ignatius Loyola

Part One
Listening to Your Story

"Come to me, all you who labor and are burdened, and I
will give you rest. Take my yoke upon you and learn
from me, for I am meek and humble of heart;
and you will find rest for your selves.
For my yoke is easy, and my burden light."

Mt 11:28–30

Entering Your Sacred Story

Sacred Story prayer, modeled on St. Ignatius's classic examination of conscience, is a proven path to spiritual growth. It is the narrow road but the one taken by many saints and ordinary laity in the Church's history. If you are ready to make Christ the center of your life, you will find no better daily spiritual prayer discipline. Divine love is an abiding relationship that God invites you to share daily. Listen to the wisdom below to help prepare you to enter this relationship with God before you begin Week 1. Here are some "rules of engagement":

✠ If you are looking for quick fixes to spiritual or psychological problems, you will soon lose heart. The full healing of your wounds, and the path to complete peace, only begins on this earth. You will achieve no final victory for what ails you this side of eternity. However, you will find the path to that final victory, and it is here that you will find peace.

✠ If you seek only external confirmation of religious or political biases, you will be frustrated. Surrendering fixed ideologies and a judgmental heart is required fare on your Forty Weeks journey.

✠ If you live principally by rules and laws, or if you avoid all rules and laws, you will be surprised. Those who live by laws alone will encounter the fierce Love that exceeds all laws. And those who reject laws will discover that Love has unambiguous boundaries of right and wrong.

✠ If you are being asked to do these spiritual exercises to fulfill someone else's plan, or for any sort of program requirement, kindly tell your sponsor, "No, thank you." Unless you engage Forty Weeks in complete freedom of heart, you will fail in the practice and undermine its purpose.

So, who should engage this prayer journey? St. Ignatius wanted people with generous hearts who were aware that they needed God's help.

✠ Jesus proclaimed that the sick needed a physician, not the well (Mk 2:17). We are all sick, and only those willing to see their spiritual ills will submit to the Divine Physician's healing embrace in these exercises. If you know you are ill and believe you cannot get better without God's help, welcome.

✠ Jesus calmed the storm that terrified His disciples (Mk 5:35–41). Engage Sacred Story prayer if you are distressed about the chaos in your life and believe God is calling you to a secure shore.

✠ Jesus can heal chronic illness, but He has come to forgive us our sins and open to us eternal life (Lk 5:17–26). Engage in these exercises if you want to experience Jesus's power to forgive your sins.

✠ Jesus encouraged John the Baptist and his followers not to take offense at Him when their faith in Christ brought them suffering and threats (Mt 5:2–6). Engage these exercises if the practice of your faith is causing you to suffer persecution for Christ's sake. Hold fast to belief in Him as the Son of God, and take no offense.

✠ Jesus invited the weary and the overburdened to find rest in Him (Mt 11:25–30). Engage these exercises if you are weary with your life and find yourself overburdened.

✠ Jesus invited the rich young man to surrender his possessions and follow Him (Mk 10:17–25). Engage these exercises if you are ready to let go of what is holding you down and willing to follow a new path.

✠ Jesus invited Zacchaeus to come down from his tree and follow Him home (Lk 19:1–10). Engage these exercises if your privilege, position, and places of honor have not brought you the peace, security, and hope they promised.

✠ Jesus invited the woman of Samaria to drink the living water that wells up to eternal life (Jn 4:4–42). Engage these exercises if you are ready to surrender the cynicism of failed love and relationships, ready to forgive, and ready to move forward with your life.

✠ Jesus chided the work-anxious Martha to allow Mary to sit at His feet (Lk 10:38–42). Engage with these exercises if you are ready to sit still awhile, each day, and listen to the Kingdom within.

✠ Jesus invited Peter to join Him in His work (Lk 5:10–11). Engage these exercises if you trust that your sins, addictions, and failures do not limit Jesus's desire to take your hand in discipleship as He writes your sacred story.

✠ Jesus demanded to know the names of the Gerasene's demons (Mk 5:1–20). Engage these exercises if you are weary of your spiritual, psychological, and material demons. Welcome these exercises if you are willing to name them, with Jesus by your side, and allow Him to exorcise and heal the spiritual and psychic darkness—the habits, sins, and addictions—that rob you of freedom and peace.

✠ God invited the Blessed Virgin Mary not to fear but to say yes and participate in the eternal plan of salvation (Lk 1:26–38). Engage these exercises if you are ready to let your heart be Christ's home and so labor with Him for universal reconciliation.

✠ Jesus invited His disciples to dine with Him (Jn 15:1–17). Enter Sacred Story prayer if you desire unbounded love, joy, peace, and a share in Jesus's glory—and His sufferings.

✠ Jesus invited all those wishing to follow Him to deny themselves, pick up their cross daily, and follow Him (Lk 9:23). Engage these exercises if you can willingly allow Christ to reveal your narcissism and by His grace, transform your life into sacred story.

✠ Jesus invited His disciples to keep a vigilant heart, to reject carousing and drunkenness, and to avoid getting trapped in the anxieties of life, lest they be surprised on the day of the Son of Man (Lk 21:34–36). Engage these exercises if today is your day to hearken to the Son of Man and to return to God with all your heart.

ℰↃ

Many of us have never taken the time to listen to Jesus's story by reading, prayerfully, one of the four accounts left for us by His early followers. Before advancing to Week 1, we will read one of the four Gospels. Only read one of them, but read it reflectively and prayerfully in a place of restful solitude. This place can be at home or some other favorite place you love to be alone in peace and quiet. (Perhaps it will be your place of prayer for these next forty weeks.)

Which Gospel should you read? Matthew writes to convince the Jews that Jesus is indeed the promised Messiah, the Davidic King, foretold by the prophets. Mark's focus is to reveal Jesus as the true Son of God who suffered and died to achieve complete victory over sickness, sin, and death. Luke, the physician, writes to reveal Jesus as the promise and hope of the poor and the weak. And John reveals Jesus as the Logos, the Word of God, who preexisted creation with the Father as the One who would save us.

Read the Gospel that immediately speaks to your heart at this time in your life. Don't rush your reading; there is no hurry. You might read one chapter per day, or several, until you have read the entire Gospel. Relish the story of the One who holds you and all creation in being.

Jesus is real and wants to become part of your daily life. He wants a relationship with you. He waits to be your hope, your forgiveness, and your peace. Open your heart to Him as you read His sacred story.

‽

NOTES

Week I

FIRST

I will choose one or two times each day to set aside for a fifteen-minute space of contemplative rest and reflection. This should be a place of quiet, free of technology—a place apart.

SECOND

I will be specific about the time of day and the place (or places) where I can find these moments of reflective quiet. I will take a moment to ponder where these will be and see them in my imagination.

THIRD

I will take my fifteen-minute quiet moments this week to read through the lesson that follows and to meditate on the Sacred Story Affirmations.

Set your heart to the path you are to take. Trust it. The path leading to Christ in the Sacred Story practice has some simple rules that will help you immensely.

I will not read ahead.
I will awaken to the present moment.
I will take each day and each exercise as it comes.
I cannot do Sacred Story better by going faster.

You will have a new prayer exercise for every week of this journey. The exercises for this first week offer discernment principles that will help you along your way. Listen to the exercise, and pay attention to your feelings. Engage the prayers and exercises of Sacred Story with your whole being— with your "mind in your heart." Be a thinking, reflective "feeler" and believer. Awaken!

Remember, you are a pilgrim (journeying alongside Ignatius himself) in this prayer journey. The Lord Jesus will reward you for your courage and your resolve. Christ promises to be faithful to you! He will help you every single step of the way, because He came, lived, and died so you might have abundant life and bear fruit that endures to eternity. Thank Him in advance for the great blessings and insights you will receive. Live a life of gratitude to God for all life's blessings and gifts.

CR

The "Sacred Story Affirmations" sketch most of the realities you will encounter in your spiritual journey with Sacred Story prayer. As your first spiritual disciplines of this process, take some days to reflectively contemplate these affirmations for your Sacred Story practice. Use your fifteen-minute prayer times for this purpose. Take as many days as you desire, and listen attentively to them. Do not limit the number of days or sessions you spend with them. Your heart, by its peacefulness, will lead you forward to the next exercise at the right time. Trust God's grace working in your heart to lead you.

As you listen to the affirmations, be attentive to all the persons, events, and issues in your life. Be especially attentive to the things that cause fear, stress, anxiety, anger, or grief. When these emotions surface, notice how and if they connect with the affirmation that you are contemplating. Always listen with your mind in your heart to the events, issues, and persons in your life story. Be curious. Listen to how or why these events, issues, and persons may be linked to the spiritual, emotional, and moral dimensions of your experiences. Again, pay particular attention to those that might stimulate grief, anxiety, stress, anger, and fear.

Sacred Story practice focuses attention on things that are both delightful and difficult to experience. But as St. Ignatius learned, focusing attention on the difficult things is very fruitful. These aspects of your life history have the potential to rob you of hope, joy, love, and freedom. You can experience deeper, lasting peace by letting difficulties arise and allowing the Divine Physician to heal you. We have nothing to fear with Christ by our side. Take as long as you desire to reflect on the affirmations of your sacred story

CB

SACRED STORY AFFIRMATIONS

My sacred story takes a lifetime to write.

Be not afraid! Fear comes from the enemy of my human nature.

The pathway to God's peace and healing runs

through my heart's brokenness, sin, fear, anger, and grief.

God resolves all my problems with time and patience.

శ్ర

I will have difficulties in this life.

There are just two ways to cope with my difficulties.
One leads to life; one to death. I will choose life.

శ్ర

"Impossible" is not a word in God's vocabulary.

Sacred Story practice leads to my freedom and authenticity,
but it does not always make me feel happy.

శ్ర

My life's greatest tragedies can be transformed
into my life's major blessings.

Times of peace and hope always give way
to times of difficulty and stress.

Times of difficulty and stress always give way
to times of peace and hope.

శ్ర

I will not tire of asking God for help,
since God delights in my asking.

The urge to stop Sacred Story practice
always comes before my greatest breakthroughs.

૭

God gives me insights,
not because I am better than others, but because I am loved.

The insights and graces I need to move forward
in life's journey unfold at the right time.

૭

My personal engagement with Sacred Story accomplishes,
through Christ, a work of eternal significance.

Inspirations can have a divine or a demonic source.
I pray for the grace to remember how to discern one from the other.

૭

Christ, who has walked before me, shares my every burden.

Christ, who has walked before me, will help me resolve every crisis.

Christ, who has walked before me, knows my every hope.

Christ, who has walked before me, knows everything I suffer.

Christ, who walks before me, will always lead me home to safety.

૭

I will strive to curb temptations to react to people and events.
I will ask myself what causes my anger and
irritation at people and events.
I will seek to identify the source of my anger and irritation.

I will give thanks for what angers and upsets me,
for identifying their source will help to set me free.

I will strive to listen, watch, and pray. Listen, watch, and pray.
I will listen, watch, and pray!

៛

Everyone has been mortally wounded spiritually, psychologically,
and physically by Original Sin and the loss of paradise.

Journeying with Christ to the roots of my sins
and addictions will help break their grip.

I will not waste time worrying about my sins and failures. I will use my
time wisely and ask God to help me understand
the source of my sins and failings.

I will trust that Christ came to heal all my wounds.

៛

I alone control Christ's ability to transform my life
into a sacred story. The process begins when I ask
for the grace to honestly name my sins and addictions.

The process continues when I invite Christ to illuminate my narcissism.

Only God's grace and mercy can write my sacred story.

៛

I will strive daily to pick up the cross, for it leads to my life.

The closer I get to holiness, the more I will see
and feel sin's disorder in my life

The more I experience sin's disorder,
the more tempted I will be to disbelieve my life as sacred story.

The way through the temptation is
to surrender my powerlessness to God.

☙

It is never too late to open my heart to Christ and
live my life as sacred story.

Christ, who is close to the brokenhearted, restores my lost innocence.

The path to my sacred story is
Creation, Presence, Memory, Mercy, and Eternity.

☙

Your heart is prepared, and you have awakened to the path you are to take. Trust it. Remember: Do not read ahead. Do not exercise ahead. Awaken to the present moment. Take each day and each exercise as it comes.

❧

༄

I am starting a Relationship that will carry me
for the rest of my life.

I will learn the fundamentals and strive
to open my heart to God.

I trust that God will lead me.
I believe that my sacred story will unfold in truth,
in powerlessness, and with my patience.

I believe that Jesus awaits me with His
grace, mercy, and forgiving love.

What do I need for this journey?
A generous heart,
the willingness to take fifteen minutes to pray daily,
and the humility to always ask God for help.

༃

Dr. Schuchts' Reflection ~ Week One

Affirmations

This first week of the *Forty Weeks* is focused on "Affirmations." Notice inside the word "affirmation" is the word "firm." In essence, the purpose of these affirmations is to firmly undergird you with God's strength as you begin this spiritual journey, so that you become increasingly more "rooted and grounded" in Christ. (See Eph. 3:16).

This first chapter is filled with pearls of wisdom, gleaned from the Scriptures and Church teaching, and repeatedly tested by St. Ignatius in his own journey of spiritual growth and discernment (before and after becoming a priest). They are thumbnail sketches of many of St. Ignatius' valuable Rules for Discernment of Spirits.

These Affirmations have also been confirmed by many who have walked this path with Jesus and St. Ignatius, including Fr. Bill Watson, who has discovered the value of these rules throughout his priesthood, both personally and in guiding others.

As you continue through the *Forty Weeks*, I pray that these affirmations will become deeply rooted in your own mind and heart, so that you too will be able to know them to be true in the depths of your being. In the process, I believe you will experience deep and lasting freedom in your life, and as a result be better equipped to bring freedom to many others through your ministry as a priest of Jesus Christ.

You may be asking yourself "how can these affirmations take root in my mind and heart"? Notice that Fr. Bill encourages you to "reflectively contemplate" and to "listen with your mind in your heart." I hope that catchy phrase caught your attention as it did mine. To listen with your mind in your heart is to enter deeply into reflective contemplation. This kind of prayer stands at the center of Ignatian spirituality and is a cornerstone of our Catholic faith.

Here is what the Catechism has to say about praying with our hearts:

"According to Scripture it is the heart that prays... The heart is our hidden center, beyond the grasp of our reason and of others; only the Spirit of God can fathom the human heart and know it fully... The heart... is the place of truth... the place of encounter" (CCC 2562-2563).

This speaks to me of our need for an encounter with God, first drawing upon our human reasoning capacities, and then transcending them. Only the Spirit of God can lead us into the depths of our hearts to encounter the living Christ.

This is how the Catechism describes contemplative prayer:

"Contemplation is a gaze of faith, fixed on Jesus. 'I look at him and he looks at me'.... His gaze purifies our heart; the light of the countenance of Jesus illumines the eyes of our heart and teaches us to see everything in light of his truth and compassion" (CCC 2715).

I believe these insights from the Catechism will be a trustworthy source of guidance for us as we embark on this *Forty Weeks* journey together. Reading these affirmations and memorizing them is a good beginning, but much more is needed for them to penetrate the depths of our hearts.

These affirmations will only become firm in us when they become real to us. This realization takes place in prayer grounded in our daily human experience. As we fix our eyes on Jesus, we will see ourselves, including all of our sins and wounds, in the light of his truth and compassion.

None of us can see ourselves clearly without being illumined by the Spirit of Truth. And we will not have the courage to look honestly within our own hearts, unless we know we will be met with Jesus' compassionate gaze.

Through the light of the Holy Spirit we can become more and more "attentive to the things that cause... fears, stress, anxiety, anger or grief" and connect them to the affirmations we are contemplating. In this way, we can experience Jesus' healing and transformation in our lives.

Here are a few examples to illustrate how these Affirmations can become more firmly rooted in our hearts, through contemplative prayer.

Let's begin with this Affirmation describes our common human condition after the fall: "Everyone has been mortally wounded spiritually, psychologically and physically by Original sin and loss of paradise."

After reading this affirmation I asked the Holy Spirit to illumine my mind and heart. Immediately, I began to contemplate an image of Adam and Eve in paradise, resting in blissful communion with the Father, Son, and Holy Spirit. In this image, I get a sense of their wholeness and deep abiding peace. Then, I imagine the rupture that takes place as they listen to the "father of lies" and break communion with the Triune God and each other.

I see them alone and disoriented. They are deeply wounded spiritually, psychologically and physically. Then through the light of the Holy Spirit I see myself, in identification with Adam, struggling with my own spiritual, psychological and physical ailments.

Can you see how praying contemplatively in this way allows us to reflect on these Affirmations with our minds in our hearts?

Here is another example: "I will trust that Christ came to heal all my wounds." Praying with this affirmation, I ask the Holy Spirit to show me what he wants to reveal to me. I am aware of my doubt and hopelessness, seeing many areas of my unhealed wounds (spiritually, psychologically and physically). I reflect on all the times I have prayed for healing for certain debilitating wounds in my life.

I feel discouraged that many of these are not yet healed. At this point, left to myself, I can too easily turn inward and remain discouraged and filled with doubt in the midst of this evidence of all the areas where "Jesus hasn't healed me." Clouded by doubt and discouragement (inspirations of the father of lies), it is very difficult to "trust that Christ came to heal all my wounds."

Self-pity is lurking in the shadows. But, I have a choice. Do I give into it, or am I willing to bring my discouragement to Jesus? As soon as I choose to look up away from myself and towards God, the Holy Spirit turns my gaze away from my self and towards Jesus, the Physician of my soul and body (CCC, 1509). First, I see him on the Cross, bloodied and beaten. I am reminded of the phrase from Mt. 8:17, after Jesus cured everyone who came to him: "He took away our infirmities and bore our diseases."

Next, I am brought into a contemplative experience of identifying with the man at the Pool of Bethesda (John 5), feeling his hopelessness and self-pity. I am struck by Jesus' question to the man: "Do you want to be healed?" And then I am amazed by the fact that after 38 years of believing that he wouldn't be healed, Jesus instantly healed him.

Identifying with his joy, I am reminded of the different times I felt hopeless, but then Jesus came through and healed me, sometimes in amazing ways. I end the time of prayer with thanksgiving and hope. I am now stronger in my conviction: "I will trust that Christ came to heal all my wounds."

Can you see how you can pray this way throughout the Forty Weeks? I encourage you to ask the Holy Spirit to highlight one of the Affirmations and then lead you in contemplative prayer.

You can begin with these two affirmations: "I will not tire of asking God for help since God delights in my asking" (pg. 18). "I will trust that God will lead me." (pg. 21)

Don't be discouraged. Remember that "The pathway to God's peace and healing runs through your hearts brokenness, sin, fear, anger and grief" (pg.18). "Christ is close to the brokenhearted" (pg. 21).

"Be not afraid: Fear comes from the enemy of [your] human nature".

Immaculate Heart of Mary pray for us so that our hearts may be fully aligned with the Sacred Heart of your son Jesus.

෫ට

NOTES

Week 2

FIRST
I will choose a place of contemplative rest and reflection. It will be a place apart—a technology-free zone!

SECOND
I will make a decision on whether to take one or two fifteen-minute prayer breaks a day. Regularity is key to sustainable disciplines of any kind, and this is especially true of a prayer relationship with Christ.

THIRD
During my fifteen-minute quiet moments this week, I will slowly and thoughtfully read part 1 of St. Ignatius's conversion story. I will commit to read reflectively and take my time. I will ask the Spirit to inspire me to fully see and hear Ignatius's story, especially as it relates to my life.

I will pray for an open mind and heart.
I will not read ahead.
I will awaken to the present moment.
I will take each day and each exercise as it comes.
I cannot do Sacred Story better by going faster.

ജ

This second week is related to the conversion story of St. Ignatius. Your prayer exercise for this week is to read and ponder the beginning of St. Ignatius's sacred story. Pay careful attention to what in Ignatius's experience touches your own unique history. Thank Christ in advance for the blessings and insights you will receive.

Read and ponder. You may be inspired to reflect on the affirmations from last week. Be attentive to any memories that might arise and the feelings that stir as you pray this week. St. Ignatius was very clear in his teachings that careful attention to your internal spiritual movements marks the beginning of discernment. This heart-focused attention attunes your radar to the voices of the spiritual world.

❦

Part 1: St. Ignatius and His Legacy

Until his thirtieth year, Ignatius Loyola was unconscious of the sacredness of his life. Instead, he was sincerely devoted to life's pleasures and vanities. He was a gambling addict, sexually self-indulgent, arrogant, hotheaded, and insecure. Ignatius's mother died when he was an infant, and his father died when he was sixteen.

By our contemporary measures, Ignatius's family was dysfunctional. Was this person a possible candidate for sainthood? It did not look promising. But God does not judge by human standards. It is God's nature to pursue all who have fallen asleep through sin, addiction, and selfishness. God judges the heart; with unbounded grace and patient mercy, God reaches into the ruins that sin makes of our lives and transforms them into sacred stories.

Ignatius, with all his narcissism, psychological problems, and sinful vices, was awakened by God's great love. A failed military campaign and a shattered leg forced him into a lengthy convalescence back at Loyola castle, his family home. Ignatius's time of recuperation provided an opportunity for Love to shine a light on much more serious and life-

39

threatening wounds that were spiritual, emotional, and psychological in nature.

These wounds were supported by the evolution of a destructive, sinful narcissism. For thirty years, Ignatius's narcissism had rendered him unconscious to his true human nature and oblivious to his life as sacred story. The pleasures he indulged in and the power he wielded functioned like a narcotic to numb the pain of his hidden spiritual and psychological wounds. His sinful vices and self-indulgent pleasures had blinded him to the possibilities of a fruitful life guided by a well-formed conscience.

God's grace reached into the reality of Ignatius's life and awakened in him a desire for innocence. His long-buried aspirations for living authentically suddenly became his prime motivation. He noticed it first while convalescing at Loyola. He became aware of new desires and a different energy as he daydreamed while reading stories of Christ and the saints. Pondering the saints' lives, he imagined himself living in a similarly selfless way.

He compared these new daydreams to his usual vain, narcissistic ones. The old daydreams drew energy from a life of sin, addiction, and vice, while the daydreams of selfless generosity produced their own energy. Ignatius also noticed a significant difference between the feelings produced by the two sets of daydreams. The vain fantasies entertained him when he was thinking about them. But he noticed that when he set them aside, he felt empty and unsatisfied.

The new holy daydreams also entertained him when he was thinking about them. Yet when he set these aside, he remained content and felt an enduring calm and quiet joy. By paying close attention to the ultimate affective results of these two sets of daydreams and discerning their difference, Ignatius made a discovery that transformed his life and the history of Christian spirituality.

Ignatius' Awakening Mirrors His Unique Examen Prayer

Ignatius's Awakening Experience Mirrors →	*His Examen Prayer*
A GRACED EXPERIENCE OF GOD'S LOVE OPENED IGNATIUS TO ↓	GIVE THANKS FOR FAVORS RECEIVED ↓
A DISSATISFACTION WITH VAIN FANTASIES, WHICH LED TO SURRENDERING TO HOLY DAYDREAMS, CHARACTERIZED BY CONSOLATION, WHICH IN TURN ↓	PRAY FOR GRACE TO SEE CLEARLY ↓
CAUSED HIM TO REVIEW HIS LIFE AND ACTIONS, LEADING TO ↓	GIVE A DETAILED ACCOUNT OF CONSCIENCE: GENERAL AND PARTICULAR ↓
GRIEF WITH YEARNING FOR PENANCE AND REPENTANCE FOR HIS PAST SINS, CULMINATING IN ↓	ASK PARDON FOR ONE'S FAULTS ↓
IGNATIUS'S PASSION TO AMEND HIS LIFE AND A DESIRE TO LOVE GOD WHOLEHEARTEDLY.	RESOLVE AND AMEND TO SERVE GOD

The Voice of Conscience

Ignatius discovered that the new, selfless aspirations were influenced by divine inspirations. He further discovered that these inspirations reflected his true human nature and that the vain fantasies had deadened his conscience. His narcissistic daydreams led him away from enduring peace, because they masked his authentic human nature. The old daydreams were powerful, ego affirming, and familiar. He knew in his heart that living their fantasy was the path to self-destruction. On the one hand, he would be judged successful by the standards of the world—a world that measured success in terms of riches, honors, and pride. On the other hand, he would be judged a failure by the standards of the gospel—standards that advocated a life of spiritual poverty, humility and consequential service.

Ignatius was awakened to the emotional wisdom and spiritual truth of his new daydreams. He became aware of the significant damage that his old lifestyle had done both to himself and others. What had been awakened in him was the divine gift of conscience, and with it, Ignatius experienced profound regret and sorrow for having wasted so much of his life on self-indulgent pleasures and fantasies, seductions that could never bring him lasting peace and satisfaction. He began to understand that living in pleasure and fantasy destroyed his authentic human nature and silenced his deepest desires.

Divine inspiration led Ignatius to seek forgiveness for wasting his life and abusing his innocence. Grace enabled him to take responsibility for his sins against God and his authentic human nature. Divine inspiration provided Ignatius with the desire, energy, and courage to renounce the thoughts, words, and deeds of his sinful habits. Grace, received through the sacrament of Reconciliation, heightened Ignatius's consciousness and enabled him to imagine a new path for his life, and new ways to express his gifts and talents.

As usually happens when people respond to the grace of conversion, Ignatius's new aspirations confused and disconcerted many of his closest family members and friends. Nonetheless, he acted on these aspirations. Ignatius was now able to understand a path to God, a pattern of conversion that countless thousands would imitate.

A Menacing Fear Unmasked

After some months of living in the light of these new positive virtues, habits, and divine inspirations, Ignatius was suddenly gripped by terror and panic. How could he manage to live the rest of his life without the pleasures of the past? It was easy to live virtuously for some months, but for the rest of his life? This was a real crisis, because Ignatius began to wonder if this was an impossible goal.

Ignatius had two vital insights about this menacing fear. First, he realized it was a counter-inspiration prompted by the enemy of his true human nature. Second, he saw that the counter-inspiration tempted him to return to his old narcissistic vices and habits. Seduced by their powerful influence, Ignatius would abandon all hope for a life of virtue. In essence, Ignatius was tempted to surrender living the authentic life that had finally brought him peace. He sensed an evil source inspiring this menacing fear, and he challenged it head-on: "You pitiful thing! Can you even promise me one hour of life?"

A Decisive and Enduring Commitment to Remain Awake

Not knowing how he would endure, Ignatius dismissed the counter-inspiration and its evil author by recommitting to this new wakefulness for the remainder of his life. This was Ignatius's major insight: never trust the messages prompted by menacing fears! Counter them with a firm commitment to stay the course, to awaken and remain conscious.

This decisive, enduring commitment to persevere restored tranquility, and his fear abated. Ignatius had discovered, unmasked, and confronted the deceiver. In this, Ignatius learned another lesson about speaking truth to power that would guide his new life and help shape his first set of foundational discernment principles.

Ignatius's Experiences Reveal His Discernment Principles

Ignatius's Experiences →	Discernment Principles
AN ENEMY VOICE EVOKED IGNATIUS'S FEAR OF A LIFELONG STRUGGLE WITH HIS SINFUL HABITS. ↓	THERE IS CONSCIOUS FEAR AND ANXIETY OVER SURRENDERING SINFUL AND ADDICTIVE HABITS. ↓
IGNATIUS REJECTED THE "ENEMY OF HUMAN NATURE" AND CONFRONTED THIS ENEMY'S FALSE PROMISES. ↓	ONE CONFRONTS THE THREATENING "VOICE" OF SIN AND ADDICTION WITH THE TRUTH THAT THEY BRING DEATH, NOT LIFE. ↓
PEACE WAS RESTORED AFTER IGNATIUS TRUTHFULLY NAMED SIN AND ADDICTION AS DEATH DEALING.	FINALLY, PEACE RETURNS AND ANXIETY DISSOLVES.

Ignatius had to face these same fears many, many more times. Eventually he knew they were false fears, inspirations of the enemy of his human nature. Most importantly, he gradually learned how to defuse them, and to defend against them. It is vital that we understand this lesson from Ignatius: anyone who changes his or her lifestyle through a divine awakening and who, by grace, consciously and consistently enters his or her sacred story will encounter the same menacing fears. You can be strongly tempted to fall asleep and slip back into old habits and vices. When you are faced with these menacing fears—when, not if—confidently recommit to the path of life, and to the Author of life. The fears, in time, will subside. The enemy of human nature will always be disarmed.

Our spirit, our body, and God's grace at work in us compose a holy trinity. God made us this way. All three parts working cooperatively are necessary for holiness and human growth. In the paradise depicted in Genesis, the perfect cooperation of this trinity of human nature rendered us immortal. By turning from the fullness of God's grace, our immortality was lost; the perfect balance of the divinely crafted trinity of human nature—body, spirit, and God's grace—shattered. Christ's incarnation and death opened the way to immortality once again.

Our Christian life is a labor of love. In order for God's love to heal us, we must do our part to open ourselves to His graces. This requires conscious and ongoing effort to abstain from sinful, addictive habits in thoughts, words, and deeds. There is a need to pray for God's grace, and first we must awaken to that grace.

With that same grace, we have the strength to resist and abstain from sinful, addictive attitudes and behaviors, both spiritual and material. God's grace infuses our spiritual disciplines, activating the trinity of our human nature. Grace helps us climb out of the spiritual, mental, physical, and emotional ruts of our bound self. In doing so, God graces us with a future of increased hope, holiness, and balance.

ꜿꙅ

I am starting a Relationship that will carry me
for the rest of my life.

All relationships require time and patience.
I will strive for patience and ask for God's help
when I don't understand a lesson.

I will learn the fundamentals and open my heart to God.

I trust that God will lead me.

I believe that my sacred story will unfold in truth,
in powerlessness, and with my patience.

I believe that Jesus awaits me with His
grace, mercy, and forgiving love.

ꙅꝋ

Dr. Schuchts' Reflection ~ Week Two

Ignatius' Story--Brokenness and Transformation

This second week of Forty Weeks you are invited to see your own story of brokenness and transformation in light of St. Ignatius' conversion story.

St. Ignatius' story provides us with great hope, no matter what our sins, wounds or addictions. Who, besides God, could have identified young Ignatius of Loyola as a candidate for sainthood?

Before his spiritual awakening at Montserrat, Ignatius' heart was far from God. Until then, he was completely blinded by his narcissistic pride, and focused on satisfying his narcissistic (i.e. self-centered) fantasies.

Once his eyes were opened and he discovered that the path of Christ left him consoled and the path of narcissism left him empty, he developed a deep desire to encounter the living Jesus, and to have his innocence and freedom restored.

Ignatius Provides a Mirror for Us

Ignatius' story provides a mirror for each one of us to look honestly at ourselves, humbly facing how we rely on our sins and addictions to medicate and cover our wounds, and then how we try to save ourselves in our narcissism.

By seeing how Ignatius hid behind his narcissism, we can each look more directly at our own blinding pride and begin to face the sins and idolatries that have been hidden by our chronic self-deception and self-righteousness.

In Be Healed, I shared about this journey in my own life, which is ongoing (see chapters 2 and 4).

Later in chapter 6, I identified the seven deadly sins and the specific idolatries that are associated with each of them.

As you review this list can you identify Ignatius' deadly sins and the idolatries underlying them?

From our	Deadly Sin	Object of Idolatry
	Pride	Self/Accomplishments
	Envy	Status/Possessions/Talents
	Gluttony	Food/Drink/Drugs
	Lust	Sex/Relationships/Beauty
	Anger	Power/Control/Justice
	Greed	Wealth/Security
	Sloth	Comfort/Ease

reading of Week 2 of Forty Weeks, it appears to me that Ignatius struggled with the deadly sins of anger, lust, and pride. On a daily basis Ignatius slavishly "worshipped" these "gods" of power, sex and self-reliance.

Sadly, each of these deadly sins and idolatries eventually became Ignatius' prison, as his compulsive addictions and narcissistic pride crippled his life.

But we miss a vital part of Ignatius story if we only "judge" Ignatius by the outward fruit on his tree.

Looking in the Mirror

Can you see how Ignatius' Life Story is a mirror for looking at our own story?

Can you see how areas of your life and priestly ministry have been crippled by your own sins and addictions? And are you growing in understanding of how you have medicated your wounds by these idolatries?

Can you understand how the people you minister to are similarly bound by their sins and addictions, and how these are rooted in their wounds? (See chapter 7 of Be Healed for more on this).

As I have discovered, I am sure you also realize, you will only be able to help others find freedom and healing to the extent that you face your sins and addictions and allow Jesus to free and heal you.

I can relate to Ignatius' running from his wounds early in his life. Like Ignatius, I did not face my own wounds until I was in my 30's. Though I was a therapist trained to see the wounds of others, I was blinded to my own sin, wounds and narcissistic pride.

Immaculate Heart of Mary pray for us so that our hearts
may be fully aligned with the Sacred Heart of your son Jesus.

℘

NOTES

Week 3

FIRST
I will find a place each day where I can pull aside for a fifteen-minute space of contemplative rest and reflection, free from technology's distractions.

SECOND
I will review my decision on whether I will take one fifteen-minute prayer break or two fifteen-minute prayer breaks a day.

THIRD
During my fifteen-minute quiet prayer periods this week, I will gradually read through part 2 of St. Ignatius's conversion story. Reading reflectively, I will take my time. I am reading for spiritual insights about Ignatius's sacred story and my own. Prayerful reading, known in the Catholic Tradition as lectio divina (holy reading) is done slowly. Resisting the efficiency pressures of the modern age, I realize Sacred Story is not about going faster, but deeper.

I will not read ahead.
I will awaken to the present moment.
I will take each day and each exercise as it comes.

51

I cannot do Sacred Story better by going faster.

Welcome to the third week of our pilgrimage. The exercises for this week continue with the conversion story of St. Ignatius. As you listen to St. Ignatius's history, reflect on your own. As you read, recall that Ignatius woke up to the fact that there were two plots in his daydreams: Plot "A" entailed the goals and fantasies rooted in his wounded heart and in following narcissistic dreams. Plot "B" entailed fantasies of a heart rooted in Christ and discovering healing and peace by following holy dreams. You are invited to search your own daydreams and fantasies for signs of these two plots. Consider your life as you listen to Ignatius's story. God used him to guide us. Each person has the same challenge of finding the narrow path that leads to our true human nature.

You have two options for how to pray with this week's text. Some like to read during the fifteen-minute periods, while others prefer to read the whole text on Sunday and then focus on smaller sections during the fifteen-minute prayer periods for the rest of the week. Do whatever is best for you. Your goal is to listen to Ignatius's story and be attentive to any issues that seem important to you. Listen to Ignatius's story, and pay attention to whatever stirs in you, be it hope and peace or anxiety and fear. Doing this sharpens your spiritual radar for things that make your heart say, "Pay attention!" Thank Christ in advance for the blessings and insights you will receive.

Part 2: A Journey to the Heart

Ignatius's decisive and enduring commitment to his conversion launched him directly into the center of his heart's brokenness and the pride masking those wounds. After leaving home, Ignatius traveled to Montserrat and spent three days reviewing his life. It was at this time that he made a general confession of all his past sinful deeds. This first life confession initiated an enduring habit of weekly confession and communion. In this written confession, Ignatius consciously detailed his sinful attitudes, behaviors, and passions: gambling addiction, sexual self-indulgence, arrogance, and violent outbursts of temper. It took all three days to write the story of his past life.

Yet he discovered that simply detailing and confessing his sinful habits and addictions did not disarm them. That would require going deeper, to their source in his heart and history. Only in these deepest recesses could he confront the pattern of spiritual and psychological dysfunction that was most responsible for eroding his freedom and distorting his authentic human nature.

It is this inward journey that fully awakened his conscience. It was only at this depth that he discovered his authentic human nature and regained the creativity of childlike innocence. We do well to understand the tipping point of Ignatius's life from his root vices and narcissism to his new life of wakefulness, light, peace, and hope. This is how his story unfolded.

Ignatius's new, pious habit of regular confession evolved into a destructive, obsessive, and compulsive torture. He confessed and reconfessed past sins multiple times, never feeling he had gotten to the bottom of his immoral deeds. This excruciating spiritual and psychological torment lasted for months. He was so anguished by his obsessive guilt that numerous times he wanted to commit suicide by throwing himself off the cliff where he prayed.

Well aware of the emotional damage caused by this obsessive confession habit, he still could not let it go. Instead he initiated new, harsher physical disciplines and spiritual regimens. His goal was to gain complete control and self-mastery over his immoral and dissolute past. He wanted to remember every detail of his past sins so he could be perfectly cleansed. But nothing worked!

Finally, exhausted and disgusted with his efforts, he realized he intensely despised the spiritual life he was living. Ignatius had an urgent and compelling desire to "stop it!" This thought alarmed Ignatius, and his spiritual radar went on high alert. Ignatius discerned that the inspiration came from another source, but what could it be? He discovered the inspiration's origin and author only by understanding where the inspiration was taking him. It occurred to him that the inspiration was leading him in the same direction as the menacing fear he had previously experienced. Inspired to abandon his newly awakened life, Ignatius was being tempted to abandon the peace, the service to others, and the virtuous life of his sacred story. But how had this counter-inspiration succeeded in gaining entry? Ignatius's decision to stop reconfessing his past sins reveals the enemy's strategy.

Surrendering Control to Embrace Powerlessness and Innocence

Ignatius's decision to stop his damaging confession habit appears inconsequential. But the choice was the most significant spiritual decision in his entire life. It was also the most difficult, because that one choice meant fully surrendering his life to God. It meant admitting his powerlessness over his sins and in humility allowing God, not himself, to be the source of his holiness.

Reflecting on the temptation to walk away from his new Christian life, Ignatius received an insight that the burdensome, destructive habit of reconfessing past sins was rooted in a pride to try and save himself. This pride forced him to his knees. On seeing this, he "awoke as if from a dream" and was given the grace to stop the habit.

Looking at his life spiritually and psychologically, it appears that behind the sexual misdeeds, addictive gambling, and violent temper, there was a controlling, narcissistic pride and a broken heart. Our narcissistic control is solidified by the searing spiritual and psychological pain of lost innocence—the pattern of sins we inherit from the Original Sin, along with those sins committed against us early in life and later those sins committed by us.

Our narcissism, if you will, godifies us, severely restricting our ability to respond to the true God. We fill the void of our wounded, broken hearts with self-centered strivings for attention, power, and control. Our narcissism is a false identity, an anti-story. It blinds us to our authentic human nature and the deepest desires of our heart. It blinds us to our sacred story.

Ignatius's first life confession at Montserrat documented the visible manifestations of this deep distortion in his human nature. The Divine Physician next led Ignatius to the source of those visible sins. It was his wounded human nature that fueled the controlling, narcissistic personality. The pattern of visible sins, vices, and addictions was only the tip of the iceberg. It is vital to remember that Ignatius's weaning from the narcotics of aggression, addictions, and dissoluteness opened a portal to his broken heart—his wounded human nature—where he could fully confront his powerlessness and brokenness. It is here that he finally met Christ face to face. It is here, in accepting Christ's forgiveness, that healing love begins. It is here that Ignatius admitted his powerlessness to save himself and surrendered control of his life to God. This is the spiritual paradigm of powerlessness.

Ignatius's struggle with the obsessive habit of reconfessing past sins was the symbol of his hidden root sin of pride. Christ labored hard to meet Ignatius right where he was, in this harrowing place. Ignatius's frenzied, damaging re-confessing of past sins was only the latest manifestation of the same hidden narcissism that had distorted his first thirty years of life.

The same sin had been in full view on the battlefield at Pamplona, when Ignatius forced his will on the commander and all the other knights to engage a suicide mission against a far more numerous and well-armed militia. Ignatius's pride earned him a shattering defeat and a shattered leg. Fortunately, his defensive pride was shattered by God's grace awakening him "as if from a dream."

After his frightful struggle with scruples following his confession at Montserrat, Ignatius finally acknowledged his powerlessness and surrendered control of his life to God. God had waited all of Ignatius's life to transform his deepest desires into a sacred story whose legacy would endure to eternity. This surrender defines Ignatius's second set of foundational discernment principles

An outpouring of mystical grace flooded Ignatius at this point. More importantly, a humble and obedient spirit was beginning to emerge which enabled him to respond to the slightest movements of God's grace in his thoughts, words, and deeds. In this humility and docility, he discovered a life of service that changed the Church and the world. Later in life he reflected on this discovery:

There are very few who realize what God would make of them if they abandoned themselves entirely to His hands, and let themselves be formed by His grace. A thick and shapeless tree trunk would never believe that it could become a statue, admired as a miracle of sculpture...and would never consent to submit itself to the chisel of the sculptor who, as St. Augustine says, sees by his genius what he can make of it. Many people who, we see, now scarcely live as Christians, do not understand that they could become saints, if they would let themselves be formed by the grace of God, if they did not ruin His plans by resisting the work which He wants to do.

Ignatius's Experiences Reveal His Discernment Steps

Ignatius's Experiences	Discernment Steps
Ignatius's struggle with scruples hid his vainglory. ↓	THE INITIAL CONFRONTATION WITH ONE'S ROOT SIN ↓
Ignatius constantly reconfessed to seek salvation by willpower alone. ↓	THE EFFORT TO CONTROL ONE'S ROOT SIN ONLY BY PERSONAL EFFORT OR FORCE OF WILL ↓
Ignatius experienced suicidal impulses, disgust, and the desire to walk away from his newfound faith. ↓	DESPAIR AND DESIRE TO GIVE UP FAITH WHEN HUMAN EFFORT ALONE FAILS ↓
Ignatius traced the spirit of disgust to a demonic source. ↓	INSIGHT THAT DESIRE TO REJECT THE SPIRITUAL JOURNEY IS A TEMPTATION ↓
Ignatius abandoned his compulsive confessing of past sins.	THE ADMITTING OF POWERLESSNESS TO SAVE ONESELF AND THE SURRENDERING OF PRIDEFUL ACTIONS

The proud narcissist, the man who was master of his own universe, became a humble and obedient servant of the universe's true Master and Creator. To arrive at this point, Ignatius had to admit his powerlessness. He had to surrender control over his life and the distorted aspects of his human nature that had evolved over the years. He had to learn how to live out of his newly emerging authentic self, his true and free human nature, a nature that had been hidden behind his wounded heart. Because of this, Ignatius also had to learn how to dismantle the narcissism that had evolved over the first thirty years of his life. The counter-inspirer, the enemy of his human nature, had cleverly concealed his true human nature, and Ignatius had to begin life over again, this time allowing God to reveal to him his authentic self. This was why, after the resolution of this greatest of his life's crises, Ignatius experienced himself being taught by God. It was, he said, exactly like "a child is taught by a schoolmaster."

The Divine Inspirer and the Counter-inspirer

This harrowing crisis taught Ignatius a most vital lesson about counter-inspirations. The willpower and resolute commitment to live virtuously for the rest of his life could be manipulated and turned against him by means of subtle inspirations. What seemed like a holy, pious, and noble practice—a serious approach to confession—devolved into a damaging habit that made him loathe his spiritual life, and in frustration, inspired him to abandon it. He learned that the counter-inspirations of the enemy of his human nature could act like "an angel of light." These inspirations appear holy but when followed, they end in disaster, distancing one from God and from one's authentic self.

Ignatius gained clearer knowledge of the two spiritual forces that inspire and seek to guide the evolution of one's story. He gathered what he had learned from "speaking truth to power" (to the enemy of human nature) and what he had learned from surrendering control of his life to God into guidelines for discerning these different inspirations. For now, it is sufficient to say that the Divine Inspirer is the author of one's original innocence, that is, one's authentic and free human nature. The Divine Inspirer works gently in and through every situation, especially the misfortunes associated with the damaging spiritual and psychological ordeals of life.

It is the nature of the Holy Spirit to offer forgiveness and provide shelter from the enemy of human nature, whose sole purpose is to destroy innocence. The Divine Inspirer forgives sins, restores lost innocence, mends broken and wounded hearts, releases captives, sets the oppressed free, and illumines one's sacred story and true human nature (Lk 4:18).

The counter-inspirer also works through all the events of one's life and relationships. His work is evident in the distortions of spirit and mind, the deep wounding caused by the evolution of sin from the Original Sin and also sin inherited from one's family and culture. The counter-inspirer works to corrupt innocence and deform one's spiritual, emotional, physical, and psychological nature—one's true human nature. Jesus condemned the violation of the innocent and the childlike. No human being can escape the machinations this evil breeds in one's body, mind, and spirit. Since the Original Sin, this evolutionary force has infected every person and consequently, all of human history.

The counter-inspirer conceals our original wounds, counseling and guiding our steps to build a false identity, an anti-story, characteristically identified by a distorted ego and defended by narcissism. Our narcissistic pride rationalizes the habits, vices, addictions, and lifestyles that form our anti-story. The counter-inspirer renders us unconscious to our sacred story and to our true, divinely shaped human nature.

God led Ignatius through this distorted evolution back to the lost innocence of his true human nature. To get there, Ignatius had to confront his pattern of spiritual and psychological distortions born from by his narcissistic pride. It was a mighty castle that he had built on the shifting sands of a child's wounded innocence, on a child's lonely, broken heart. God provided Ignatius the inspiration and grace to allow that castle to crumble. The shattering of his powerful defenses and the unmasking of his prideful, narcissistic pattern proved to be the tipping point of Ignatius's entire conversion process.

Wakefulness, Holiness, and Heightened Consciousness

Ignatius's conversion from his anti-story and his full awakening to his sacred story was not a single event but rather a gradual process. His full evolution from a vain egomaniac to a saint took the rest of his life. This is evident in his Autobiography. In three linked narratives recounting personal near-death experiences, Ignatius reveals his growth in holiness, a process that evolved over a long, twenty-eight-year period.

In the first account, he is filled with fear of judgment, because he understands that pride is still a strong temptation for him. In the second account, he is no longer afraid of death, but instead, he is filled with sorrow for his delayed response to God. In the third account, grace floods his heart, and he is filled with an intense devotion and desire for eternal union with God. These three episodes mirror the three classical stages of mystical growth: purgation, illumination, and union. The three episodes also convey the reality of Ignatius's patience with the process of his spiritual growth:

A Lifelong Commitment to Christ in the Church

It took Ignatius the remainder of his life to develop into the saint we know today. His was a gradual, steady evolution from a sinful narcissist in control of his own life to an innocent, obedient servant of God. He discovered and embraced the power and energy of living in the holy trinity of his authentic human nature—spirit, body, and God's grace, working in unison. Growth in holiness requires desire, patience, and daily effort to awaken to our authentic human nature. It takes time for grace to penetrate the influence of our anti-story so that our sacred story can more fully emerge. There are no shortcuts to holiness, not even for saints.

Ignatius' Three Near-Death Experiences Mirror
The Classic Process of Spiritual Growth

Ignatius's 3 Near-Death Experiences →	Universal Principle →	Mystical Path
(1) 1522 Ignatius, justifying himself, anxiously recoiled and focused on his sinfulness. ↓	PANIC OVER ONE'S SALVATION DUE TO WEAKNESS AND SINFULNESS →	PURGATION ↓
(2) 1532 Ignatius, no longer fearful, regretted not having responded sooner to God's graces. ↓	SADNESS AT SLOWNESS OF ONE'S RESPONSE TO GOD'S LOVE AND INVITATION TO INTIMACY →	ILLUMINATION ↓
(3) 1550 Ignatius felt intense joy at the thought of dying and being with God. →	AN ARDENT, ALL-EMBRACING LOVE OF GOD AND DESIRE FOR COMPLETE UNION WITH THE TRINITY →	UNION

If you desire to surrender your anti-story and open to your sacred story, grace will awaken you, like Ignatius, to places in your heart's memories you might not wish to visit. The awakening will begin like Ignatius's. It starts with an honest identification of the visible manifestations of those spiritual and psychological distortions in the particulars of your human nature. These distortions disclose your lost innocence and a heart broken by the Original Fall and the cumulative sins of your family, clan, and culture. Ignatius started this process with his life confession. He truthfully identified the habits, addictions, sins, and compulsions characteristic of his lost innocence and broken heart. Open yourself to the graces of God that will illumine the distinctive narcissistic elements fueling your sinful, compulsive behaviors. Ignatius needed much grace to overcome his defenses and unlock this hidden truth about his life. Everyone who embraces the invitation to walk this path can confidently rely on the same grace to navigate this vital part of the process.

Finally awakening to your sacred story will take you to the places in your heart where your innocence is wounded, your true human nature is distorted, and your heart is broken. Awakening to your sacred story will reveal the outlines of your anti-story. You will need to honestly evaluate the narcissistic pattern in your own life, identifying the pleasures, powers, and habits that act as narcotics, blocking the pain of your broken heart and lost innocence.

This pattern that masks your authentic self and your true human nature is the pattern of your false self. It is the deceit of the anti-story that hides the radiance of your authentic human nature and the sacredness of your life story. This was Ignatius's experience. By divine inspiration, he discovered his false-self masquerading as a pious, conscientious penitent.

Once he reached this point, Ignatius awakened, "as if from a dream," to his sacred story. By so doing, he was graced to unite mind and spirit, action and contemplation, the eternal in the present moment, and so to see the Divine Presence in all people and in all creation. His new consciousness of God so energized him that he could daily enter the stream of his sacred story, enabling him to reengage life's duties and obligations with a serene heart and with clarity of purpose. He courageously allowed God to write his sacred story over the remainder of his life—hourly, daily, weekly, monthly, yearly.

The vitality of Ignatius's personal relationship with God—in Father, Son, and Spirit—was possible through the grace and gratitude he experienced in the constant encounter with his personal sinfulness and disordered passions. These graced encounters always brought illumination, insight, energy, and hope, never discouragement, fear, or despair.

A proud, dissolute, insecure narcissist finally found serenity and security in God's full love, acceptance, mercy, and forgiveness. Interestingly enough, this happened in and through Ignatius's powerlessness and weaknesses, and perhaps even because of them! That which so marred his early life became the very source of his strength and sanctity. Ignatius discovered, like St. Paul, that in his weaknesses and sin, he was strong in Christ (2 Cor 12:10). It will be the same for you.

I am starting a Relationship that will carry me for
the rest of my life.

All relationships require time and patience.
I will strive for patience and ask for God's help
when I don't understand a lesson.

I will learn the fundamentals and open my heart to God.

I trust that God will lead me.

I believe that my sacred story will unfold in truth,
in powerlessness, and with my patience.

I believe that Jesus awaits me
with His grace, mercy, and forgiving love.

Dr. Schuchts' Reflection ~ Week Three

Ignatius' Life Story--Sin and Addictions

This week you are invited to enter more deeply into Ignatius' life story, and thus deeper into the journey into your own heart. This journey is the best possible formation for your ministry as a priest of Jesus Christ. As you grow in freedom, you will be able to genuinely help others find true and lasting freedom.

Before applying this week's material to your personal life, I want to pause for a moment to reflect on your ministry as a priest, where you deal with people, like Ignatius, who are bound in sin or addiction.

Sins and Addictions

When people come to you for confession who struggle with repetitive sins or addictions, how do you help them? They may come to you for confession and receive absolution, but they don't seem to make much progress. Why not? Is the sacrament ineffective? We know by faith, this isn't the problem, because the sacrament contains all the graces and power of Christ's redemptive sacrifice and resurrection.

So, what is the problem? St. Ignatius shows us by his life story: "Simply... confessing his sinful habits and addictions did not disarm them."

Like St. Ignatius, all those struggling to overcome addictions or habitual patterns of sin may be saints in the making. But have you noticed that they rarely find freedom until they do the things that Ignatius did?

- They must desire freedom and actively pursue it,
- They must acknowledge their powerlessness to heal themselves and seek God's grace.
- They must make a firm and enduring commitment to a process of healing and recovery.

65

As you discovered this week in your reading, these are the same basic steps that St. Ignatius followed in his conversion process. They are also the fundamental steps that form the basis for the 12-step programs that are most effective in treating addictions. In fact, from what I have learned, the founder of AA, "Bill," had a Jesuit spiritual director.[2]

Lasting Freedom

Did you notice in the readings this week that Ignatius' commitment to Christ and his conversion process was *decisive and enduring*? Though Ignatius could not save or heal himself, his perpetual willingness was essential.

And yet his commitment to Christ did not instantly free him. Instead it propelled him into his brokenness. Though Jesus could have instantly delivered Ignatius of his addictions and sins, he didn't. Why not? He was after something much more essential. He wanted to restore Ignatius' relationship with the Father, first and foremost, and then restore his innocence and bring him into true and lasting freedom. Isn't this what holiness and sainthood consist of?

And isn't this what we all long for--to be made pure and innocent, and to have the joy of intimacy with Christ and one another? Yet, like Ignatius, we too easily lose hope.

Heart Restrictions

Through this account of Ignatius journey, Fr. Watson shows us that the "visible sins, vices and addictions were only the tip of the iceberg." They were part of Ignatius' false self, covering his sin and weaknesses. Buried beneath the facades Ignatius had constructed, an ugly narcissistic pride and the painful effects of a broken heart remained hidden.

Ignatius is a mirror for us. We each have a false self, which covers the deeper inadequacies and sins. Underneath that, we each suffer from a broken heart. We all run from our pain and shame. We numb and constrict the pain by restricting our hearts.

Fr. Watson tells us that Ignatius restricted and numbed his heart through his "narcissistic pride." This barrier around his heart kept him (and others) from seeing or feeling his brokenness. It also kept him cut off from experiencing God's love and joy.

Every person you minister to in confession, in pastoral counseling, or in the other sacraments, is in the same boat. No matter how nice or ugly their clothes, cars, and homes, each has a broken heart which needs healing. Every person covers it with a false front.

The same is true for you and me. Are you aware of the restrictions in your own heart, which keep you from experiencing gratitude, joy, peace and love? I am gradually becoming more aware. I yearn to receive more of God's love and to give it freely to everyone I encounter. But my heart is restricted. I want to live every moment in peace and joy, but the restrictions of my heart make the "rivers of living water" seem like a trickle. Can you identify with this struggle?

This is why we all need to follow the path of conversion and healing that Ignatius walked. This is a journey into the Sacred Heart of Jesus, who leads us into the depths of our own hearts. It is in this way that you become Christ's presence to a broken and hurting world.

This is your fundamental calling as a priest of Jesus Christ, to lead people into this journey into the heart of Christ and their own hearts.

Journey into the Heart

This is the key point in this week's readings. We, like Ignatius, will continue to try to save ourselves, unless we face our brokenness and powerlessness. Only then will we see our need for a living Savior.

This journey is a journey into the depths of our hearts as Fr. Watson notes: "It was only at this depth that he discovered his authentic human nature and regained the creativity of child-like innocence." And so it is with us, brothers.

Advice from Your Brother Priests

Priests walking this journey with Ignatius were asked the question: "What is one thing you learned from Part Two of St. Ignatius' story that you could translate into some advice you would give to a fellow priest?" Here is what a few of your brother priests had to say:

✠ *Our spiritual journey is a journey in our heart, challenging us to be honest toward ourselves, to be aware of our wounds and to let the Holy Spirit start to heal us.*

✠ *The important thing I found is to remember that I cannot fix myself. I have to pray to the Lord for the grace to surrender my ego and will to the Lord in order that He can transform my heart and my life. I have to give my 'Yes' to let God do what he needs to do.*

✠ *The addictive/compulsive patterns in our lives are 'numbing agents' for pain in the heart. Entering into the brokenness with Christ leads to healing the pain.*

✠ *We can't just keep confessing the symptoms of our broken hearts. We all must journey deep into our own hearts and in the heart of Christ in order to receive the healing He has in store for us.*

Immaculate Heart of Mary pray for us so that our hearts may be fully aligned with the Sacred Heart of your son Jesus.

℘

NOTES

Week 4

FIRST

I will review my faithfulness to my daily fifteen-minute time(s) of contemplative rest and reflection. If my commitment has wavered, it may be helpful to write down the specific location and the time(s) of day. I ask God for the grace to recommit to this practice, which is the most important dimension of Sacred Story prayer. I will resist the temptation to judge myself harshly when I fail to live up to the ideal. Each day, I will do my best to be faithful to the commitment I have made.

SECOND

I will purchase a small spiral notebook (if I have not already done so) should I need more space for my journaling than is provided in the NOTES section at the end of each week. It will be needed later. However, you may find the Notes pages at the end of each week sufficient for your short daily journal entries.

THIRD

During my fifteen-minute quiet moments this week, I will read through part 3 of St. Ignatius's conversion story. It is spiritual reading. I will read and reread reflectively and take my time. I will invite God to be my companion as I read. I will ask the Lord to help me listen with my heart and be attentive to what moves me spiritually. I will use the process that works best for me. If I can better reflect on the material during my fifteen-minute prayer periods by reading it all first on Sunday, then I use that method. It may be helpful to highlight the sections of the readings that created hope and/or anxiety, and bring those sections to reflection and prayer.

I will not read ahead.
I will awaken to the present moment.
I will take each day and each exercise as it comes.
I cannot do Sacred Story better by going faster.

☙

Welcome to the fourth week of our pilgrimage together. The exercises for the fourth week move from the conversion story of St. Ignatius to your own story. You are invited to make a commitment to join with St. Ignatius, and all the holy women and men in the Church, to give your life to Christ for this great work of reconciliation.

Listen to the call and pay attention to whatever stirs in you, be it hope and peace or anxiety and fear. Doing this sharpens your spiritual radar for things that prompt your heart to say, "Pay attention!" Thank Christ in advance for the blessings and insights you will receive.

Part 3: The Call to Universal Reconciliation

As with Ignatius, God extends to us an invitation to awaken to the pattern of spiritual, emotional, and psychological dysfunction that has formed our anti-story. God invites us to awaken to our lives as sacred story and to produce fruit that endures to eternity. The awakening and growth will reveal where our freedom is compromised and how we close our hearts to our authentic human nature.

Christ compassionately shows us how our selfishness and pride have corrupted our creativity, robbing us of the joy of innocence. God's invitation is gentle. God's awakening is merciful. Rest assured that God's passion is to pursue us, rescue us, heal us, and bring us back to our original innocence. God's passion is personal. God's passion is love. God's passion is Christ Jesus.

God's intention is to gradually heal and transform our thoughts, words, and deeds. For every thought, word, and deed influences our history in the direction of an anti-story or a sacred story. Every thought, word, and deed—for good or ill—touches all people in my life, the entire world, and all of creation, shaping history's final chapter.

The effects of sin and narcissism—as well as the effects of virtue and selflessness—have individual, social, physical, spiritual, and ecological ramifications that reach to the ends of creation. For everything and everyone is one in Love—one in Christ Jesus—through whom and for whom everything was made (Rom 11:36).

Every thought, word, or deed, no matter how discreet, has positive or negative significance in the interconnected web of life that God has fashioned through Christ. It is Christ's being—His Sacred Story—that links each of our individual sacred stories. It is in Christ that the entire cosmos is joined together. God in Christ has made us responsible for and dependent upon each other and upon the earth that sustains us.

The Christ of the cosmos—through whom and for whom everything was made—became man and confronted, absorbed, and defused all the destructive force of evil's evolutionary anti-history running through human nature and the created cosmos. Christ reconciles in Himself everything in the heavens and on the earth to bring peace to all by the blood of His cross. His Sacred Story redeems and renews every chapter in our history, individual and collective.

Christ Jesus passionately awaits our participation to join His work of universal reconciliation. Our willingness to accept the path of conversion entails truthfully identifying our sins, dysfunction, and addictions. It entails experiencing and admitting our powerlessness to save ourselves. It requires the patience of a lifetime while Christ writes our sacred story.

My participation in Christ's work of reconciliation is the only worthy vocation and the only labor that produces fruit enduring to eternity. My accepting the invitation unlocks the very mystery of life.

When I accept the invitation, Christ promises to share His universal glory. Accepting the invitation to intentionally enter my sacred story has momentous consequences.

Now Is the Time to Wake from Sleep

Our time on this earth is so very brief. Since the time of Christ's birth, life, death, and resurrection, our story can only be measured and valued in light of His eternal mission of Reconciliation. Intentionally entering my sacred story will, over time, enable me to know God more intimately and serve God more generously. Like Ignatius, I am called to awaken from sleep—to awaken to wholeness and holiness. I was created and infused with the gift to awaken to a life that reverences the God who, in Christ and the Holy Spirit, is present in all creation: every person and everything.

Awakening to my sacred story, as Ignatius did, calls for courage, in the cleansing of the spirit and psyche that it initiates. The process requires discipline in the face of temptation and monotony. It requires consciously asking, even begging if necessary, for God's graces. It requires time and patience, deliberately choosing each day to be faithful to time and space for God. Awakening requires the patience of a lifetime. Embraced and trusted, the journey is rich with blessings beyond our wildest expectations. Encountering Christ daily in sacred story forever changes life, relationships, the earth, and eternity.

73

What is needed for the journey will be provided each day. In your journey through the memories and experiences past and present, you are promised the power and mercy of the Love that maintains and guides the entire cosmos. It is this Love that waits to transform your sins, addictions, angers, fears, grief, guilt and shame. It is this Love that restores your broken heart into a vessel of forgiveness, light, and peace. The more embedded and impenetrable the web of darkness, compulsion, sin, and addiction in your life, the more strategic and magnificent is God's grace in breaking its grip, for nothing is impossible with God (Lk 1:37).

On this journey, you will gain personal and real knowledge of sin and mercy, creation and eternity. You will come to know, experientially, our gracious God, present in Christ's Body in the Church, in the sacraments, in yourself, in others, and in all creation. Some of your insights will come in a flash; others will unfold over weeks, months, or years. From now on, the whole process of your life is about waking from sleep (Eph 5:14; Rom 13:11), bending to the real, to the authentic, to your true human nature, living and working for fruit that endures to eternity.

Your Sacred History

Your life (and each person's life) is inextricably interwoven with and integrated into Christ's Sacred Story in ways both mysterious and sublime. It is mysterious, because the ways of this world are not the ways of the Kingdom. What is deemed valuable and successful in this present age is in fact foolish and useless in the spiritual life. It is sublime, because the most private sufferings offered to God, the faintest cries for mercy and forgiveness, and the simplest acts of care, kindness, or generosity done for one's enemy, God's beloved poor, and His magnificent creation, are written in gold in the Book of the Lamb. These are the thoughts, words, and deeds that will endure to eternity.

There are no shortcuts to the story's unfolding. Conversion is lifelong but measurable when I intentionally, daily, consistently, and faithfully enter my sacred story. My story begins where Ignatius's began, in the grace of the call to conversion. My conversion will begin to take shape when I accept that call and follow the pattern of Ignatius's own conversion. I will discover things that disquiet, create shame and confusion, and unlock hidden angers, fears, and grief. I will encounter a heart broken, and innocence and paradise lost.

But most important, in all of this, I will be held, sheltered, and guided by the only thing necessary, Christ's love. I will be given strength to speak truth to power. I will be given grace to see and honestly name those sins, habits, and addictions that bring death—spiritual, physical, psychological—and not life. Then, as I surrender to my powerlessness in favor of God's power, the Divine Physician will rewrite my life as sacred story.

Surrendering control of my life to the care of the Divine Physician by admitting my powerlessness to save myself will enable me to be vulnerable, creative, innocent, and humble. Once my heart is open, the Spirit of God will continue to write my sacred story. My lifetime of patience will bear fruit that endures to eternity. My pilgrim journey, like Ignatius's, follows the proven and time-tested mystical path to wholeness and holiness. There are no shortcuts. Christ Jesus Himself has traveled the path. He will guarantee my journey's safe passage and carry my burdens, failures, shame, broken heart, and confusion.

I will hold in my heart the humble example of Jesus washing my feet. He endured humiliations, torture, and a disgraceful death so that I can find hope and healing for everything in my life that needs healing, forgiveness, and redemption. From the beginning of time His Sacred Story is mystically imprinted into the souls of His chosen people and the Church. Through the pattern of His Story, I, the Church, and all people can have their history rewritten as sacred story.

I will intentionally enter my life narrative for fifteen-minute intervals once or twice each day. My story, linked to Christ's Sacred Story and to all people and to all creation, runs from my birth in all my thoughts, words, and deeds to shape my destiny here and in the hereafter. Sacred Story prayer will help me attune to Creation, Presence, Memory, Mercy, and Eternity. When I encounter the fears, stresses, angers, temptations, failures, addictions, and sins in my day, I can briefly attune to Creation, Presence, Memory, Mercy, and Eternity and ask for the grace to see my whole story. By so doing, I invite the Divine Physician to heal me and awaken my heart to its true human nature.

Christ extends the invitation: His love, at the heart of the universe, awaits my response. I pray for the courage and generosity to enter with Christ into my sacred story.

CB

I am starting a Relationship that will carry me
for the rest of my life.
All relationships require time and patience.
I will strive for patience and ask for God's help
when I don't understand a lesson.
I will learn the fundamentals and open my heart to God.
I trust that God will lead me.

I believe that my sacred story will unfold in truth,
in powerlessness, and with my patience.
I believe that Jesus awaits me with
His grace, mercy, and forgiving love.

SO

Dr. Schuchts' Reflection ~ Week Four

St. Ignatius' Story and Your Sacred Story

During this fourth week, you are invited to reflect more deeply on how St. Ignatius' conversion story mirrors your own Sacred Story. In this fallen world, we all have an anti-story that attempts to thwart our sacred story. Our anti-story is formed in narcissistic pride, which is driven by our sin, identity wounds and addictions.

But we are not doomed by any part of our anti-story. We are continually given the grace, through the sacraments and prayer, to become whole and holy in union with Jesus. His grace, the power of the Holy Spirit flowing in us, is what transforms our anti-story into a Sacred Story.

The more we surrender to Christ, the more we are enabled by grace to discover our true identity and mission. This is how we discover our Sacred Story.

Having a clear sense of your identity and mission is extremely important in thriving as a person and a priest. I have met many priests who have a clear sense of their identity and mission when they are celebrating the sacraments. But many lose sight of their Sacred Story when they are relaxing at home or engaged in social situations.

This is why it is so critical to allow your entire person to be fully integrated into Christ. The conversion story of St. Ignatius allows us to see how this journey progresses from anti-story to Sacred Story.

Anti-Story—False Identity

Our anti-story is based in a false identity which keeps us under the influence of the "father of lies." As we live from this false self, we come to understand ourselves, like Ignatius did, through the lens of our failures, sins, addictions, and wounds. Or worse yet, we deceive ourselves through our narcissistic pride, while denying the damage caused to us and others through our sins, wounds, and addictions.

When we are operating from this false identity, it affects everything we think, say and do. Every thought, word, and action flows from this identity, and in turn forms it. When living from our anti-story, we end up perceiving God, others, and ourselves through a distorted filter. As a result, our desires also become disordered.

This is apparent in the life of St. Ignatius. His desires for love, connection, and joy were derailed early in his life. His childhood wounds, coming from the losses he experienced as young child, as well as the unhealthy environment he grew up in, left him seeking comfort and connection in disordered ways.

Ignatius ran from these devastating wounds and influences that were too much for him to face. As a result, he found solace in his sins and addictions. These disordered desires were kept in place and hidden by his "destructive and sinful narcissism."

Ignatius turned to those deadly sins and addictions for pseudo-salvation, rather than turning to God who alone eventually provided him with the genuine hope, power, love, and esteem he so desperately needed.

Wounds Underlying Sin & Addictions

Judging from the little I know about Ignatius life, I would make an educated guess that underlying his deadly sin of Anger (and corresponding idolatry of power) Ignatius had gaping wounds of fear and powerlessness.

Likewise, under his all-consuming Lust (and corresponding idolatry of sex, women, and beauty), I would imagine that Ignatius was medicating deep wounds of rejection and abandonment.

Finally, underlying Ignatius' fierce Pride (and corresponding self-adulation), I believe Ignatius had deep wounds of shame and hopelessness, which manifested in his narcissism, and came to the surface in his compulsive confessions and suicidal wishes.

These influences all contributed in defining Ignatius' anti-story. But thankfully, Jesus continued to pursue Ignatius and gave him the grace to convert his anti-story into a Sacred Story. He promises the same for each of us.

Your Sacred Story

In the end, Ignatius did not define himself by his sins, wounds and addictions. Rather he discovered his own Sacred Story hidden in the life of Christ. And he was only able to do this when he accepted the fact that he could not save himself from these challenges.

As I reflect on Ignatius' story as a mirror of my own and yours, I am reminded of the hope-inspiring words of St. John Paul II from World Youth Day, 2002: *"We are not the sum of our weaknesses and failures. We are the sum of the Father's love for us and the very real possibility of becoming the image of His Son."*

Reflect on that in your own life. **You are not the sum of your weaknesses and failures**. You are not defined by your sins and addictions. You are not destined to live from the identity formed in your wounds. The father of lies can always try to deceive you and keep you bound (and always will try to do this), but that is not **who** you are.

You are the sum of the Father's love! Like Ignatius, you are on the way to becoming a great saint. You have a very real possibility of becoming the image of the Son-Jesus.

You are already baptized, confirmed, and ordained into this identity of Jesus Christ. That is your true identity! As you continue your journey to wholeness and holiness during these forty weeks and beyond, you will see yourself becoming more and more like Christ in your thoughts, words and deeds.

As you face your powerlessness and call out to Jesus to save you, you will gradually discover your true identity in Christ. You are, by God's grace, living into your own unique Sacred Story.

Here are some words of encouragement from your brother priests who are journeying with you on your healing journey to discover your Sacred Story:

✠ *We have wounds and sins but we are not sin itself. Sin doesn't destroy our identity as beloved.*

✠ *The more we surrender to Christ, the more we are enabled by grace to discover our true identity and mission.*

✠ *It is liberating to come to the realization that I have been operating out of an "anti-story" most of my life. That where I belong is ultimately within Christ's Sacred Story makes complete sense, and that I must give myself to traveling there step by step.*

✠ *Sometimes due to identity lies we can feel more comfortable with our anti-story than our Sacred Story. Our Sacred Story is the only true accounting of our relationship with God.*

*Immaculate Heart of Mary pray for us so that our hearts
may be fully aligned with the Sacred Heart of your son Jesus.*

℘

NOTES

Week 5

FIRST

I select my fifteen-minute quiet time(s) for the week ahead. I visualize where I will go each day and at what time(s). I ask God for the grace to make those appointments throughout the week, in a technology-free zone.

SECOND

From this point forward, I will bring my notebook to my prayer sessions for the remainder of the forty weeks.

THIRD

My fifteen-minute prayer times this week consist of two exercises:

1. I ask for the inspiration to discover the name of God that speaks directly to my heart. It can take two or more days to discover the name that unlocks my heart to God's love and mercy. If God does not inspire me in the first two days, I will set this exercise aside and move to the second exercise. But I will continue to ask for the inspiration for the rest of the week to find the name. I will thank God in advance, because God will give me the inspiration I need to reveal the name that speaks to my heart. I will thank God in advance for this important grace.

2. For the remainder of the week, I listen to the three parts of Ignatius's conversion story in light of my own story. A simple spiritual reflection associated with this exercise is described below.

I will not read ahead.
I will awaken to the present moment.
I will take each day and each exercise as it comes.
I cannot do Sacred Story better by going faster.
I will ask God to help me.

☙

Take a moment to ask God for this grace: "Lord, open me to the knowledge of my own heart." The heart is where the important work of prayer takes place. The mind reveals facts. The heart reveals the truth of my being. The heart is how Scripture describes the most important aspects of the human condition. Here are a few examples:

✠ The heart reveals the state of corruption caused by sin (Gen 6:5; Jer 17:9–10; Mt 15:9).[3]

✠ The heart is where the process of conversion and forgiveness takes place (Ez 36:26; Mt 18:35; Rom 2:29).

✠ The heart is the point of convergence, where self-condemnation comes face-to-face with hope in God's power (1 Jn 3:19–20).

✠ The heart's purity enables one to see God (Mt 5:8).

✠ The heart is the locus of compassion (Lk 7:13).

✠ The heart is the custodian of memory and contemplation (Lk 1:29; 2:19, 51).

✠ The heart is the vessel holding the secrets that illuminate the true meaning of life (Mt 6:21; Lk 24:32; Ps 85:9).

✠ The heart is defined as the center of human consciousness and action, wherein God discerns the rightness or wrongness of my thoughts, words, and deeds. The heart is the center from which each person will stand before God and render the ultimate account of their thoughts, words, and deeds (Heb 4:12–13).

✠ The heart perceives love as the ultimate end, gift, and purpose of being (1 Cor 13).

✠ The testimony of Christ in Scripture speaks to the heart's desire for innocence, based on the weariness of life, and the burdens it carries, resulting from corruption (Mt 11:28–30.).

✠ Christ also promises to respond to the heart searching for Him and gives the conviction that He can be found by those who seek Him (Lk 11:9–11).

Seek knowledge of the heart, and ask God for the grace to open a pathway to your heart. Seek also knowledge of God's heart, present in Christ's Sacred Heart. This grace will help to unite your heart to the heart of Christ. "Lord, open me to the knowledge of my own heart."

For the first two days of fifteen-minute prayer periods this week:

Once you are settled in your place of prayer, ask for God's inspiration for this time. Then ask, in words from your heart, to be inspired to discover or remember the most intimate and/or meaningful name for God the Father, Son, and Spirit that you have used in prayer.

The name will resonate deeply in your heart and reflect God's relationship to you and your personal relationship with God. The following may be helpful:

Father, Loving Father, Almighty Father, Our Father, Father God, Loving Creator, Creator God, God of Love, My God, Holy God, Father of the Poor, God of All Mercy, God of All Compassion, Father of Jesus, Lord

Jesus Christ, Lord Jesus, Christ Jesus, Dear Jesus, Adorable Jesus, Adorable Christ, Good Jesus, Jesus, Merciful Savior, Jesus My Savior, Son of God, Dearest Lord, My Lord, My Lord and My God, Sacred Heart of Jesus, Lamb of God, Good Shepherd, Crucified Savior, Holy Spirit, Spirit of Jesus, Spirit of the Lord, Loving Spirit, Holy Spirit of God, Love of God, Divine Spirit, Creator Spirit, Creator God

Ask for the grace to discover the name for God that touches your heart most intimately. You will know the right name, because it has the power to unlock your trust and your love and to stir your affections.

Write the name for God in your notebook when you discover it. From this point forward, use this name when you address God. God delights when you speak directly from your heart.[4]

For the remainder of the fifteen-minute prayer periods this week:

Review Ignatius's story and your own. Use this question as the focus for the exercise: "Like Ignatius, have I discovered the one area of my life that convinces me, beyond any doubt, that I cannot save myself and must rely on God to save me?"

Recall parts 1 and 2 of St. Ignatius's narrative. In your prayer times, review the sections of his story that resonate with your own story. In these prayer periods, recall those parts of his story that moved your heart in one of two ways:

1. "What spontaneously evoked anxiety in me as I listened to Ignatius's story?" I will reflect on why this anxiety was provoked. In my notebook, I will record what evoked my anxiety and why.

2. "As I listened to Ignatius's conversion story, what inspired or gave me hope about my life?" I will reflect on why I was inspired or hopeful. In my notebook, I will record what inspired me and why.

For the last fifteen-minute prayer period at week's end:

Using my notebook jottings, I will sift through the entries and ask for the grace to identify the one issue or idea that caused me the most anxiety. I will record this in my notebook. Then I will write down why I felt the anxiety. I may not know why something causes anxiety, so if it is not clear yet, I will not be anxious about that. Instead, I will invite God into this unknown area: "Lord, why did this make me anxious?"

In my notebook I will also record what I discovered that offered me the most hope or inspiration and why. If I don't know, I will invite God to reveal this to me: "Lord, why did this cause me to have hope?"

I will be brief and specific in my notebook entries. My reflection plus my writing exercises ought not to extend beyond the allotted time of fifteen-minutes that encompasses my prayer period.[5]

❧

I am starting a Relationship that will carry me
for the rest of my life.

All relationships require time and patience.
I will strive for patience and ask for God's help
when I don't understand a lesson.

I will learn the fundamentals and open my heart to God.

I trust that God will lead me.
I believe that my sacred story will unfold in truth,
in powerlessness, and with my patience.

I believe that Jesus awaits me with His grace, mercy, and forgiving
love.

❧

Dr. Schuchts' Reflection ~ Week Five

Encountering God in our Hearts

During this Fifth week, we began by looking at the importance of our hearts, as it is revealed in Scripture. Remember, our spiritual heart is the faculty God gave us to encounter Him and to experience his love (CCC 2563). A pure and steadfast heart can apprehend God.

This is why we started the week asking God to open a pathway to our heart. Then we prayed for "the inspiration to discover the name of God that speaks directly to my heart."

The particular name which God revealed to you highlights a unique aspect of His love for you. The Catechism informs us that "when God gives us his name, he is handing himself over to us" (CCC 203).

Pause a moment to let that sink in. The Father Almighty, who created all things seen and unseen, desires to give himself to you, in a very personal way. He is entrusting himself to you through the name He revealed to you.

As you speak His name, ask Him what he desires for you by giving you this particular name. How does this name affirm your true identity and help define your Sacred Story?

As you reflect on this personal name of God, ponder some of the ways he has revealed himself to you over the years in keeping with this name. How have these encounters shaped your understanding of God along with how you see yourself and others?

One of your brother priests, in journeying through this fifth week, made the following observation:

✠ *"The way I experience God, the way He reveals Himself to me and interacts with me, seems to be very connected to how I understand my vocation and call to minister to others. That is to say, in my life God has zealously pursued me and I am beginning to discover in myself zeal to pursue those who do not know Him."*

I find it interesting that science is now discovering that our physical hearts have the capacity to know, i.e. we have receptors in our hearts. Stress (anxiety) closes off these receptors, whereas love and hope allow our hearts to become more open.

That is one of the reasons we are paying attention to anxieties and hopes this week. To encounter God, our hearts need to be receptive to Him.

During the second part of the week, you were instructed to monitor your daily anxieties as well as your inspirations and hopes.

Hopes and Inspirations are beautiful experiences of consolation in God's love. We leave encouraged and filled with the Spirit and able to trust God more.

Anxieties on the other hand, reveal areas of your life where you are not yet secure in God's love. In paying closer attention to the sources of these anxieties you can learn where you are not yet abiding in trust with Him. These sources of anxiety are warning signals showing you where and how you feel threatened. Listen to them!

When we are anxious we tend to do one of two things- we either turn towards God in surrender to receive greater trust and security from Him, which in turn brings inspiration and hope. Or we turn inward and increase our self-reliance and narcissistic pride. This second response may give us temporary relief, but in the long run it only further increases our anxiety.

In my life, I have gone through seasons where I have become aware of heightened anxiety. Often these seasons turn into times of great spiritual growth. One of those seasons occurred when I was in my early thirties.

Though it was highly challenging at the time, I can look back now and realize that this period of heightened anxiety marked the beginning of a profound conversion experience and opened me up to receive a life-changing encounter with God where I experienced much inspiration that resulted in lasting hope.

But I must admit at the time it wasn't much fun and I didn't see much hope. Rather, I felt frighteningly out of control and found it hard to connect with God. In fact, this time period began with panic attacks, which terrified me and left me feeling very alone.

I noticed a few things during that season of my life which have become life lessons. I discovered that my anxiety was an important signal about areas of my life which were not yet in alignment with God. It signaled some deep areas of wounding, much like Ignatius discovered in his life.

When I tried to control or medicate my anxiety (with my sugar addiction, intellectualizing or sports) it only got worse in the long term. But when I surrendered my anxiety to God, sooner or later, it dissipated.

In the long run, this time of heightened anxiety led me right into the arms of God. This week a few of your brother priests shared similar experiences:

✠ *"While away from the church (20 years), and after a weekend of beating myself up over an important work-related event that had gone awry, I spontaneously knelt and prayed before going to bed, and once in bed, realized a divine peace flooding my entire body, and the assurance of 'everything will be okay.'"*

✠ *"I was on a 30-day silent retreat and during the retreat I had an experience of Jesus and Mary embracing me on the day my dad left home after my parent's divorce. The Lord showed me he was right there with me never taking his loving gaze off of me. I still live in that gaze."*

✠ *I realized that my anxieties have caused me to become self-reliant. I need to turn back to the Lord and surrender my life to Him instead of trying to take everything on by myself.*

✠ I saw how anxieties can be revealing God's loving invitation to open my heart to Him. How losing control on my life gives me peace and trust.

Immaculate Heart of Mary pray for us so that our hearts may be fully aligned with the Sacred Heart of your son Jesus.

≪≫

NOTES

Week 6

FIRST

I will plan my fifteen-minute quiet time(s) for the week ahead. I will visualize where I will go each day and at what time(s). I will ask God for the grace to help me keep those appointments throughout the week. I will seek a technology-free zone—a place apart.

SECOND

I will have my notebook at hand for each prayer period.

THIRD

The prayer exercise for this week is composed of two parts. I will take half of the week's prayer periods for the first part and the other half of my prayer periods for the second part:

Once settled in prayer, I will ask God to reveal to me the most important persons, life events, and/or issues that generate gratitude, hope, and love in me.

Then I will ask God to reveal to me the most important persons, life events, and/or issues that evoke anger, fear, or grief in me.

I will not read ahead.

I will awaken to the present moment.
I will take each day and each exercise as it comes.
I cannot do Sacred Story better by going faster.
I will ask God to help me.

This week, I will say this affirmation aloud once daily:
I ask God to reveal to me the most important people,
life events, and/or issues in my story up to this point.

༄

Each of us has persons, issues, and life events that shape our life story, our history. We are conscious of some of these pieces, while others are buried deep in our memory. We seek grace to understand those things that, in negative and positive ways, most strongly shape our thoughts, actions, feelings, and beliefs linked to God, the world, and ourselves. These persons, life events, and issues are often linked to the spiritual plotlines in our life story, leading toward or away from God.

This week, we seek God's grace to awaken to our affective memories. That is, we want to recall persons, life events, and issues and feel the emotional weight—the heart value—they have in our history. Because these significant elements often evade our conscious awareness, we need to rely on grace to reveal them.

Naturally, I seek insight into the closest, most intimate circle of people and events in my life story—my parents, family, friends, and important events. I will be attentive to the feeling these memories evoke.

For one life event, I might feel fear (something that has the power to generate the anxiety I know as fear). For another life event, my predominant feeling might be anger (something that hurt me or a loved one). For one person, I might feel mostly love (someone who has cared deeply for me). For another person, I might feel anger (someone who hurt me in some way). For one issue, my predominant feeling might be grief (the loss of a loved one, or a missed opportunity that grieves my heart). For another issue, my experience might be gratitude or hope (an issue that has positively transformed my life for the better).

Pray that God enlighten your mind and heart to know each person, issue, or life event and the single predominant feeling (fear, anger, or grief; gratitude, hope, or love) each inspires.

For your prayer periods this week, sit apart in your quiet place. Find a comfortable position that permits you to be alert. Breathe deeply for a few minutes, mindful that God's love sustains your very life. Next, using the personal name for God you identified last week, ask God to enlighten your memory and imagination so that the most significant people, issues, and life events come into your mind and heart.

As you become aware of each, pause briefly to write down the name of the person or the issue or life event that comes to memory. Next to each of these, write a single word for the most predominant feeling that arises in your heart. A word of caution here: do not succumb to the temptation to analyze or judge the feelings as they arise.

For the first half of the week, use the first chart to ask God to inspire you to remember the elements (person, issue, or life event) that generate gratitude, hope, or love. Pray that those elements most important to your history come into your mind and heart.

For the second half of the week, use the next chart to ask God to inspire you to remember the people, issues, or life events that generate fear, anger, or grief. Pray that those elements most important to your history come into your mind and heart.

TEN PARTS OF MY LIFE HISTORY THAT GENERATE
GRATITUDE, HOPE, OR LOVE

Persons / Life Events / Issues	*Gratitude / Hope / Love*
1.	1.
2.	2.
3.	3.
4.	4.
5.	5.
6.	6.
7.	7.
8.	8.
9.	9.
10.	10.

TEN PARTS OF MY LIFE HISTORY THAT GENERATE
FEAR, ANGER, OR GRIEF

Persons / Life Events / Issues	*Fear / Anger / Grief*
1.	1.
2.	2.
3.	3.
4.	4.
5.	5.
6.	6.
7.	7.
8.	8.
9.	9.
10.	10.

Cʒ

I am starting a Relationship that will carry me
for the rest of my life.

All relationships require time and patience.
I will strive for patience and ask for God's help
when I don't understand a lesson.

I will learn the fundamentals and open my heart to God.

I trust that God will lead me.

I believe that my sacred story will unfold in truth,
in powerlessness, and with my patience.

I believe that Jesus awaits me with His grace,
mercy, and forgiving love.

ʂɔ

Dr. Schuchts' Reflection ~ Week Six

Affective Memories

In this Sixth Week, you have been asking God for the grace to awaken *affective memories* by revealing to you the people, events, and issues that have had a significant impact throughout your life.

These *affective memories* have profoundly shaped your life-both positively and negatively. They form key elements of your Sacred Story, as well as defining aspects of your anti-story.

Whether you realize it or not, these experiences, both past and present, profoundly influence your ongoing affections and attitudes towards God and others. They form the core of your identity and self-awareness, influencing how you view yourself and how you have come to understand the world around you.

Are you aware of how these memories shape your perceptions of life and influence the movements of your heart as you make your way through your daily activities?

Science has validated that every experience beginning in the womb is recorded in our brains and remains part of our memory and identity. Every cell of our body contains the effects of these memories- both positive and negative. Whether we are conscious of them or not, these affective memories play a key role in our daily thoughts, emotions, and reactions to ongoing circumstances.

During the first part of the week you identified those people, events, and issues that generate gratitude, hope, and love. Many of these are the people who have loved you and the impactful events that shaped your Sacred Story in a positive way.

Whether or not you were aware of God's presence in the people and circumstances you identified this past week, they were conduits of God's blessings throughout your life.

God in himself is "Eternal Blessedness" (CCC, 1). All that He does in our lives, directly and through others, expresses His personal love for us.

Those people, events, and issues that you identified later in the week which elicited fear, anger, or grief may be foundational elements of your anti-story. These people, events and issues are an inevitable result of living in a broken world. Eventually, all of our experiences can become a source of gratitude and hope, as we see God's hand of love through every circumstance.

This foundation of trust is the ultimate basis of our hope and gratitude. As your brother priests wisely observe, God transforms the worst parts of our anti-story into the most beautiful aspects of our Sacred Story.

He converts our mourning into joy, inspires mercy and justice in the areas in which we experience anger, and works through our fear to bring us into greater security and trust. Though we often blame God for the difficulties in our life, He is rarely the cause of those events which bring fear, anger, or grief. God is good and full of love. He is the giver of every good gift (Ja. 1:18).

Jesus assures us that he came to bring abundant life, and it is the "thief" who comes to "steal, kill and destroy." (Jn. 10:10). Satan steals our joy and plants seeds of destruction in our minds and hearts. St. Ignatius in his Spiritual Exercises warns us that we are most vulnerable to the enemy of human nature's influence in areas of our weaknesses and wounds.[6]

This is why we need to pay attention to our affective memories, both positive and negative. With the good memories we respond with gratitude, love and hope.

With the Holy Spirit's aid, we need to bring all of our "negative" affective memories into the light of Christ's redemption. The Father promises to work all these things together for our good and his glory. Even the memories of our anti-story become a vital part of our Sacred Story.

Your brother priests summarize this week's exercises beautifully:

✠ *God never leaves us and is able to bless every personal encounter, issue, struggle, and event that we live through. He is constantly at work in our lives if we have the eyes to see it and will help us through any situation to become the saint He wants us to become. He is near us, involved in our lives, closer than we can imagine.*

✠ *It makes sense that all of our experiences and memories contribute to who we are. It also makes sense that we do not know the true effect that we have upon others.*

✠ *My healed wounds, united with Christ's, can become a fountain of love for all I encounter. My past misery is the greatest gift I have to offer as a priest and father. My empathy, compassion, and love for the people of God flow from my wounded life. Praised be Jesus Christ!*

✠ *Eventually, all of our experiences can become a source of gratitude and hope, as we see God's hand of love through every circumstance.*

Immaculate Heart of Mary pray for us so that our hearts may be fully aligned with the Sacred Heart of your son Jesus.

℘

NOTES

Week 7

FIRST

I will review my fifteen-minute quiet time(s) for the week ahead and visualize where I will go each day and at what time(s). I will ask God for the grace to keep those times sacred. I will have my notebook at hand for each prayer period. I will always use my personal name for God.

SECOND

During my fifteen-minute quiet prayer this seventh week, there are two prayer exercises. I will take the first half of the week's prayer periods for the first exercise and the second half of my prayer periods for the second exercise.

THIRD

1. I will ask God for the grace to identify how the Ten Commandments fit into my life as a gift to bring awareness, healing, balance, and God's peace.
2. I will ask God for the grace to identify the deepest hope of my heart for my life and my future.

I will not read ahead.
I will awaken to the present moment.
I will take each day and each exercise as it comes.
I cannot do Sacred Story better by going faster.

I will ask God to help me.

This week, I will say this affirmation aloud once daily:
The Ten Commandments are a profound gift from God
to the chosen people and to all humankind.

ೞ

Read 1 and 2 before starting your prayer sessions this week:

1. For the first half of the week:
Use the Decalogue Examination of Conscience to better understand your life story and the gift of healing and balance that God desires for you. Pray that your imagination be graced so that the most important issues in the Commandments, those that illuminate your history (your story), will come into your mind and heart. Pray to "see" what you have never seen before. Pray to see your life as God sees your life.

The Commandments were given to the Chosen People in a Covenant that was sealed with a blood sacrifice. The Church reflects that the power of the animal sacrifice sealing the Covenant receives its power from Christ's blood, which it foreshadows. The Commandments, as gift, are a foundation for God's work to repair our broken human nature, to forgive us, and to reopen the way to eternity: the work of Christ's death and resurrection. It is no wonder then that laws enshrining the Commandments' truths have transformed stories of violence and injustice to stories of civility and justice for countless millions of people in the last three millennia.

For this exercise, we are reflecting on the Commandments to enhance our understanding of their richness and wisdom. The exercise will help to clarify how each Decree carries its own responsibilities and boundaries. These Decrees revealed by God remind us of the truth about God, humanity, and oneself. They are a gift to guide our way home so our thoughts, words and deeds bring life, not death.

Before concluding your prayer period, use your notebook to record where in your life you have missed the mark in living the decree you reflected on. Be specific, honest, and courageous. Ask for the grace of integrity and openness to embrace the truth of your own experience.

This may be a helpful format to follow as you reflect on each decree: Identify the decree (and the sub-themes in the decree) as mild, moderate, or strong, depending on the challenge this specific decree presents to you. For example, you may write "6th—moderate, especially regarding [issue]" or "4th—mild regarding [person]" or "7th/10th—strong regarding [event]." Use codes if you prefer to safeguard confidentiality and augment honesty.

Note: The purpose of this exercise is to simply identify your challenges with the Commandments. With Christ by your side, watch with curiosity and detachment, without self-blame. God sees beyond any patterns of sin and failure you have, or think you have. God knows you for whom you are. God loves you. God is the Divine Physician who desires to help you honestly see your life as it is so He can bring forgiveness, healing, freedom and peace.

2. For the second half of the week:
Pray for the grace to remember the books, stories, songs, events, movies, and art that have the power to bring you to tears. The shortest phrase in Scripture is "Jesus wept" (Jan 11:35). Pray to remember the turn of phrase, the lyric, the dialogue, the word spoken to you, the melody, and the image that has touched your heart so profoundly that your only response is to weep. What causes us to weep holds significance in our history and informs our story. Pray to remember and feel what moves you to tears.

The Gospels record that Jesus wept twice. He wept over Jerusalem, for failing to recognize that the time of its deliverance was at hand (Lk 19: 41–44). And He wept over the death of His good friend Lazarus: "See how he loved him," the people said (Jn 11:33–6). Both instances reveal Jesus's deep longing for humanity's reconciliation and peace. It is Christ's desire to bring freedom from death's grip, that death which resulted from humanity's disobedience. Jesus's weeping expresses the deepest longings of His heart. His tears reveal His mission in life, a mission He received from the Father, for those He loves.

Tears reveal the deepest longings of our hearts, too. They are a window to the heart and soul. Ask God for the grace to remember and understand what brings you to tears, what breaks your heart or expresses your heart's longings for healing and peace.

Use your fifteen-minute prayers in the second half of the week to recall what causes you to weep, that is, what brings you to tears and expresses the deepest longings of your heart. Do not spend more than fifteen minutes for each of your prayer periods. For your prayer, sit apart in a quiet place. Find a comfortable position that permits you to be alert. Breathe deeply for a few minutes, mindful that God's love sustains your very life.

Next, using the personal name for God you identified, ask God to enlighten your memory and imagination so that you can remember and understand what brings you to tears, and why. How is your life mission— your story—revealed in your tears? What stories, movies, books, songs move you to tears, and what can God help you understand about your life from them?

Before your prayer period ends, write down what caused your tears and why it caused your tears (if it is clear). Reflect further on what this might possibly reveal to you about your story. Do your tears reveal your deepest longings and God's desire to bring you hope and peace?

THE DECALOGUE EXAMINATION OF CONSCIENCE[7]

First Decree: I am the Lord your God, you shall have no strange gods before me.

Is God the center of my life? Have I displaced God with my career, work, concern for wealth and pleasure? Does the worship and honor of God take shape in my weekly religious practices? Do I pray often? Do I turn to God for forgiveness often? Have I resorted to relying on superstition, the occult, or astrology in place of asking for God's assistance?

Second Decree: You shall not take the name of the Lord your God in vain.

Do I casually take God's name in vain? Do I have a habit of swearing in jest or in anger? Do I use God's name to damn other people? Do I nurse hatred of God in my heart? Do I harbor anger toward God for the difficult things in my life or in the world? Do I reverence God in my heart?

Third Decree: Remember to keep holy the Sabbath day.

Do I make every effort to prepare myself for the Sunday liturgy? Do I make every effort to attend the Sunday liturgy? Do I allow social or sporting events to displace or limit my attendance at the Sunday liturgy? Do I limit unnecessary servile work on Sunday? Is Sunday a true day of spiritual rest and refreshment?

Fourth Decree: Honor your Father and Mother.

Do I give proper reverence to my mom and dad for the gift of life? Do I thank them? Do I spend time with them? Do I strive to forgive the shortcomings of my parents? Do I hold anger or grudges against them in my heart? Do I try to respond to them with love and charity? Do I attend to them in their sufferings and weaknesses? Am I patient with their infirmity as they age?

Fifth Decree: You shall not kill.

Have I ever killed someone or participated in actions that have led to other's death? Do I strive to overcome the prejudices I have against individuals or groups? Do I resist acting on my prejudices so as not to harm persons with my words or deeds? Do I act with cruelty toward others? Do I risk my life or the lives of others by using illegal drugs? Do I risk my life or the lives of others by driving recklessly or intoxicated? Do I strive in words and deeds to promote the value of life from conception to natural death? Have I ever helped someone terminate a pregnancy or end his/her own life? Do I strive to do everything I can to uphold the value of each person? Do I harbor satisfaction in my heart at the death of those people whom I consider evil? Do I vote for politicians/civil servants because of their positions to protect and promote abortion, euthanasia, capital punishment or preemptive war? Do I mourn the loss of all human life, no matter the cause of death?

Sixth Decree: You shall not commit adultery.
Ninth Decree: You shall not covet your neighbor's spouse.

Do I protect my covenant relationship and uphold its sacredness? Do I strive daily to support my spouse? Do I turn to other persons for emotional support to make my spouse envious? Do I denigrate my spouse by comparing her/him to others? Do I speak harshly about my spouse behind his/her back to gain the affections of others? Do I uphold the sacredness of my covenant commitment by never seeking the sexual attention of those to whom I may be attracted? Do I uphold my covenant by never engaging in any sexual activity with someone other than my spouse? Do I use pornography or masturbation to arouse my sexual appetites? Do I denigrate the spiritual integrity of persons by focusing on their physical beauty or appearance? Do I protect my covenant relationship by not purposely fantasizing about sexual relations with someone other than my spouse? Do I hold sacred the gift of sexuality for marriage? Do I strive to cultivate purity of heart as a sign of God's own single-heartedness? Do I reverence sexual intercourse first and foremost as the gift most akin to God's creative energies, a gift of love to create a human life destined for an eternity with God? Do I casually inhibit God's presence in this divine gift with drugs or medical procedures when there is no legitimate reason?

Seventh Decree: You shall not steal.
Tenth Decree: You shall not covet your neighbor's goods.

Do I cheat on papers and exams to steal a better grade? Do I take things that do not belong to me? Do I keep things I have borrowed? Am I honest in my investments, taxes, and all my financial dealings? Do I use legal loopholes in tax laws or business practices to harvest financial rewards that ultimately hurt the less fortunate? Am I honest and truthful in my business dealings, even if it means I may lose profits or customers? Do I vandalize or harm property or goods that do not belong to me? Do I envy those who have more than I do? Do I let concern for wealth and comfort take center place in my life? Do I live lavishly because I have the resources to do so? Do I spend money on luxury goods I do not need? Do I live with envy of those who have more than I do? Do I respect the limited resources of the earth as a divine inheritance to benefit all people? Do I give a percentage of my earned income to the poor? Do I strive to live so as to minimize waste and protect the environment? Do I examine my investment patterns to discern if companies I own, or in which I have stock, are treating their employees justly and are protecting the environment in their practices? Do I ever put the drive for profits ahead of the welfare of persons or the environment?

Eighth Decree: You shall not bear false witness against your neighbor.

Do I uphold the honor of other people's reputations? Do I avoid spreading gossip and avoid seeking gossip from others? Do I share information about people with third parties, even if it is true, when that information threatens the person's reputation? Do I avoid spreading lies or rumors about other people? Do I challenge people who gossip and spread damaging information about others? Do I avoid and denounce TV, radio, magazines, and newspapers that employ the tactics of personality destruction and malicious gossip to sell news and generate profits? Do I tell others what they ought to do instead of getting my own house in order?

CB

I am starting a Relationship that will carry me
for the rest of my life.

All relationships require time and patience.
I will strive for patience and ask for God's help
when I don't understand a lesson.

I will learn the fundamentals and open my heart to God.

I trust that God will lead me.

I believe that my sacred story will unfold in truth,
in powerlessness, and with my patience.

I believe that Jesus awaits me with
His grace, mercy, and forgiving love.

ᘓ

The Ten Commandments and Our Deepest Desires

At first glance, the two exercises for this week seem to be on opposite ends of the spectrum. On one side, we have the Ten Commandments, which highlight God's order and justice. These are the boundaries which keep us on the path of healing.

On the other, we are encouraged to become more aware of the deepest desires of our hearts, which are at times revealed by the books, movies, television shows etc. which bring us to tears.

The effect of looking at these together is very powerful. One is Law, the other is Grace. One brings up our fears and shame. The other brings up our deepest longings for love and fulfillment. Yet, as Fr. Bill points out--both are for our healing and holiness. They are directed to the same end-union with God.

Let me offer some illustrations from my own experience of looking at these exercises this week. I noticed as I was observing my reactions to the Ten Commandments, the Fifth Commandment caught my attention.

As I paid attention to the movement of grace, I began to reflect on some of the ways that I "kill" my own heart as well as the hearts of those I interact with daily. This happens when I hold onto resentments. (In the Sermon on the Mount Jesus identified resentment as a violation of the Fifth Commandment).

Later in the week, I noticed that I was brought to tears watching a television show-*Undercover Boss*. If you're not familiar with this reality show, the general plot is usually the same. The president or CEO of the company goes undercover to experience the work conditions of the people that work for the company.

At the end of every show, the boss (who is now revealed to his employees) rewards those who have done good work, and generously responds to their unique personal needs, which he discovered while he was undercover.

This is the point in the show where I usually tear up. Watching the boss's kindness touches me deeply. Watching the employees cry, out of their gratitude, touches something deep in my own heart.

As the exercises this week point out, there is something in this show that reveals the deepest desires of my heart. I want to be the recipient of this unexpected grace. And my heart longs to give this unexpected kindness to others.

It took me awhile, but I eventually realized that this merciful kindness and generosity is the flip side to the Fifth and Tenth Commandments, which set boundaries on our tendency to be unkind to one another.

Perhaps this is why Jesus takes the commandments one step further and commands us to love our enemies and extend extra kindness to those who treat us spitefully. Kindness and generosity are both expressions of God's love.

Is there anything in all this that calls to your deepest desire as a person and priest of Jesus Christ? Can you imagine if it were possible for you to go undercover into the homes and lives of your parishioners?

Picture yourself thanking them for living the Gospel and then finding ways to meet their deepest unmet needs. Wouldn't that bring you both to tears, and fulfill the desires of your fatherly heart?

I believe this is what Jesus desires for each one of us. At the end of our life, we are not going to be judged solely on our failures-how we violated our true nature (as reflected in the Ten Commandments). We will also be rewarded for the good we have done-the ways we went out of our way to be generous and kind to others.

One of the movies that touched me deeply and brought me to tears is called "Mr. Holland's Opus." It is a story of a music teacher and father of a disabled child, who laid down his career ambitions for his son and students. (He wanted to write an Opus).

Day after day, his own dream is delayed as he serves his family and students. He goes through his entire career without ever writing his musical masterpiece. But in the process, he discovers that God has written a greater masterpiece through his many sacrifices.

In the final scene he finally sees the fruit of the little ways he chose love over self. All the people he touched throughout his life are there-and he is overwhelmed to see the impact. This is his true Opus.

When I saw that movie I cried deeply, getting a glimpse of the rewards waiting for us in heaven, seeing all the people our lives have touched.

As a priest of Christ and father of many, this is your life. This is what it will be like when you see all the people you have touched deeply by your sacrifices. You are the "undercover" Jesus who expresses God's kindness and generosity to so many.

As an image of the Father, you teach them the Commandments to keep them directed towards God's holy order. You also inspire them to attend to the deepest desires of their own hearts, so that they yearn for Holy Communion, which is only fully realized in the Beatific Vision.

The Commandments are boundaries which are intended keep us on the right path. The desires of our hearts keep us centered on that target for which we aim all of our lives.

These are a few observations from your brother priests on their reflections from week 7:

✠ *The 10 Commandments are not limits on our freedom or joy. They are rather guides that protect us from unnecessary pain, suffering, and self-destructive behavior.*

✠ The commandments from God are ways to love Him and protect our love and our feeling loved

✠ Reflecting on our tears (or lack of tears) makes us open to the graces of God. Tears soften our heart, make us vulnerable and receptive.

✠ I recognize that my tears are a path to healing and freedom. I don't mind being vulnerable because that is a sign of the spiritual poverty I need to be an effective minister.

Immaculate Heart of Mary pray for us so that our hearts may be fully aligned with the Sacred Heart of your son Jesus.

℘

NOTES

Week 8

FIRST

I will select my fifteen-minute quiet time(s) for the week ahead and visualize where I will go each day and at what time(s). I will ask God for the grace to keep those times sacred throughout the week, in a technology-free zone. I will always use my personal name for God.

SECOND

I will have my notebook on hand for each prayer period.

THIRD

My fifteen-minute quiet prayer this week consists of two prayer exercises. I will take the first half of the week's prayer periods for the first exercise and the second half for the second exercise. If I find it more beneficial, I can combine the two with the alternate exercise.

First Spiritual Exercise: I will ask God for the grace to become aware of any habitual vices that obstruct my quest for holiness and interfere with the freedom God desires for me.

Second Spiritual Exercise: I will ask God for the grace to become aware of any addictions I possess that are eroding my quest for holiness and the freedom God desires for me.

Alternate Spiritual Exercise: I will ask God for the grace to see the connections between any habitual vices that erode my freedom and their link with addictive behaviors in my life story.

I will awaken to the present moment.
I will take each day and each exercise as it comes.
I cannot do Sacred Story better by going faster.
I will ask God to help me.
I will awaken to my spiritual nature and to the inspirations that inspire faith, hope, and love.
I will awaken to the inspirations that inspire cynicism, impatience, and lusts. I will wake up!

This week, I will say this affirmation aloud once daily:
I believe that understanding the source of my vices and addictions can lead to greater joy, authenticity, and holiness.

☙

Read 1, 2, and 3 before starting any prayer sessions this week:

The two powerful spiritual diagnostics for this week's lesson offer you the potential for great enlightenment. Vices and addictions reveal valuable information about our life stories. If we seek medical advice for pain, the doctor asks us where we hurt. Christ, the Divine Physician, sees our vices and addictions as manifestations of where we are hurting and our unsuccessful attempts to anesthetize our hurt. The Gospel calls them "sinful," because they manifest habits that erode our true human nature and our faith, hope, and love. The doctor calls them destructive, because they ruin our lives and relationships.

If you can honestly identify addictions and vices in your life story, you are on a path to freedom. If you prayed to Christ, the Divine Physician, to wake up to the connections between them in your life story, you should rejoice. Because your healing, leading to interior freedom, can now begin. Christ came to save sinners, not the righteous, and Sacred Story is about allowing Christ to help us identify where we need His healing graces. This is the great gift He wants to give to us. Be not afraid. Christ knows you are working with him to wake up.

Pray with words from your heart that will enable you to see what you have not seen before and to see connections between aspects of your life story. A word of caution: resist the temptation to be judgmental, anxiously plan corrective therapies, or get lost in fear. If you find yourself slipping into any of these, gently stop the exercise, and refocus your heart. These two exercises, like all the others, are to be approached with a compassionate, honest eye. It may be helpful to recall that you are reflecting on these components of your life narrative with the Divine Physician by your side. The goal is simply to wake up! Watch and pray!

1.For the first half of the week:
Pay attention to the vices (pride, gluttony, lust, sloth, envy, avarice, anger). They are sometimes called capital sins (from caput, the Latin word for head) because they are root habits or vices that lead to many other problems. All of us are subject to vices, which have the ability to hook us mildly, moderately, or strongly.

Simply identify your capital sins/vices. Ask Christ, the Divine Physician, to help you understand their source and context in your life history. Ask for the grace of deeper understanding, and then with Christ, observe your life with compassionate curiosity, and with objectivity. God sees beyond any vices you have, or think you have. God knows you for whom you are and loves you. Jesus, the Divine Physician, watches compassionately and carries the burden for all your vices. He desires that you gain greater understanding and freedom. He has great compassion and patience for those seeking His help and healing.

At the end of each prayer period, mark down in your notebook all the capital vices that trap you and to which you are susceptible. Be brief in your writing, but specific. List how intensely (mildly, moderately or strongly) they ensnare you. For example: Gluttony—moderately when I'm anxious.

2. For the second part of the week:
Pay attention to your addictions. Ignatius had addictions to gambling and possibly to sex. Everyone has addictions (whether mild, moderate, or strong) to one or more things. Our addictions reveal valuable diagnostic information that is worth bringing to the Divine Physician.

Do not exceed your fifteen-minute limit for each prayer period. For your prayer, sit apart in a quiet place. Find a comfortable position that permits you to be alert. Breathe deeply for a few minutes, mindful that God's love sustains your very life. Next, using the personal name for God you identified, ask God to enlighten your memory and imagination so that you can see any addictions you have in the context of your life story.

Before completing your prayer period, record any addictions that surfaced. Be brief and specific. Identify each addiction by name and frequency: Seldom, Often, or Constantly. For example, you may write:

Television—S   Exercise—O   Gambling—C

3. Alternatively:
You can combine the above spiritual diagnostics into a single prayer exercise. Here is how you might do it: For your first two prayer exercises of the week, pray for the grace to honestly recognize the vices and addictions that erode your freedom and compromise your true self. Write them out in your notebook as indicated above, listing the vices as mild, moderate, or strong and the addictions as seldom, often, or constantly.
Begin the rest of the prayer sessions in the standard manner. During your prayer session, review what you wrote in your notebook, and ask Christ, the Divine Physician, in very personal words, to help you discover the

connections between the vices and addictions. For example, you may notice that when you are angry, you might move toward one or another addictive behavior. When you are envious, you might be drawn to other addictive behaviors, and so on for the other vices.

Recall that the grace you are asking for is the inspiration to understand the vices and addictions in and of themselves, and more importantly, to identify the connections between them as they manifest in your life story. When, through grace, you begin to wake up to the links between the thoughts, words, and deeds of your life story, then growth in holiness and authenticity can occur.

Before the end of each prayer period, record any discoveries you make between the vices and addictions that God reveals to you. Thank God for the courage to honestly see yourself as you are. Thank God for the grace to wake up to live in greater freedom.

THE SEVEN CAPITAL VICES

Pride

Pride is an unrestrained and improper appreciation of our own worth. This is listed first because it is widely considered the most serious of the seven sins. Pride—narcissism—was the foundation of Adam and Eve's sin that made them fall for the serpent's temptation to "be like gods." Adam and Eve displaced God, the Creator, as the arbiter of truth and goodness. They, who were creatures, made themselves gods, the final judges of truth and goodness. Their action led to the loss of paradise and to a world of sickness and death. Pride often leads to the committing of other capital sins. Pride is manifest as vanity and narcissism about one's appearance, intelligence, status, wealth, connections, power, successes and all the other things that one uses to stand apart from others and from God.

Greed

Greed is also known as avarice or covetousness. It is the immoderate desire for earthly goods and power. It is a sin of excess. The object of one's greed need not be evil. The problem lies in the way a person regards or desires an object, making it a god and investing it with inappropriate value. Greed can inspire such sinful actions as hoarding, theft, fraud, tax evasion, environmental waste, or unethical business practices.

Gluttony

Gluttony comes from the Latin word meaning to gulp down or swallow. It is the sin of overindulgence and usually refers to overconsumption of food and drink. Gluttony can be eating too soon, too expensively, or too much. St. Alphonsus Liguori explained that feeling pleasure in eating is not wrong. Because food tastes good, we are delighted by this gift. It is not right, however, to eat with pleasure as the only motive and to forget food's function in sustaining vitality and health.

Lust

The sin of lust refers to corrupted desires of a sexual nature. Sexuality is a gift from God and pure in itself. However, lust refers to the impure thoughts and actions that misuse that gift. Lust deviates from God's law and sexuality's sacred purpose of allowing woman and man to participate in God's creative nature. Indulging in the sin of lust can include, but is not limited to, fornication, adultery, bestiality, rape, masturbation, pornography, and incest.

Sloth

Sloth is often described simply as the sin of laziness. However, while this is part of sloth's character, its true face is spiritual laziness. The sin of sloth means being lazy and lax about living the Faith and practicing virtue. Paraphrasing the Catholic Encyclopedia, we could say that sloth means aversion to labor or exertion. St. Thomas calls it sadness in the face of some spiritual good that one has to achieve. In other words, a slothful person is bothered by the effort to sustain one's friendship with God. In this sense, sloth is directly opposed to charity.

Envy

The sin of envy or jealousy is more than just someone wanting what others have. Sinful envy leads one to emotions or feelings of upset at another's good fortune or blessings. The law of love naturally leads one to rejoice in the good luck of one's neighbor. Envy opposes such love. Envy is named among the capital sins because of the other sins to which it leads.

Anger

Anger or wrath may be described as excessive and powerful feelings of hatred and resentment. These feelings can manifest as a passionate denial of truths expressed by others. Anger can also manifest in the form of denying truths about one's own life and impatience with the procedure of law. Anger is manifest, too, in the desire to seek revenge outside of the workings of the justice system. Anger, in essence, is wishing to do evil or harm to others. The transgressions born of vengeance are among the most serious, including assault, murder, and in extreme cases, genocide and other crimes against humanity. Anger is the only sin not necessarily associated with selfishness or self-interest, although one can be angry for selfish reasons, such as jealousy.

അ

A Short Primer on Addiction

The word addiction is used in many contexts. Common usage of the term has evolved to include psychological dependence. In this context, the term goes beyond drug addiction and substance abuse problems. It also refers to behaviors that are not generally recognized by the medical community as addictive problems, such as compulsive overeating or hoarding.

When the term addiction is applied to compulsions that are not substance-related, such as problem gambling and computer addiction, it describes a recurring compulsion one engages in despite the activity's harmful consequences to one's individual physical, mental, social, or spiritual health.[8]

Other forms of addiction could be habitual defrauding or tax evasion, money addictions, work addiction, exercise addiction, habitual overeating, habitual shopping, sex addiction, computer addiction, email addiction, video game addiction, pornography addiction[9], television addiction, and social media addiction.

Gabor Maté sums up addiction's profile: "Addiction is any repeated behavior, substance-related or not, in which a person feels compelled to persist, regardless of its negative impact on his life and the lives of others." According to Maté, addiction can be identified by the following four traits:

> 1. compulsive engagement with a behavior or a preoccupation with it,
>
> 2. impaired control over the behavior,
>
> 3. persistence or relapse despite evidence of harm, and
>
> 4. dissatisfaction, irritability, or intense craving when the object—be it a drug, activity, or other goal—is not immediately available.

ՀՁ

I am starting a Relationship that will carry me
for the rest of my life.

All relationships require time and patience.
I will strive for patience and ask for God's help
when I don't understand a lesson.

I will learn the fundamentals and open my heart to God.

I trust that God will lead me.

I believe that my sacred story will unfold in truth,
in powerlessness, and with my patience.

I believe that Jesus awaits me with
His grace, mercy, and forgiving love.

ՀՁ

Dr. Schuchts' Reflection ~ Week Eight

Vices and Addictions

This eighth week you are invited to honestly examine your vices and addictions, in the light of Christ's holiness, compassionate gaze, and merciful love.

Remember he sees you in your wholeness and does not define you according to your sin. He understands that behind every disordered desire, there are good and holy desires and unmet developmental needs.

Jesus sees with great compassion what you can only partially see; i.e. how your areas of wounding have become the fertile ground for your vices and addictions. He understands more than you do, how these vices and addictions reveal areas where you are hurting.

Without awareness of Jesus' compassion, this exercise can be especially challenging. We all have a natural aversion to facing our sins and weaknesses. We end up hiding in darkness and avoiding Christ's love and light. (See Jn. 3:16-21).

When we get a glimpse of our brokenness, we have a tendency to want to minimize or justify it. We certainly don't want to let anyone else see these shortcomings in our lives.

Part of the reason for our reluctance I believe is that our fallen human nature has a natural inclination to view these vices and addictions mistakenly, as *our core identity*. Too often we see our fallen-ness through the lens of self-condemnation and discouragement.

This is the clearly the work of the enemy of our human nature, who wants to keep us enslaved to our sin, and bound in shame and hopelessness.

He begins his work early in our childhood by wounding us when we are still vulnerable, and then giving us license and enticing us to comfort ourselves through specific vices and addictions that assuage our pain.

These vices and addictions become false comforts. For the Holy Spirit of Jesus and the Father alone can truly heal, fulfill and comfort us. In the long run, our vices and addictions leave us empty and isolated--cut-off from vital relationships with God and others.

Isolation is the breeding ground for our addictions, and the inevitable consequence of our vices. From isolation, we are lured into self-indulgence to ease the pain of our loneliness, which in turn brings about deeper shame and withdrawal--aloneness.

The more we give into the lure of these temptations, the more we become vulnerable to the enemy's lying voice, accusing us that we are bad and no longer worthy of love.

Moreover, we come to believe that we are hopelessly stuck in these sins and compulsions, and that things will only get worse, no matter how hard we try.

Though these internal reactions feel true to us, they are destructive lies from the enemy. When we encounter these lies of shame and hopelessness, they are signals to us that we are in the grip of desolation or strongholds and therefore we should consciously turn to Christ.

Strongholds are "vice-grips" keeping us trapped and unable to free ourselves. This is precisely why and where we need a Savior. Jesus is the only one powerful enough to release us from these traps and to reveal truth and love in place of the lies we believe.

The word "vice" has many synonyms that paint a bleak picture: evil, immorality, depravity, iniquity, idolatry etc. They are certainly the antithesis of the virtues that are associated with Christ and his priesthood.

As priests, it can be even more difficult to acknowledge these vices and addictions, because of the standard of holiness in Christ which you are called to represent to the world.

But the opposite is also true. Like St. Ignatius, as you bring these vices and addictions into HIs light, you become all the more potent in your priesthood. His grace is perfected through your powerlessness and humility.

The more you surrender these "vice-grips" and find freedom in Christ, the more you are able to bring hope to the people you serve. Knowing personally the reality of Jesus' power to save, you will have confidence that others can find a similar freedom.

Rather than becoming obstacles to your holiness and priestly ministry, these weaknesses of character can become the very means through which Jesus works in and through you.

The following are some insights and words of encouragement that your brother priests desire to share with you this week:

✠ *As I reflected upon specific behaviors and actions, I was shown the bigger picture: patterns of belief and actions over long periods of my life. I could see God showing me these larger, common themes that I was not as readily aware of without looking at the detail in this prayerful way.*

✠ *I was struck by the reflection on how the enemy can wound us as children and how that can lead to seeking false comforts. These false comforts can seem so pleasing while at the same time being short lived and shallow.*

✠ *Sin inherently robs us of our freedom. It leads to more sin, to addiction, and to vices.*

✠ *A deeper realization of how I have allowed myself to believe that certain vices were part of my core identity. A recognition of the need to reject these identity lies and the connected vices.*

Immaculate Heart of Mary pray for us so that our hearts may be fully aligned with the Sacred Heart of your son Jesus.

ℰℭ

NOTES

Week 9

FIRST

I will select my fifteen-minute quiet times for the week ahead and visualize where I will go each day and at what times. I will ask God for the grace to keep those times sacred throughout the week. I will have my notebook at hand and spend no more than fifteen minutes in each formal prayer session. I will always use my personal name for God.

SECOND

My fifteen-minute quiet prayer this ninth week consists of six simple prayer exercises, one each for Monday through Saturday. I can use my Sunday prayer time to read over the prayer exercises and set my heart for the week ahead. If I am doing two prayer sessions a day, I have the option to engage each exercise twice.

THIRD

I will begin each fifteen-minute prayer period by sitting in a comfortable position. Speaking God's name, and with personal words from my heart, I ask to be open to my own heart and life story as I enter the short time of prayer. If I focus better by breathing deeply and saying God's name with each inhale and exhale, then I will do so. I will pray with personal words from my heart to see what I have not seen before, and to see connections among aspects of my life story. I am invited to watch these components of my life narrative with the Divine Physician by my side. Christ invites me to wake up in my life.

I will awaken to the present moment.
I will take each day and each exercise as it comes.
I cannot do Sacred Story better by going faster.
I will ask God to help me.
I will awaken to my spiritual nature
and to the inspirations that inspire
faith, hope, and love.
I will awaken to the inspirations
that inspire cynicism, impatience and lusts.
I will wake up!

This week, I will say this affirmation aloud once daily:
I believe every thought, word, and deed of mine
carries a force that can change me, others, and history.

ᛒ

The six spiritual diagnostic exercises for this week's lesson offer you the potential for more enlightenment. Spend your fifteen-minute sessions this week listening to your heart. Ask God for the grace to discern the key elements in your life story linked to the following: gratitude; relationships; spiritual, social, and financial values; and people you need to forgive or whose forgiveness you need to accept. Take one day for each of the six spiritual diagnostics. Deciphering these can help you see the two plot-lines (like Ignatius's prideful, self-centered story and his spiritual, selfless story) in your life history more clearly. Be sure to ask for God's assistance to "see" each of these six elements. Use the personal name for God to ask for this grace for each day's prayer.

Monday
GRATITUDE

I ask God for the grace to remember the one experience, event, or person for which I am most grateful. It could be a kindness someone showed me. It could be a loving gesture from a parent, friend, husband, wife, or child. It could be something that did not happen to me—some danger or threat, sickness or accident that was avoided or minimized. It could be some significant event in my life that moved me in a new direction. It could be a spiritual experience that opened me to a deeper hope and joy in my life. What comes to mind? I will pray for the grace to recall the feelings I felt at the time of the event and take note of the reasons why. I pray to see connections in my responses to other prayer exercises as they occur. Before I finish my prayer, I will write my memory and why it inspires gratitude, in one sentence.

Example: At first, I thought having a brother with Down's Syndrome would be a great burden to our family, but it brought our family together in a way we had never been before, teaching us the true meaning of life and love.

Tuesday
RELATIONAL GOAL

I ask God for the grace to identify the most important relational goal I can imagine for my life story. It could be with God, my spouse, my children, my family, or a close friend. This is the one relational goal that if I accomplished it, I would believe that my life was fulfilled. I will look for connections in my responses to other prayer exercises as they occur to me. Before I finish my prayer, I will write my relationship goal and why it would define my relational success, in one sentence.

Example: My family situation growing up was less than ideal, and I have always wanted to achieve success in life by working hard to be a great husband and father.

Wednesday
SPIRITUAL GOAL

I ask God for the grace to understand my most hoped-for spiritual goal for my life story. It could be with God, my spouse, my children, my family, or a close friend. It is the one spiritual goal that if I accomplished it, I would believe that my life was fulfilled. I will look for connections in my responses to other prayer exercises as they occur to me. Before I finish my prayer, I will write my spiritual goal and why it would define spiritual success for me, in one sentence.

Example: I know I can be lazy and a bit self-centered, and so success in my spiritual life would be to pray daily and always try to do something for someone I see who needs help.

Thursday
SOCIAL GOAL

I ask God for the grace to understand my most hoped-for goal that represents the positive social impact of my life story. It is the one social goal that if I accomplished it, or helped accomplish it, I would believe my life was fulfilled. I will look for connections in my responses to other prayer exercises as they occur to me. Before I finish my prayer, I will write my social goal in one sentence and why it would define social success for me and the world.

Example: I want to be known for making a difference in the world by standing up for those in society who are the most powerless and forgotten and to be fearless in doing so.

Friday
FINANCIAL GOAL

I ask God for the grace to understand my most hoped-for financial or economic goal or ambition for my life story. It is the one financial goal that if I accomplished it, or helped accomplish it, I would believe my life was fulfilled. I will look for connections in my responses to other prayer exercises as they occur to me. Before I finish my prayer, I will write my financial goal in one sentence and why it would define financial success for me.

Example: When I was younger, making lots of money seemed important, but now, I hope I can work to live and not live to work, and hopefully teach my children the same values.

Saturday
FORGIVENESS

I ask God for the grace to understand the one person who would be most grateful to receive my forgiveness. I also ask God for the grace to understand the one person whose forgiveness I would be most grateful to receive. Before finishing my prayer, I will write two short sentences below, one for each person, describing why gratitude would be present in each instance of forgiveness.

Example: It has been hard for me to forgive my parents for divorcing, and success in this area would be to ask God for the grace to not hold on to anger but to forgive them as Jesus forgave on the cross.

☙

I am starting a Relationship that will carry me
for the rest of my life.

All relationships require time and patience.
I will strive for patience and ask for God's help
when I don't understand a lesson.

I will learn the fundamentals and open my heart to God.
I trust that God will lead me.

I believe that my sacred story will unfold in truth,
in powerlessness, and with my patience.

I believe that Jesus awaits me with His grace, mercy, and forgiving
love.

80

Dr. Schuchts' Reflection ~ Week Nine

Joy, Hope, and Freedom

Did you notice the sharp turn in our focus in this ninth week? We moved from facing our sins, weaknesses and failures in week eight, to now looking at sources of our joy, hope and freedom.

Of the six spiritual exercises from week 8, the first was on gratitude (joy) the next four concerned goals (hope) and the last one invited us to forgive (freedom). Do you recognize these as essential aspects of your Sacred Story?

Gratitude is the virtue of living in the present moment, with trust in the Father's abundant provision (Mt. 6:25-34). The more we can see and receive the good gifts which the Father is always providing, the more we are able to genuinely experience fulfillment and joy in our daily lives.

Gratitude is also the antidote for our vices, because in gratitude we assume a posture of open hands and open hearts. All the vices, in contrast, are attempts at grasping for what we need, because we are afraid we will miss out. In that, our hearts become closed.

Joy, the fruit of gratitude, is the signal that we are fulfilled and that our basic relational needs have been satisfied. The psychologists and neurologists who developed the *Life Model* contend that joy is our most fundamental relational need.[10]

When our joy capacity is lacking we are much more prone to seek substitutes- i.e. addictions. The areas of addiction you identified in week 8 are symptoms of depleted joy levels. The lower your joy, the more prone you are to addictions.

Our addictions eventually lead us in despair. We need to battle this with hope. The relational goals identified this ninth week are very concrete expressions of choosing to have hope for the future. Most of those goals were relational--highlighting our relationships as the basis of our joy and hope.

We need to keep looking toward the future with hope because God has promised us that as we continue to persevere, our hope will not be disappointed. St. Paul expresses this eloquently: "... and hope does not disappoint because the love of God has been poured out into our hearts, through the Holy Spirit that has been given to us" (Rom. 5:5).

Arguably the most important exercise of the week was the final one on forgiveness. Forgiveness is the key to our healing and is the means to true freedom. We cannot be free until we are able to forgive God, ourselves, and others from our hearts.

One of the primary ways that Jesus reveals the Father's mercy is by offering us His forgiveness. But Jesus also warns us that we can only receive God's mercy to the extent that we are willing to forgive from the heart.

It is not that the Father withholds his forgiveness from us as a kind of retaliation. Rather, our forgiveness opens our own hearts to receive all that the Father desires to pour out to us. When our hearts are closed we cannot receive his love.

Here is the way the Catechism expresses the relationship between offering forgiveness and receiving God's mercy:

"Now-- and this is daunting--this outpouring of mercy cannot penetrate our hearts as long as we have not forgiven those who have trespassed against us.... In refusing to forgive our brothers and sisters, our hearts are closed and their hardness makes them impervious to the Father's merciful love; but in confessing our sins, our hearts are open to grace" (Catechism, 2840).

Notice the words the Catechism uses to describe our hearts when we are unwilling to forgive or be forgiven. Our hearts become "closed", "hard" and "impervious to the Father's merciful love."

When our hearts are closed we are not able to receive what God is always pouring out. We end up joyless, with bitterness rather than gratitude, and hopeless rather than hopeful. This sick condition of our hearts makes us vulnerable to vices and addictions.

The opposite is also true. As we forgive and receive forgiveness, we open our hearts to receive more and more of the Father's love. We become then channels of living water, bringing joy and freedom to many others.

This is the greatness of your priesthood. You teach the people of God how to trust God, with gratitude. You instill hope by keeping our eyes focused on the good things to come. And you become the primary agents of God's forgiveness and mercy through the sacraments.

But as you know, you can't authentically communicate what you have not yourself received. The sacraments are inherently powerful, but they become more effective as your hearts are transformed (see Catechism 1098).

As you grow in gratitude, hope and forgiveness, your message and ministry become increasingly more potent. The Holy Spirit longs to pour his life through you--so that you can bring others into the joy, hope and freedom that you yourself have discovered.

These observations are from your brother priests who accompanied you on Week 9:

✠ *Without gratitude everything I do becomes a chore.*

✠ *Forgiving and accepting forgiveness is the best way to be grateful toward God whose Son died for us.*

✠ *Reflecting on life goals in the context of prayer revealed to me some of the deepest desires of my heart and of God's desires for me.*

✠ *I need to both forgive those who have wounded me in the Church and*

... be aware of the call to help others, especially my parishioners, to do the same.

Immaculate Heart of Mary pray for us so that our hearts may be fully aligned with the Sacred Heart of your son Jesus.

જી

NOTES

Week 10

FIRST

I will select my fifteen-minute quiet times for the week ahead and visualize where I will go each day and at what times. I will continue to ask God for the grace to keep those times sacred. I will have my notebook at hand, and I will spend no more than fifteen minutes in each formal prayer session. I will always use my personal name for God.

SECOND

My fifteen-minute quiet prayer this tenth week is composed of simple prayer exercises for Monday through Saturday to help me find links in my life story. I may use my Sunday prayer time to read over the prayer exercises and diagnostic charts so I can set my heart for the week. If I am doing two prayer sessions a day, I will have more reflection time.

THIRD

I will begin each fifteen-minute prayer period by sitting in a comfortable position. I will speak God's name, and with personal words from my heart, I ask to be open to my own heart and life story. I will ask for the grace to see connections between aspects of my life story. I am invited to watch these components of my life narrative with the Divine Physician by my side. Christ invites me not to be afraid but to wake up in my life—my spiritual life. I will watch and pray with Christ.

I will awaken to the present moment.
I will take each day and each exercise as it comes.
I cannot do Sacred Story better by going faster.

I will ask God to help me.

I will awaken to my spiritual nature
and to the inspirations that inspire faith, hope, and love.

I will awaken to the inspirations
that inspire cynicism, impatience, and lusts.
I will wake up!

This week, I will say this affirmation aloud once daily:
I affirm that everything that has happened to me
and everything I have experienced in my entire life
is present in my memory.

❧

Read this page and the next before starting any prayer sessions this week.

Whether you have or have not done the exercises for weeks 6 through 9, you can still do this week's exercises. If you wrote notes for the past weeks, refer to them. If not, take this exercise as a stand-alone piece, and sometime later, go back and do the weeks you passed.

For week 10, there are five diagnostic charts to contemplate. These charts are designed to help you pray for graced insights from God to better understand your life history. The five diagnostic charts are as follows:

1.List of the vices and Commandments

2. Chart for listing key elements in your life story

3. Chart with four elements in your life story where you can pray for

insights to see links or connections

4. Chart that shows the progressive levels of sin's impact on Ignatius's spiritual and material being, and the way that originating sins and wounds lead to core sin, and finally to the fruit of these sins (those that are most visible or manifest in his story), and

5. the same chart as above, repeated with blank spaces for you to fill in your own unique experiences

The data from your life diagnostic charts will be helpful to you throughout the year. You are only in the beginning period of attempting, with God's grace, to see your sin history more clearly. Your goal is to better understand how to listen to your sacred story.

Remember, Christ watches with you with love, patience, compassion, and infinite mercy. Be not afraid! What follows are suggestions for how best to use the fifteen-minute prayer sessions in this tenth week of Sacred Story prayer.

INSTRUCTIONS FOR EACH DAY'S PRAYER PERIOD

Sunday: I contemplate briefly the list of vices and Commandments and all the diagnostic charts and ask God for the grace of openness to see both the trees (unique elements of my life history) and the forest (the unique elements that when combined, form a single life story).

Monday: I fill in the first diagnostic chart with at least one element for each of the statements provided.

Tuesday: I fill in the second diagnostic chart, with the goal to write at least three of the five things requested in each category.

Wednesday: I contemplate the diagnostic chart I filled in on Tuesday, praying to see if there are any obvious links among Commandments, vices, addictions, persons, and/or events. I draw lines linking those connections that are clear to me.

Thursday: I contemplate the diagnostic chart of how sin impacted the life of St. Ignatius and try to see the links in his original (root), core (trunk), and manifest (fruit) sins.

Friday: I contemplate the elements from the diagnostic charts I filled in earlier in the week and pray for the grace to see more clearly how sin has impacted me at the roots, trunk, and fruit of my life. For each of the blank spaces on the last chart, I write those elements (at least one each) that I believe are present in my life as original sins (root), core sins (trunk), and manifest sins (fruit).

Saturday: I contemplate the charts I filled in this week and ask for God's grace to see any connections that will aid me in my Sacred Story journey. I ask for God's grace to be open this entire forty-week journey so I can begin to see my life story in its entirety.

LISTS OF VICES AND COMMANDMENTS

VICES

PRIDE   ENVY   GLUTTONY   LUST   SLOTH   GREED   ANGER

COMMANDMENTS

First	I am the Lord your God; you shall have no strange gods before Me.
Second	You shall not take the name of the Lord your God in vain.
Third	Remember to keep holy the Sabbath day.
Fourth	Honor your father and mother.
Fifth	You shall not kill.
Sixth	You shall not commit adultery.
Ninth	You shall not covet your neighbor's spouse.
Seventh	You shall not steal.
Tenth	You shall not covet your neighbor's goods.
Eighth	You shall not bear false witness against your neighbor.

LOOKING FOR LINKS IN MY STORY

Monday: I fill in the first diagnostic chart with at least one element for each of the statements provided.

A COMMANDMENT THAT CHALLENGES ME	
VICES THAT ENSNARE ME	
ADDICTIONS I LIVE WITH	
PERSONS/EVENTS THAT GENERATE FEAR, ANGER, OR GRIEF	
PERSONS/EVENTS THAT GENERATE FAITH, HOPE, OR LOVE	
STORYLINES IN BOOKS/ MOVIES THAT ALWAYS BRING ME TO TEARS	
WHAT ALWAYS MAKES ME ANGRY	
WHAT ALWAYS MAKES ME GRATEFUL	
WHAT ALWAYS INSPIRES FEAR IN ME	
MY ULTIMATE FAITH GOAL	
THE AREA OF MY LIFE MOST OUT OF CONTROL	

LOOKING FOR LINKS IN MY STORY

Tuesday: I fill in the second diagnostic chart, with the goal to write at least three of the five things requested in each category.

FIVE COMMANDMENTS I AM MOST CHALLENGED IN LIVING	FIVE VICES THAT ENSNARE ME	FIVE ADDICTIONS I LIVE WITH	FIVE PERSONS/EVENTS THAT CAUSE FEAR, ANGER, OR GRIEF

Wednesday: I contemplate this chart praying to see any obvious links among Commandments, vices, addictions, persons and/or events. I draw lines linking those connections that become clear to me.

Thursday: I contemplate the diagnostic chart of how sin impacted the life of St. Ignatius and try to see the links in his original (root), core (trunk), and manifest (fruit) sins.

LINKS IN ST. IGNATIUS'S STORY

THE FRUIT

(manifest fear, anger, and grief,
moral weaknesses, vices, addictions, and sinful habits
that are the most visible to you)
*Ignatius's addictive gambling,
reactive anger, and
sexual self-indulgence*

THE TRUNK

(disobedience and narcissism,
along with their fear, anger, and grief,
that form the superstructure of your daily life,
feeding on originating sins and events)
*Ignatius's arrogance,
blinded conscience, and
narcissism*

THE ROOTS

(ancient, originating events
that form a foundation
for patterns of disobedience and narcissism,
along with their fear, anger, and grief)
*Original Sin that wounded Ignatius's heart and soul;
distinctive family/clan sins and early life events that
wounded him spiritually, psychologically, and physically*

Friday: I contemplate the elements from the diagnostic charts I filled in earlier in the week and pray for the grace to see more clearly how sin has impacted me at the roots, trunk, and fruit of my life.

For each of the blank spaces on the chart below, I write those **elements** (at least one each) that I believe are present in my life as original sins (root), core sins (trunk), and manifest sins (fruit).

MY MANIFEST SINS—THE FRUIT FROM MY TREE

MY CORE SINS—THE TRUNK OF MY TREE

MY ORIGINAL SINS—THE ROOTS OF MY TREE

ೞ

I am starting a Relationship that will carry me
for the rest of my life.

All relationships require time and patience.
I will strive for patience and ask for God's help
when I don't understand a lesson.

I will learn the fundamentals and open my heart to God.

I trust that God will lead me.

I believe that my sacred story will unfold in truth,
in powerlessness, and with my patience.

I believe that Jesus awaits me with His grace, mercy,
and forgiving love.

ഏ

Dr. Schuchts' Reflection ~ Week Ten

Links in Your Life Story

This tenth week is intended to provide you with a more in-depth understanding regarding how the various aspects of your life story are inter-connected. You are invited, through the illumination of the Holy Spirit, to see the *fruit*, *trunk* and *roots* of your tree.

From beginning to end, the Scriptures use the image of a tree to represent our spiritual life. In the book of Genesis, two trees are mentioned—the Tree of Life and the Tree of Knowledge of Good and Evil. These are contrasted again in Psalm 1 and by Jesus in Matthew, chapter 7. The Tree of Knowledge of Good and Evil is the bad tree that cannot bear good fruit, because it is rooted in self.

The *fruit* on this deadly tree are the manifest sins, vices and addictions that rob us of the joy of life. They are the symptoms of a spiritual disease that has infected all of us through Original Sin. St. Paul calls these visible patterns of sin "works of the flesh" (Gal. 5: 19-20). They are the manifestation of us trying to find fulfillment apart from God.

Over the past several weeks, you have been slowly examining this fruit on your tree in light of the Ten Commandments and Capital Sins. God gives his Holy Law to us as a gift so that we can see our sin clearly and recognize our need for salvation and healing (see Rom. 7 and 8).

The *trunk* of the tree is the core sin of narcissism-which is just another way to speak about our self-centered pride, including all the ways we rely upon ourselves for salvation rather than turn to God. As we explore the roots, we see a whole pattern of generational sin that is passed down to us, beginning with Original Sin.

In addition to the generational influences which affect us deeply, we can also see how the patterns of sin in our life create wounds of fear, hopelessness, shame etc. These wounds are the result of our own personal sin as well as the sins of those around us, from the time we were conceived until the present.

In St. Ignatius life story, we see how all of these are linked together:

The fruit on his deadly tree were the manifest sins and addictions, such as his reactive anger, compulsive gambling, and sexual self-indulgence.

The core sins of narcissism at the trunk of his tree were evident in his arrogant pride, blinded conscience, and his futile attempts to save himself. We know less about Ignatius root issues but we can surmise from his family history and patterns of sin, he was running from pervasive fear, rejection, shame and abandonment.

Our own life stories are a little more difficult to see objectively. But as you look over your reflections this week, you should be able to identify many elements of your tree.

What are the "works of the flesh" in your life? What are the vices at the trunk which undergird your self-reliance? What wounds did you discover as you explored some of your root memories?

Can you see how the roots of your tree feed the trunk, which then gives sustenance to the rotten fruit in your life? This knowledge will be extremely beneficial for you as you go deeper into your own healing journey. This understanding should also help you tremendously in your priestly ministry.

As you discover the roots in your own tree, you will naturally be equipped to help others see their deeply rooted patterns of wounding and sin. Your pastoral ministry will continue to become more effective. In your homilies you will be able to speak to the deeper longings and brokenness in your people and give them hope. In the sacrament of reconciliation, you will be able to help penitents reach new levels of freedom as you lead them to discover their own trees.

151

Your brother priests speak to this reality in working through the material on this tenth week:

✠ *Knowing the links in my own brokenness helps me walk with others to understand their own, especially in the confessional. Often the sins that we confess are linked with other factors that keep us bound.*

✠ *I learned that our vices are linked to our addictions in various different ways through the different events and relationships in our lives.*

✠ *Meditating upon myself with the light of the Holy Spirit helped me see my heart and all memories, wounds, habits, weaknesses, hopes, joys...as part of the bigger picture of God's plan for me. A plan where there is meaning and grace even in challenges and darkness.*

✠ *As I begin to acknowledge my vices I am able to see the impact that it has on many aspects of my life. By God's grace, I desire freedom from these things.*

Immaculate Heart of Mary pray for us so that our hearts may be fully aligned with the Sacred Heart of your son Jesus.

ॐ

NOTES

Week 11

FIRST

I will select my fifteen-minute quiet time(s) for the week ahead and once again visualize where I will go each day and at what time(s). I will ask God for the grace to keep those times sacred. I will have my notebook at hand for each prayer period for this week. I will spend no more than fifteen minutes in each formal prayer session. I will always use my personal name for God.

SECOND

My fifteen-minute quiet prayer this eleventh week is a simple prayer exercise for Sunday through Saturday. I will write a letter to Christ Jesus asking for His help and healing for my life story. The letter is my confession of faith in Him who comes to heal me and forgive me. The letter is also a snapshot of my whole life. It is my opportunity to tell Christ where I have been wounded by sin and life's difficulties, how I struggle for wholeness, and why I need Jesus's help and forgiveness. I will ask Jesus to be my Savior.

THIRD

My prayer sessions this week only can be longer than fifteen minutes, because I am writing a letter. Nevertheless, I still begin each prayer period by sitting in a comfortable position. I will use my favorite name for Jesus

154

specifically (such as Christ Jesus, Lord and Savior, Redeemer, etc.) for this week's personal prayer, because Christ is the Person of the Trinity who won my freedom from sin and death. This week, He is the one to whom I am speaking.

I will awaken to the present moment.
I will take each day and each exercise as it comes.
I cannot do Sacred Story better by going faster.
I will ask God to help me.
I will awaken to my spiritual nature and
to the inspirations that inspire faith, hope, and love.
I will awaken to the inspirations that
inspire cynicism, impatience, and lusts. I will wake up!

This week, I will say this affirmation aloud once daily:
Lord Jesus Christ, you experience great joy when I allow you to forgive my weakness and sinfulness, because you lived, died, and rose again so that I might have new life in you.

☙

A LETTER TO CHRIST JESUS

You may be wondering how you will make use of the prayer exercises from the past few weeks. This will become clearer as your journey continues. Have faith that your efforts will be spiritually fruitful. You are not expected to see the complete picture in everything you have done so far. We have been on a treasure hunt of sorts, pulling together many diverse elements of our life story. The process of piecing the parts together will happen throughout the rest of your life—both by your careful attention and by the grace of God. So, have patience and trust. As time goes on, everything you have done up to this point will take on greater meaning for you (if you follow the lessons in order and ask for God's help).

For this week's exercise, to prepare your whole-life confession, you can refer to some of what you wrote in the previous weeks.

What do we mean by whole-life confession? A whole-life confession is different from a confession of your whole life. It is not helpful, nor is it required, to twice confess sins and faults you have already confessed. The opportunity of a whole-life confession is to look at connections and patterns of sin and failure across your whole life—what we have been working on these past weeks. You are invited to ask for God's help to see a holistic picture of your life—your story—with Christ as your Divine Physician and healer.

Think of this confession as your report to Christ—based on your spiritual diagnosis—after these weeks of prayerful reflection. You can confess current issues and past issues that have been overlooked. As you do this, you are telling Christ the chronic patterns of sin and weaknesses that your prayer and reflection, with the help of God's grace, has awakened in you. And importantly, you are telling Him how these issues are linked to your life story—your history.

Consider this reflection from Pope St. John Paul II:

> It must be recalled that...this reconciliation with God leads, as it were, to other reconciliations, which repair the other breaches caused by sin. The forgiven penitent is reconciled with himself in his inmost being, where he regains his innermost truth. He is reconciled with his brethren whom he has in some way offended and wounded. He is reconciled with the Church. He is reconciled with all creation.[11]

As you look at your life story with Christ, the Divine Physician, address Him directly, and acknowledge why you need Him as your Savior. This could be the very first time you have reviewed your life, seen clearly why you cannot save yourself, and directly asked Jesus to be your Savior. What a profound grace to know why you cannot save yourself and to ask

Christ for this tremendous gift! A profound grace, indeed!

Look at this from Christ's perspective, too. There is no greater gift you give to Christ than your sinfulness and weaknesses as you ask for His healing love, mercy, and forgiveness. By doing so, you take seriously the gift of His life, passion, death, and resurrection. You are telling Jesus you need His cross to be healed. You are thanking Jesus for suffering and dying for you so you can be renewed in Him. This is the real focus of the Christian life! Jesus really loves you and wants to hear what you have to say to Him. He waits with compassion and great longing to hear your story. He waits to carry your burdens and to offer you His forgiveness.

> The Pharisees and their scribes complained to his disciples, saying, "Why do you eat and drink with tax collectors and sinners?" Jesus said to them in reply, "Those who are healthy do not need a physician, but the sick do. I have not come to call the righteous to repentance but sinners." (Lk 5:30–32)

With Jesus as your Divine Physician, a whole-life confession makes perfect sense. He understands you and everything about your life. He has an intense desire to hear your life story and wants to respond as your Savior. Your letter is a statement of your need and a confession of your sins and patterns of sin, as well as a request for forgiveness, healing, and hope. What follows are a few guidelines to help you prepare for this simple, holy, and graced letter:

One picture is worth a thousand words. Your life is a picture, a story. Write a letter to Christ that is no more than 1,000 words. If typed, it would be about three and a half pages, double-spaced. But you do not have to write that much. I repeat: write no more than 1,000 words.

Use personal words that are heartfelt. Early on, you identified the name for God that touches your heart. This week, if you haven't already, find the name for Christ specifically that speaks to your heart. Perhaps it is Christ Jesus, Lord and Savior, or My Lord. You are speaking to the One who won your victory and who came into the world to save you. This week, we want to speak directly to Christ Jesus. Speak to Jesus in the first person: "Please forgive...; I remember...; I suffered...; Please heal me...." Write the confessional story—your history—directly from your heart to the heart of Jesus.

Strive for honesty. Strive earnestly for courage and honesty in your letter. The letter is for you and you only, unless you choose to share it in sacramental Confession (Reconciliation). You need not impress anyone. What is significant is your courage and honesty. Be honest too, about the forgiveness you need to extend to others. Write from your heart.

You are not climbing Mount Everest. Please, pray for the grace not to turn this simple, graced letter/confession opportunity into a huge, exhausting task. You are not climbing a mountain. You are having a conversation with Christ about your life. Hear Him say this to you:

> Come to me, all you who labor and are burdened, and I will give you rest. Take my yoke upon you and learn from me, for I am meek and humble of heart; and you will find rest for your selves. For my yoke is easy and my burden light. (Mt 11:28–29)

Pray for Patience and Compassion. Awakening to your life story will take the rest of your life. It takes a lifetime for Christ's work of healing and forgiveness to embrace your heart and soul. There is no finish line or ultimate enlightenment you can reach on this earth. You will always need healing at deeper levels. You will constantly grow in love and enlightenment, selflessness and humility, until the day you pass from this earth. You will not be finished until the day the Divine Physician sits you down at His eternal banquet.

> But as for the seed that fell on rich soil, they are the ones who, when they have heard the word, embrace it with a generous and good heart, and bear fruit through perseverance. (Lk 8:15)

Set the scene in your heart's imagination. Here is how you might set your heart's imagination as you write: imagine you have been given the opportunity to be alone with Christ when He is walking from one town to another. You will have fifteen minutes with Him...alone. See the road and the other followers walking up ahead of you and the Lord. No one else can hear you. Write your letter as if you are speaking to Christ in this setting. He knows why you want to speak with Him and is ready to hear you. Before you begin talking about your life, He looks you in the eyes and says, "Soon, I will be lifted up on my cross. I am doing this for you so that you can find forgiveness, healing, and hope for the sins, weaknesses, and suffering you experience in your life. As I conquer all death and sin—as I breathe my last breath—I will hold you and your life story in my heart. You will find victory and eternal life in me and one day be with me in paradise."

> Then Jesus said, "Father, forgive them, they know not what they do." Then he said, "Jesus, remember me when you come into your kingdom." He replied to him, "Amen, I say to you, today you will be with me in Paradise." (Lk 23:34, 42–43)

What follows is a template for how you might structure your heartfelt conversation/letter/confession to Christ Jesus, the Divine Physician:

✠ "Dear Jesus, I am so grateful for all the gifts you have given to me." Spend some time writing from your heart why you are grateful. Use Jesus's name often as you write, and give very particular examples of why you are grateful.

✠ "Lord, I am profoundly aware of how some of my past experiences [life history, family, friends, work, school, neighbors] are linked to areas of unfreedom in my life and how these experiences have created embarrassing and/or discouraging habits and rooted patterns of sinfulness." Spend some time looking back over your life, and offer particular examples that capture the links and patterns of sins, addictions, vices, and Commandments where you are challenged and desire spiritual growth. If you cannot discern patterns yet, simply speak about these areas individually. If there are central people in your life story who are linked to these destructive patterns, mention them to Christ. If you are confused about some of the things you do, tell Jesus what they are, and then ask for His help to better understand why you do what you do. From your heart, ask Christ's grace to gain greater freedom from these sins, patterns of sin, habits, and vices.

✠ "But Lord, there is one central pattern of sin that causes me the most embarrassment, shame, confusion, and discouragement." Spend some time being very specific in your conversation with Jesus about this pattern of sin in your life and why it is so difficult for you. Tell Jesus the particular circumstances when you seem to fall under its spell the most and the circumstances that surround your failures. Tell Jesus how you feel when you fail. If there are specific incidents of this pattern of failure that you have not confessed, tell them to the Lord, and ask for His healing and forgiveness.

✠ "Lord Jesus, I have come to realize that I cannot save myself, and I ask for your compassion. I ask that you be my Savior. Rescue me and be with me all the rest of my days." Spend some time speaking with Jesus, in very particular words, about why you have come to realize you cannot save yourself and why you need His grace—why you need Him to be your Savior. Tell Him in very clear words why you know (because of x, y, and z) that you cannot save yourself. Tell Him about any persons you cannot forgive and what they did to you. Tell Him why it is difficult for you to forgive them. Tell Jesus that with His grace, you can desire to forgive them and in time, be able to forgive them. Ask for that grace. Ask the Lord to keep His attention on the core issues in your life (name them) that constantly trip you up, and pray that you never tire in seeking His forgiveness and that you never lose hope in yourself or in Him. Ask the Lord to be your Savior.

✠ "Lord Jesus, I thank you that you have given me the courage to face any fears I had and to trust you with my life in this healing sacrament of your redeeming love." Close your letter/conversation/ confession with very personal words from your heart, thanking Jesus that He has heard your prayer and that He will always be your Savior. With heartfelt words, thank Jesus that He understands your life, and ask that He continue to walk with you, give you grace, and be with you till the end of your days. Ask Jesus for the grace to serve Him more each day with everything you think, say, and do. Ask for the grace to work for fruit that will endure to eternity.

✠ "Thank you Jesus for being my Savior." Close your heartfelt letter by thanking Jesus for being your Savior. Ask for His continued grace as He writes your sacred story.

℘

I am starting a Relationship that will carry me
for the rest of my life.

All relationships require time and patience.
I will strive for patience and ask for God's help
when I don't understand a lesson.

I will learn the fundamentals and open my heart to God.

I trust that God will lead me.

I believe that my sacred story will unfold in truth,
in powerlessness, and with my patience.

I believe that Jesus awaits me with His grace, mercy,
and forgiving love.

℘

Dr. Schuchts' Reflection ~ Week Eleven

Letter to Jesus (Whole-Life Confession)

During this 11th week, you are invited to write a letter to Jesus, integrating all you have been reflecting upon since you began *Forty Weeks.*

Leading up to this activity of making a Whole-Life confession, you have acknowledged the many gifts and graces of your life story and also sought insight from God on distortions in your story-- the poisonous fruit of vices and addictions—flowing from wounds to the root and trunk of your life's story.

You now have a clearer understanding of how the Original Sin of self-centeredness and pride (narcissism) have sustained these patterns of sin in your life. You have also gained a deeper understanding of how your wounds become the fertile soil in which your sins and patterns of addiction grow.

Through all of this time of prayer and reflection, your trust in Jesus has been growing deeper as well. You are realizing more and more that he did not come to condemn you for your sins and addictions, but that He desires to free you and bring to fulfillment your life's greatest desires.

Jesus' desire is for you to be rooted and grounded in his love (Eph. 3: 17). He wants you to bear the fruit of love, joy, peace, patience, goodness, faithfulness and self-control in your life (Gal. 5: 22-23).

With this knowledge and increased trust, you are ready to write your letter to Jesus, expressing your gratitude, confessing your sins, and asking him to heal you of the underlying shame, insecurity, and fear that robs you of fulfillment.

This letter to Jesus is a beautiful tapestry of your life. It is a confession, offered from the depths of your heart, but it is so much more than a simple recitation of your sin.

You are able to share with Jesus the shame that you feel and the details of what you have done that makes you feel unworthy of his love. Allow His merciful love to dispel your shame and silence your self-condemnation.

Examining your sin and compulsions in light of your life history allows you see how your relationships have formed both your Sacred Story and anti-story. In light of these realities, you are facing how powerless you are to save yourself. Spiritual poverty is the antidote to narcissistic pride and the doorway to entering into His Kingdom (Mt. 5:3).

This is one of the reasons we can end our letters with genuine gratitude. Jesus transforms our sin and shame into His grace and glory (see Isa. 61:1-2). We are then enabled to see our life more and more as a Sacred Story.

Your brother priests offer this awareness from the week's letter-writing activity. Jesus takes our sins and wounds and transforms them into something beautiful and life-giving to others:

✠ *It's beautiful to be aware how, everything is part of God's bigger plan for my salvation and redemption. Even sins can become, and are, starting points for God's graces*

✠ *The life confession isn't just a mere recitation of sin but rather involves bringing to the Lord the whole tapestry of threads that make up your life story.*

✠ *The things we are most ashamed to talk to Jesus about are the areas that He most desires us to bring to him.*

✠ *My wounding is so paternal; out of my wounding I want to love and be a great father to those I serve. That is my deepest desire.*

Immaculate Heart of Mary pray for us so that our hearts may be fully aligned with the Sacred Heart of your son Jesus.

℘

NOTES

Week 12

FIRST

I will select my fifteen-minute quiet time(s) for the week ahead and visualize where I will go each day and at what time(s). I continue to ask God for the grace to keep my times of prayer sacred and to seek a place that is technology-free. I will bring my notebook to each prayer period and commit to spending no more than fifteen minutes in each formal prayer session. I will always use my personal name for God.

SECOND

My fifteen-minute quiet prayer this twelfth week consists of one simple prayer exercise for Sunday through Saturday.

THIRD

I will keep working on my letter, or if it is complete, I will reflect on what I have written during my prayer times. I will read and reflect with Christ as my companion and stay with my letter to Christ Jesus, asking for His help and healing for my life story.

I will awaken to the present moment.
I will take each day and each exercise as it comes.
I cannot do Sacred Story better by going faster.

I will ask God to help me.

I will awaken to my spiritual nature and to
the inspirations that inspire faith, hope, and love.

I will awaken to the inspirations that
inspire cynicism, impatience, and lusts. I will wake up!
Be not afraid!

I will not make any decisions that bend into my fears and my anxieties.
They are founded on bad information and will not lead to my peace.

This week, I will say this affirmation aloud once daily:
Lord Jesus Christ, I affirm you will always transform my sin and
weakness into grace and blessings! I will not be afraid!

CB

Your letter to Jesus may or may not be complete. Use your fifteen-minute prayer times this week to continue the reflection and writing process, or if complete, reflect and pray with the letter. Bring your notebook to your prayer sessions. After each session, write one sentence for what brings you the most hope as you read your letter and one sentence for what causes you the most discouragement as you read your letter.

If you have resolved to bring your letter to confession, make an appointment with a priest for sacramental Reconciliation. Consciously commit to scheduling the appointment for some time in the next two weeks. If the priest you seek for confession is not familiar with the Forty Weeks method, explain to him what it is. Let him know that you would like to read to Christ your confession in this letter form. Tell him that you have spent twelve weeks preparing it, and thank him for letting you go to confession in this manner.

$\text{\large ♋}$

I am starting a Relationship that will carry me
for the rest of my life.

All relationships require time and patience.
I will strive for patience and ask for God's help
when I don't understand a lesson.

I will learn the fundamentals and open my heart to God.

I trust that God will lead me.

I believe that my sacred story will unfold in truth,
in powerlessness, and with my patience.
I believe that Jesus awaits me with His grace, mercy,
and forgiving love.

$\text{\large ♋}$

Dr. Schuchts' Reflection ~ Week Twelve

Hope and Discouragement- (Letter to Jesus-Part II)

During this 12th week you are continuing to focus on your letter to Jesus. The specific assignment this week focused each day on parts of the letter that brought you *hope*, as well as those areas where you felt *discouraged*.

Hope and discouragement are key indicators revealing the spiritual condition of our hearts. You might say they are spiritual heart monitors.

Have you ever known anybody that was asked to wear a heart monitor so that the doctor could track the movements of their beating heart during the day?

This week, you were given a kind of spiritual heart monitor, so that you could discern with the Divine Physician the movements of your heart involving signs of health (hope) and sickness (discouragement).

What did you discover as you monitored your heart this week? Did you pay attention to the areas where you felt discouraged in reflecting on your letter?

Though none of us enjoy feeling discouraged, we can learn a lot about ourselves by paying attention to those things that discourage us.

We begin by understanding in general what brings discouragement in our lives. Notice the three parts of the word "discouragement": dis/*courage*/ment. The main word is "courage." When we are dis-couraged, we experience a loss of courage, and thus a deflating of our hearts.

Brené Brown, who is well known for her talks on vulnerability and shame, defines "courage" this way:

> "The root of the word courage is *cor*—the Latin word for heart.

In one of its earliest forms, the word courage had a very different definition than it does today. Courage originally meant "To speak one's mind by telling all one's heart." ...Ordinary courage is about putting our vulnerability on the line. In today's world, that's pretty extraordinary."

Do you see how writing your letter to Jesus was an extraordinary act of courage? By vulnerably opening your heart to Jesus, you shared some of your deepest secrets and areas of shame. You took a big risk putting it out there.

Did you notice how your heart responded? Did you feel an increase in hope? Hope is a signal that our hearts are open and expectant of love.

When we are able to share areas of shame and hurt in a relationship and receive Jesus' love and mercy instead of condemnation, we experience an upsurge in hope. Our hearts are lifted to the heavens.

The opposite is also true. When we are afraid to share those things that weigh us down, we end up feeling more and more discouraged, until eventually we may even become depressed. This in turn becomes fertile ground for our vices and addictions.

Similarly, if we risk the courage to share something vulnerable about ourselves and are met with condemnation or indifference, we may end up feeling even more discouraged. This is deflating. We lose hope and courage.

Jesus is the one person who we can expect will receive our sharing with complete love and mercy. Believing this truth is the origin of hope. As you receive, you can also give.

Doesn't all this help you appreciate the incredible gift you offer to penitents in the Sacrament of Reconciliation? In union with Jesus, you are providing a safe environment for them to be courageous.

In Christ, you are a dispenser of hope and a banisher of discouragement.

And in light of this, here are some of the insights from your brother priests this week:

✠ *Writing my letter to Jesus has helped me to realize the intimate encounter that is the Sacrament of Confession. How wonderful that He waits for us there and uses us to share His Mercy and Love.*

✠ *I was reminded that confession is not about clearing my 'sin ledger' but rather it's about allowing Jesus to be my Savior and to heal me of the deep harm that sin causes.*

✠ *The Lord has broken many of my vices and allowed me to be free. While the temptation still comes there is no fear or anxiety about it. I just feel fortified by Christ even when I am in spiritual desolation.*

✠ *I am not sure if this connects to the letter specifically, but the grace this week was a keen insight into my wounded-ness that I had forgotten about - I lost my twin in the womb and it is increasingly clear that this is related to my insecurity, wounds, and perhaps vocation.*

Immaculate Heart of Mary pray for us so that our hearts may be fully aligned with the Sacred Heart of your son Jesus.

℘

NOTES

Week 13

FIRST

I will select my fifteen-minute quiet times for the week ahead and visualize where I will go each day and at what times. I will petition the Lord for the grace to keep sacred my times of prayer and strive to pray in a place that is technology-free, a place apart. I will bring my notebook to each prayer period and commit to spending no more than fifteen minutes in each formal prayer session. I will always use my personal name for God.

SECOND

For this week's fifteen-minute prayer sessions, I have one simple prayer exercise for Sunday through Saturday.

THIRD

I continue to stay with my letter to Christ Jesus asking for His help, insight, patience, grace, and healing for my life story. I will either keep writing or speaking to Christ, or sit with my letter in prayer. The letter is a snapshot of my whole life, and it is of supreme spiritual worth to be present to Christ with my life story. So, I will either continue writing or pray over what I have written and confessed.

I will awaken to the present moment.
I will take each day and each exercise as it comes.

I cannot do Sacred Story better by going faster.

I will ask God to help me.

I will awaken to my spiritual nature
and to the inspirations that inspire faith, hope, and love.
I will awaken to the inspirations that inspire cynicism,
impatience, and lusts. I will wake up!
Be not afraid!
I will not make any decisions
that bend to my fears and my anxieties. They are founded
on bad information and will not lead to my peace.

This week, I will say this affirmation aloud once daily:
Lord Jesus Christ, I believe you came into the world, born of Mary,
so that I may have life and have it abundantly.

ᘓ

We are a people of faith who live in the light of the Cross of Christ, the light of the Resurrection of Christ, and the light of the Second Coming of Christ. We are His sisters and brothers. We live because we are loved by God.

During these days, as you reflect on your whole-life confession, remember that confession includes grateful praise along with admission of sins and faults. Remember that Christ, the Divine Physician, came so that you can triumph through your failings and weaknesses, by His healing and forgiving grace, to produce fruit that endures to eternity. St. Ignatius once marveled that he did not think, in the entire history of the Church, there was ever someone who sinned as much as he did, who was also given so many graces. "Where sin increased, grace overflowed all the more" (Rom 5:20).

If you have not yet made your confession, you have time both to write a letter and to go to confession this week. These weeks of prayer are about

173

developing a deeper relationship with God in Christ. Do not surrender to your anxiety or perfectionism that may suggest that you have not done enough of the prayer sessions to make a confession or write a letter. If you feel you are behind, do what you can to keep moving forward.

If you have made your confession, use your fifteen-minute prayer periods this week to be with Christ and the letter you wrote to Him. Bring your notebook to your prayer sessions. After each session, write one sentence for what brings you the most hope as you read your letter, and one sentence for what causes you the most discouragement as you read your letter. Linger over the words and phrases that brought you hope and peace. Remember the experience of your confession, and allow its graces to penetrate deeply into your heart.

 C3

I am starting a Relationship that will
carry me for the rest of my life.

All relationships require time and patience.
I will strive for patience and ask for God's help
when I don't understand a lesson.

I will learn the fundamentals and open my heart to God.
I trust that God will lead me.

I believe that my sacred story will unfold in truth,
in powerlessness, and with my patience.

I believe that Jesus awaits me with His grace, mercy,
and forgiving love.

80

Dr. Schuchts' Reflection ~ Week Thirteen

Letter to Jesus (Whole Life Confession)-Part III

As you continue to mine the treasures of your Whole-Life Confession, I invite you to reflect on the Affirmation for this thirteenth week, as a way of transforming areas of discouragement into hope.

Lord Jesus Christ, I believe you came in to the world, born of Mary, so that I may have life, and have it abundantly

You were encouraged to recite this Affirmation each day, because it expresses the way to our finding hope:

Let's take each phrase of this Affirmation and allow our minds and hearts to enter more deeply into it through meditation and contemplation.

First of all, do you believe that "Jesus came into the world and was born of Mary"? For most of us, this core statement of our faith is easy to affirm. Every time we recite the Apostles Creed, we assert our faith in the Incarnation of Jesus through the womb of the Blessed Virgin Mary.

But this Affirmation can become even more real to us at a heart level, when we are able to enter into the reality of the Incarnation contemplatively, such as when praying the Joyful Mysteries of the Rosary.

In contemplative prayer, we allow our head-knowledge to become heart-knowledge. We realize in a whole new way that Jesus shares in our humanity and plays a vital part in our Sacred Story.

Similarly, can we recite the second part of the Affirmation with rational assent that Jesus came into this world so that you and I "may have life and have it abundantly"? The question is, do we really believe this in the depths of our hearts?

Theologically, we can all acknowledge this statement is true because it comes directly from Jesus' own words in the Gospel of John: "A thief comes only to steal and slaughter and destroy; I came so that they might have life and have it more abundantly" (Jn. 10:10).

Truth is relatively easy to embrace in the abstract. However, when we view this verse through the lens of our Whole-Life Confession, especially in the areas where we discovered discouragement, we are confronted with a sudden upsurge of doubt and unbelief.

Our sins, wounds, and addictions have brought death and darkness into our souls. These strongholds are the wailing sirens in our life that signal where we *are not living abundantly*.

When it comes to these "vice-grips" in our life, we all have a hard time believing Jesus came to bring *me* into abundant life. I may believe this Affirmation for another, but when it comes to these areas in my life, it is much harder to believe and hope for myself.

The longer we examine these areas of discouragement, the more we identify with this lament of St. Paul: "Miserable one that I am! Who will deliver me from this mortal body? Thanks be to God through Jesus Christ our Lord." (Rom. 8:24-25).

Did you notice that the Affirmation this week begins precisely with these words: "*Lord Jesus Christ*"? Each word in Jesus' name is packed with life-changing revelation.

The title "Lord" means that Jesus is the full revelation of Yahweh of the Old Testament. Personally, this title calls me to submit the entirety of my life to him, including and especially all my brokenness.

The name "Jesus" in Hebrew is *Yeshua* and it means: *God's Salvation*. This is the name Gabriel gave to Mary at the Annunciation. Jesus was born of Mary so he could heal us and free us from these strongholds.

The title "Christ" is translated from Messiah in Hebrew and means *Anointed One*. Jesus is the one anointed by the Spirit to bring us out of bondage and into Freedom.

On our own, we are miserable. We can't bring ourselves abundant life, no matter how hard we try. But thanks be to God, we are not on our own. Jesus Christ our Lord is the anointed one who came to deliver us.

Now recite the Affirmation again: *"Lord Jesus Christ, I believe you came into this world, born of Mary, so that I may have life and have it abundantly."*

As you speak the word *"Lord"* think of the apostle Thomas traumatized by Jesus' crucifixion and left paralyzed by fear and doubt.

Then contemplate the scene as Jesus appears to the twelve and says personally to Thomas: "Put your finger here, and see my hands; and bring your hand, and put it into my side. Do not be unbelieving but believe." Thomas answered him, "My *Lord* and my God!" (John 23:27-28).

Allow yourself to take Thomas' place. Wherever you are living from your wounded identity--perhaps paralyzed by fear and doubt, be aware of Jesus' standing before you.

Jesus presents himself to you and shows you his wounds. Quiet yourself so that you can be present in the upper room with him.

Now he says to you: "Put your finger here and see my hands; and put out your hand and place it in my side. Do not disbelieve but believe."

I encourage you to spend some time in prayer this week with your letter and bringing your doubt and discouragement into this contemplative prayer experience of Thomas in the Upper Room.

Speak out loud the words of St. Thomas: "My Lord and My God." Then recite again the Affirmation: *"Lord Jesus Christ, I believe you came into this world, born of Mary, so that I may have life and have it abundantly."*

As you prepare for that experience, I offer these words of encouragement and hope from your brother priests:

✠ *The reflection brought me into a deeper personal meditation on ways that I have not been open to receiving God's abundance due to sloth. I am realizing how I have avoided this abundance from a place of not feeling worthy of it.*

✠ *God desires to take all of the miseries of our lives and transform them through his mercy.*

✠ *Sin is profound and complex but the Lord's mercy and grace are greater. He wants to heal me and to know Him more deeply than sin affects me.*

✠ *Trusting in God's mercy, our lives are restored and we are given the grace to encourage others to fear not, but trust in Him.*

Immaculate Heart of Mary pray for us so that our hearts may be fully aligned with the Sacred Heart of your son Jesus.

೮ᴅ

NOTES

Part Two
Learning Sacred Story Prayer

"It was not you who chose me, but I who chose you and
appointed you to go and bear fruit that will remain,
so that whatever you ask the
Father in my name he may give you.
This I command you: love one another."

Jn 15:16–17

Week 14

FIRST

As I begin part 2 in Forty Weeks, I consciously determine if it is beneficial to change the number of times I pray daily. I will ask for patience to start each day with renewed commitment, even if I miss a day's prayer. If I am using a notebook separate from the Forty Weeks "Notes" pages, I will bring it to each prayer period. I will begin this week, in my notebook or on the "Notes" pages, a habit of simple daily journaling.[12] At the end of each day, I will mark one event that increased my faith, hope, and love and one event that decreased my faith, hope, and love. I will always use my personal name for God.

SECOND

I will listen attentively to my experience to discern the two plotlines in my story. I will do this by consciously attending to my fantasies and/or daydreams.

THIRD

As I begin part 2 in Forty Weeks, I will encounter several more foundational exercises. Like the exercises leading up to a whole-life confession, these additional exercises will help identify important narrative themes in my story that I can bring to my formal times of prayer.

The exercises' meaning and energy come from my asking God for help and grace—from my relationship with God.

I will awaken to the present moment.
I will awaken to my spiritual nature.
I will not make any decisions based on fear.

This week, I will say this affirmation aloud once daily:
My sacred story takes a lifetime to write.

CB

Take this full week after your whole-life confession for this Ignatian daydream/fantasy exercise. It is inspired by St. Ignatius's "awakening" while he was recovering from his battle wound. Now is the perfect time to do this exercise, because after Reconciliation, you have much more clarity and peacefulness to see, by grace, the contours of your story.

Ignatius, while recovering from battle, discovered that his daydreams and fantasies were pulling his heart in two different directions. One direction was toward vain, self-serving, self-indulgent exploits rooted in his wounded human nature. The other direction was toward holy aspirations representing his authentic human nature and the deepest aspirations of his heart. These latter daydreams had been inaudible and out of view most of his life. The black noise of temptation and a false self-portrait both deafened and blinded his heart. Aided by grace, he awoke to the existence of his fantasies and daydreams and (also by grace) discovered that only one of the two storylines expressed his authentic human nature—the deepest dream of his heart.

You will discover that many daydreams and fantasies fight for room in the conscious and unconscious spaces of your heart. No matter their differences, or the fact that they might seem unrelated, they always fall into the two storylines representing the two trajectories of your heart.

182

One set of daydreams or fantasies trend toward infinite Love, holy appetites, integration, humility, reconciliation, hope, peace, wakefulness, sobriety, and gratitude. The other set of daydreams/fantasies trend toward finite things, appetites low and earthly, disintegration, narcissism, resentment, cynicism, anxiety, unconsciousness, drunkenness, and lack of gratitude.

Begin this week by paying attention to your daydreams and fantasies. Let them see the light of day. You will find their traces everywhere:

✠ in the things you purchase, and the things you want to purchase

✠ in your favorite songs, movies, and stories

✠ in the podcast and TV programs that claim your passionate loyalty

✠ in the lives of artists, athletes, actors, saints, politicians—the heroes you emulate and admire and those you disdain

✠ in your programs of study and your job applications

✠ in the friends you have, and the friends you wish you had

✠ in the things that happened, and the things you wish had happened

✠ in the places you want to visit or make your home, and the places you want to leave and never return

✠ in the worlds you visit in cyberspace, and the ones you visit in your inner sacred space

✠ in what motivates you to exercise and discipline yourself, and what influences you to fall out of shape

✠ in the individuals and groups you love, and those whose love you reject

✠ in the people you offer forgiveness, and those you refuse to forgive

✠ in the people you envy, wishing you had their looks, talents, connections, wealth, happiness, or relationships

✠ in what causes you to practice your faith, and what causes you to forget and forgo its practice

✠ in the persons and events that stir your sexual lusts, and the persons and events that stir your childlike innocence

✠ in what opens your wallet to give to the needy, and what closes it to their need

✠ in the stories, images, and experiences that break your heart, and those that cause your heart to be joyful

✠ in the things that make you cry, and the things that make you laugh

✠ in the person or group you want to spend the rest of your life with, and the person or group you want to spend the rest of your life avoiding

✠ in what moves your heart to thanklessness, and what makes it swell with gratitude

The Prayer Exercise

Do this exercise in the context of your daily fifteen-minute prayer sessions, allowing it to permeate your actual daydreams. Your brief journal entry at the end of the day can itemize just one thing that brought you hope and peace that day and just one thing that eroded your hope and peace. In light of this fantasy exercise, focus on themes related to the two main daydreams/fantasies that you unconsciously or consciously entertain. An example: *"I daydreamed about x today and it brought me joy because...."*

Your own daydreams and fantasies may not be so sharply felt but will most likely align with the two themes described below.

NARCISSISTIC DAYDREAMS/FANTASIES

Anxiety, fear, lusts, compulsive appetites, resentment and anger, control of others, getting even/getting back, addictions, lost innocence, aggression, and vices populate these story lines. In short, they are linked to your broken heart and wounded human nature. These daydreams/fantasies generate electrical energy, excitement, and urges to things low and earthly. They inflate your ego and excite you while you are fantasizing or engaging them, but they leave you dry, empty, hungrier, and dissatisfied—even depressed—after the fact. Or out of your sadness, depression, anger, emptiness, and dryness, you may turn to them for satisfaction and release—like a narcotic—a painkiller for your heart.

GRATEFUL DAYDREAMS/FANTASIES

Peace, calm, self-control, forgiveness, surrendering angers and hatreds, appreciation of beauty and innocence, holy dreams and high ideals, inspirations to selfless love, desires for healing, and the joy of making a difference and living a meaningful life are their storylines. These storylines are linked to your God-given human nature and the deepest dreams of your heart. These daydreams/fantasies generate peace, tears, quiet hope, and aspirations to all things innocent, beautiful, and noble. They humble your heart and fill you with gratitude while you are fantasizing or engaging them, and they leave you fulfilled, content, and satisfied—even joyful—after the fact.

.

ᜣ

Lord, you will open my lips;
and my mouth will proclaim your praise.
For you do not desire sacrifice or I would give it;
a burnt offering you would not accept.
My sacrifice, O God, is a contrite spirit;
a contrite, humbled heart, O God, you will not scorn.
(Ps 51:17–19)

ᜧ

Dr. Schuchts' Reflection ~ Week Fourteen

Discerning the Two Plot Lines of Our Story

Before moving into Part II of *Sacred Story*, I want to pause briefly to review where we have journeyed so far. I believe this brief synopsis of Part I will offer you a much-needed perspective as you explore the two plot lines of your story.

In Week 1, we began with the Sacred Story Affirmations. These are the Eternal Truths illuminating our path on the way to God, leading us into the wholeness which comes from communion with Him.

In Weeks 2-5 we explored St. Ignatius story to understand how his life experiences offer a mirror to our own Sacred Story.

In discovering how Ignatius' daydreams, vices, and addictions were rooted in his wounds and narcissistic pride, we were able to more objectively identify how original sin, personal sin, and the wounds caused by these sins have shaped our personal anti-story.

Similarly, in seeing how the Father's love and mercy redeemed Ignatius and turned his anti-story into a Sacred Story, we are able to have great confidence in approaching God in our shame and brokenness. We act on this confidence by calling on him with the personal name that speaks intimately to our hearts.

During Week 6-10, we began to explore our own history of relationships, vices and addictions, in light of the Ten Commandments and Seven Deadly Sins. We identified our life goals and began to see how all the pieces fit together in preparing for our Whole-Life Confession.

Finally, in Weeks 11-13, we first wrote and then reflected on our letter to Jesus, bringing out into the light the areas of our greatest shame, while also expressing our gratitude to Jesus for accepting us as we are, and for saving us from our sins.

As you worked through this material, you were able to see how the Divine Physician is healing you through each part of your Sacred Story, continuing through to the present moment.

Everything you have been walking through personally is also forming you to participate more fully in Christ's priestly ministry, so that you can accompany others on this journey of healing and transformation.

It is only as you come to understand your own journey through the eyes of God's mercy that you are able to offer that same gift to those to whom you minister in His name—Heb 4:15.

With those foundations, we now are ready to enter into Part II, which begins by exploring the two plot lines of our story. We are called to awaken, like St. Ignatius, to the content of our daily thoughts and daydreams. Which thoughts/fantasies/daydreams reveal the mind of the world? And which ones reveal the mind of Christ?

One plot line is rooted in original sin, which manifests in self-centered pride (narcissism). The other is centered in God's creation and redemption, where our identity is rooted and grounded in God's merciful and self-giving love and truth.

The exercise for this week is very simple and straightforward, but profoundly important to our spiritual well-being. You are monitoring at the end of each day your thoughts, fantasies and daydreams. As you become more aware of your thoughts and inspirations, be conscious that your mind is the primary battleground, where Satan wages his war (2 Cor 10:5; Eph 6:12).

This internal battle is expressed most succinctly in the struggle between what St. Paul refers to as "Spirit vs. Flesh":

"For those who live according to the flesh are concerned with the things of the flesh, but those who live according to the spirit with the things of the spirit. The concern of the flesh is death, but the concern of the spirit is life and peace" (Rom 8:5-6)

187

In Galatians, St. Paul further elaborates by highlighting the "works of the flesh" (immorality, impurity, idolatry, hatreds, selfishness etc.) from the "fruit of the Spirit" (love, joy, peace, patience, self-control etc.) (See Gal 5:19-23).

As you examine your thoughts, fantasies and daydreams this week, pay attention to which ones produce the fruit of love, joy, peace and gratitude. In contrast, notice the ones that result in a consciousness of shame, fear, anger and bitterness.

Your brother priests made these observations after engaging in this self-examination all week:

✠ *I have learned that I can daydream about narcissistic things at certain moments. And at certain other moments I may daydream about grateful daydreams. This means that I am the center of a big fight between my ego and my God-given human nature.*

✠ *We often have patterns of thoughts that lead to particular behaviors. If we can be more aware of where the thoughts are coming from, we can focus on the good, repent of the bad, and more easily lead lives of holiness and great virtue.*

✠ *I realized how subtle the narcissistic daydreams or thoughts can be and how they will swallow me up if I let them. The grateful dreams made me smile and helped me to want to please God more.*

✠ *I learned the importance of journaling the first thing that comes to mind, without thinking too much!*

> *Immaculate Heart of Mary pray for us so that our hearts may be fully aligned with the Sacred Heart of your son Jesus.*

സ

NOTES

Week 15

FIRST

I will ask for the grace of patience to start each day with renewed commitment, even if I miss a day's prayer. I will have my notebook at hand for each prayer period. I will remember to spend no more and no less than fifteen minutes in each formal prayer session. At the end of each day, I will continue to note in writing one event that increased my faith, hope, and love and one event that decreased my faith, hope, and love. I will always use my personal name for God.

SECOND

I am listening this week for the way that pride (narcissism) takes shape in my daily life. I will do this by engaging an attentiveness prayer that examines the two principal forms of narcissism (passive and aggressive). On Monday, Tuesday, and Wednesday of this week, I will reflect on one type of narcissism, and on Thursday, Friday, and Saturday, I will reflect on the other.

THIRD

I will continue to draw consolation from my letter to Jesus/whole-life confession. Also, I can bring insights on narcissism from my daily life into my prayer times. Sacred Story prayer is rooted in my asking God for help.

Through grace, an intimate relationship between myself and God is being established.

I will awaken to the present moment.

I will awaken to my spiritual nature.

I will not make any decisions based on fear.

This week, I will say this affirmation aloud once daily:

Be not afraid.

Fear comes from the enemy of my human nature.

CB

Read this page and the next at the beginning of the week:

Recall how Ignatius of Loyola discovered a narcissistic pride at the root of all his manifest sins, addictions, spiritual dysfunction, and emotional imbalances. In Genesis, pride is the principal sin of Adam and Eve, or as we might define it today, narcissism.[13] The serpent tempted both Adam and Eve with eating the fruit of the forbidden tree by telling them that their "eyes will be opened" and they would "be like gods" (Gen 3:5). The rest of the story is the history of sin, sickness, and death.

The immense grief, sorrow, and guilt of paradise lost by human choice are memories burned deep in the heart of each and every woman and man who has lived, is living, or will ever walk this earth. But praise God, because it is through the wound, guilt, and grief of paradise lost that we come to understand the divisions in our hearts (Jer 17:9).

Although our sin separates us from God, it still points out the path that sets each woman and man on a journey back home to God and to our authentic self. St. Ignatius achieved his greatest enlightenment when he identified the pattern of sin in his story. Once he awoke to it, God used him powerfully in the work of redemption. God will do the same for each of us.

Awakening to our prideful narcissism is understood as a positive move toward deeper spiritual growth. It is not a depressing exercise to make us feel bad or fearful. If these negative emotions result from your prayer, set your eyes and heart on Christ Jesus, the Divine Physician. Recall that He looks on you with joy and love as you discover the things that diminish your hope and spiritual freedom. Allow Christ to work His healing graces in your story. Remember our affirmation for this week: fear comes from the enemy of human nature.

How does narcissism work? Narcissism, or pride (both words describe the same damaging spiritual darkness), makes me the center of the universe and the ultimate arbiter of all truth. Narcissism displaces God in order that I can be "like a god." From that first sin of narcissism flows humankind's banishment from paradise; the advent of pain, sickness, and death; the emergence of evolutionary evil in family structures, as evidenced by Cain's murder of Abel; and the fracturing of the human community as symbolized in the greed, competition, and overweening pride underlying the parable of the Tower of Babel.

Man and woman consciously displaced God as their center and source, and made themselves center and source. From this results the fracturing of creation's harmony. A terminal virus of sin now infects the core of all living things. The corruption caused by this virus has even altered life at the cellular, molecular, and biological level. Nothing in the created order has been left untouched or unharmed by the virus of this sin (Gen 3:17–19; Rom 8:18–27).

We are all born into it, and we all participate in it. Self-centeredness is an equal-opportunity employer. All serious Christian prayer disciplines target this core sin so that by the power of Christ's sacrifice, "creation itself would be set free from slavery to corruption and share in the glorious freedom of the children of God" (Rom 8:21).

It is spiritually valuable—exceedingly so—to understand what form of prideful narcissism your life circumstances have shaped in you. It might be helpful to realize that no side of pride's face is better than the other. Both are equally difficult to admit! Both forms of prideful narcissism displace God in our lives and serve to mask our wounded human nature— our heart's grief at paradise lost.

Prayer Exercise

With the Divine Physician's grace, ask to understand how you displace God as the center of your life. Ask to become aware of the grief, anger, and fear that grips you, and the void at the center of your heart and soul that only He can heal. The grace of a whole-life confession gives us renewed humility. It fosters a desire to open more to Christ's life and the spiritual growth, insights, freedom, hope, and peace it brings!

The following two exercises will help you identify your type of prideful narcissism. Spend the prayer periods of three days on each type (Monday, Tuesday, and Wednesday or Thursday, Friday, and Saturday). You decide which type to reflect on first and which one second.

Note that this week's prayer exercise is not to solve your prideful narcissism problem! That would be discouraging (and impossible)! It is enough for now to identify, with the Divine Physician's grace, a type of narcissism that you judge more present in your story. I want to emphasize that it was when Ignatius awoke to his prideful narcissism that God was able to really work with him. You will likely discover one or the other of these two principal manifestations of prideful narcissism at the root of all things difficult in your life.

Purposely, these two types are defined in very stark language so you can distinguish them clearly. You most likely will not feel them as strongly in your story as they are drawn here. So in your reflection and prayer, attend more to the type to which you are susceptible and not so much the intensity. Ask the Divine Physician to guide your prayerful awakening in peace, trust, and hope. These two faces of narcissism capture the principal forms of pride that life's circumstances generate in human nature wounded by Original Sin.

Cઠ

The Passive Narcissist

Take the prayer periods of three days to pray with this description of the passive narcissist. It is vital to understand this type of Original Sin's pride manifesting in human dysfunction. Note briefly in your journal what you consider significant that causes anxiety or hope. Are the passive narcissist's qualities ones that typify your negative story?

This type of narcissism rehearses and repeats the anger, fear, anxiety, and grief of old wounds and hurts. The passive narcissist complains, is grasping, is cynical, and makes excuses for everything except his own bad behavior. The passive narcissist draws attention to himself in every thought, word, and deed and says he is the center of attention in these ways: "See how I have suffered." "See how I have been victimized." "See how unfairly I am treated." "See why I behave the way I do." "See why I am justified in...."

The passive narcissist works hard to blame others for her wounds and labors mightily in every thought, word, and deed to make sure others know of her suffering. The passive narcissist takes pride and finds power and comfort in her victim status, whether it is real or perceived.

The passive narcissist works very hard to maintain her victim status and remain powerless, refusing to take responsibility for changing her situation, because changing the situation means confronting pain and offering forgiveness to those who helped her evolve this way. Changing also means losing her core identity of powerless victim. To lose this identity is to lose power and control. There are three main reasons for this.

First, losing victim status means literally losing power and control of the people and events in the passive narcissist's world. Second, he is disconnected from his authentic self, so losing the status of victim initiates an acute and fearful identity crisis, because life's meaning and definitions of success have been intimately linked with being a powerless victim. Third, as a result of the loss of power and control and the loss of his false identity, the passive narcissist will be confronted with the spiritual, psychological, and emotional wounds hiding behind the passive narcissism.

During your daily activities, pay attention to sudden anger, anxiety, fear, or grief that surfaces. Pray for graced insights to comprehend how sudden anger, temptation, anxiety, fear, or grief touch the deep spiritual, emotional, and physical wounds and Original Sins in your life. For those events that seem to jump out at you and capture your attention, consciously do this short exercise, speaking to Christ from your heart:

✠ Ask to be conscious of what you are reacting to rather than reacting impulsively, without thinking.

✠ Ask to feel the heart's fear, temptation, anxiety, anger, and grief present in the reaction.

✠ Ask for knowledge—for graced insight—to begin dismantling this immature, damaging, and self-glorifying process, which for a passive narcissist is particularly depressing and for an aggressive narcissist is particularly electrifying.

✠ Ask who or what initiated this particular pattern of reaction—of overpowering or of blaming others—and why?

✠ Ask for courage to face the negative story of being a passive victim, because facing it can cause panic when you are used to being its slave, but confronting it can bring you peace and freedom.

The Aggressive Narcissist

Take the prayer periods of three days to pray with this description of the aggressive narcissist. It is vital to understand this type of Original Sin's pride manifesting in human dysfunction. Note briefly in your journal what you consider significant that causes anxiety or hope. Are the aggressive narcissist's qualities ones that typify your negative story?

This type of narcissism also rehearses and repeats the anger, fear, anxiety, and grief of old wounds and hurts. The wounded, prideful aggressor gets even, is grasping, and is determined to best others and to justify and excuse her behavior in the process. The aggressive narcissist draws attention to herself in every thought, word, and deed and says she is the center of attention in these ways: "See how special and gifted I am." "See that you never get in my way." "See, you will never overpower me." "See, I deserve what I have, because I earned it." "See, no one will ever hurt me again."

The aggressive narcissist works hard never to let anyone best him and labors mightily in every thought, word, and deed to make sure others get the message of his superiority. The aggressive narcissist takes pride in, and finds tremendous energy in, his triumphs over others, real or perceived. The aggressive narcissist works very hard to maintain his

winner status, for his negative story is now totally associated with being the winner. To lose winner status is to lose power and control. There are three main reasons for this.

First, losing winner status means losing the power and control of the people and events in the aggressive narcissist's world. Second, she is disconnected from her authentic self, so losing the status of winner initiates an acute and fearful identity crisis, because life's meaning and definitions of success have been intimately linked with the story of being the winner. Third, as a result of the loss of power and control and the loss of her false identity, the aggressive narcissist will be confronted with the spiritual, psychological, and emotional wounds hiding behind her aggressive narcissism.

During your daily activities, pay attention to sudden anger, anxiety, fear, or grief that surfaces. Pray for graced insights to comprehend how sudden anger, temptation, anxiety, fear, or grief touch the deep spiritual, emotional, and physical wounds and Original Sins in your life.

For those events that seem to jump out at you and capture your attention, consciously do this short exercise, speaking to Christ from your heart:

✠ Ask to be conscious of what you are reacting to rather than reacting impulsively, without thinking.

✠ Ask to feel the heart's fear, temptation, anxiety, anger, and grief present in the reaction.

✠ Ask for knowledge—for graced insight—to begin dismantling this immature, damaging, and self-glorifying process, which for a passive narcissist is particularly depressing and for an aggressive narcissist is particularly electrifying.

✠ Ask who or what initiated this particular pattern of reaction—of overpowering or of blaming others—and why?

✠ Ask for courage to face the negative story of being a passive victim, because facing it can cause panic when you are used to being its slave, but confronting it can bring you peace and freedom.

THE PASSIVE NARCISSIST	THE AGGRESSIVE NARCISSIST
SELF-IDENTIFIES AS A VICTIM	SELF-IDENTIFIES AS A WINNER
IS DETERMINED TO HAVE OTHERS NOTICE HOW SPECIAL THEY ARE BY POINTING TO THEIR UNFAIR SUFFERING	IS DETERMINED TO HAVE OTHERS NOTICE HOW SPECIAL THEY ARE BY DEFEATING ALL OPPONENTS
IS CYNICAL AND EXCUSES BAD BEHAVIOR BY INSISTING IT IS JUSTIFIED BECAUSE OF HOW MUCH THEY HAVE SUFFERED	IS CYNICAL AND EXCUSES BAD BEHAVIOR BY INSISTING IT IS JUSTIFIED BECAUSE THEY HAVE EARNED IT
WALLOWS IN SELF-PITY WHEN HURT, WHETHER THE HURT IS REAL OR IMAGINED	IS VINDICTIVE WHEN HURT, WHETHER THE HURT IS REAL OR IMAGINED
BLAMES ANYONE WHO CRITICIZES OR OPPOSES THEM	THREATENS ANYONE WHO CRITICIZES OR OPPOSES THEM
PROTECTS THEMSELF FROM BEING HURT AGAIN BY KEEPING WOUNDS AS FRESH AS POSSIBLE. IF ANYTHING IS TOO DIFFICULT OR PAINFUL, THEY WILL RETREAT INTO THOSE PAINFUL MEMORIES AND TURN INWARD, AWAY FROM OTHERS	PROTECTS THEMSELF FROM BEING HURT AGAIN BY ERADICATING VULNERABILITIES. IF ANYTHING IS TOO DIFFICULT OR PAINFUL, THEY WILL ACT IN A CONQUEROR ROLE AND DOMINATE OTHERS
WINS BY EMOTIONAL MANIPULATION	WINS BY DIRECT CONFRONTATION
IS SECRETLY ATTACHED TO THEIR OWN WOUNDEDNESS	IS SECRETLY ATTACHED TO THIER POWER OF DEFEATING OTHERS
IS TERRIFIED OF TAKING CONTROL AND PERSONAL RESPONSIBILITY AND HAS DIFFICULTY ADMITTING THIS TO ONESELF	IS TERRIFIED OF SURRENDERING CONTROL AND BEING VULNERABLE AND HAS DIFFICULTY ADMITTING THIS TO ONESELF

ଔ

༅

Why, Lord, do you stand afar
and pay no heed in times of trouble?

Arrogant scoundrels pursue the poor;
they trap them by their cunning schemes.

The wicked even boast of their greed;
these robbers curse and scorn the Lord.

In their insolence the wicked boast:
"God does not care; there is no God."

Yet their affairs always succeed;
they ignore your judgment on high;
they sneer at all who oppose them.

They say in their hearts, "We will never fall;
never will we see misfortune."

Their mouths are full of oaths, violence, and lies;
discord and evil are under their tongues.

They wait in ambush near towns;
their eyes watch for the helpless
to murder the innocent in secret.

They lurk in ambush like lions in a thicket,
hide there to trap the poor,
snare them and close the net.

The helpless are crushed, laid low;
they fall into the power of the wicked,
who say in their hearts, "God has forgotten,
shows no concern, never bothers to look."

Rise up, Lord! God, lift up your hand!
Do not forget the poor!

Why should the wicked scorn God,
say in their hearts, "God does not care"?

But you do see;
you take note of misery and sorrow;
you take the matter in hand.

To you the helpless can entrust their cause;
you are the defender of orphans.

Break the arm of the wicked and depraved;
make them account for their crimes;
let none of them survive.

The Lord is king forever;
the nations have vanished from his land.

You listen, Lord, to the needs of the poor;
you strengthen their heart and incline your ear.

You win justice for the orphaned and oppressed;
no one on earth will cause terror again.
(Ps 10)

℘

Dr. Schuchts' Reflection ~ Week Fifteen

Passive and Aggressive Narcissism

The theme for this 15th week--passive and aggressive narcissism-- was especially eye opening for me the first time I engaged *Forty Weeks*. It continues to bring me self-understanding. I pray that it is equally illuminating for you.

We all have natural blind spots when it comes to seeing our narcissism. Unfortunately, that is one of the primary symptoms of the disease known as Original Sin.

I appreciate Jesus' humor in confronting our spiritual far-sightedness: *Why do you notice the splinter in your brother's eye, but do not perceive the wooden beam in your own eye? (Mt. 7:3).*

Isn't it ironic, that when we make ourselves the center of everything we can barely see ourselves at all? It's like trying to look at our nose. We see some blurry images, but not much else.

And yet we delude ourselves into believing that we can clearly see the faults and failings of others. Did you notice how easy it was to diagnose passive and aggressive narcissism in the people around you this week?

Some of the people we have difficulty with seem to revel in playing the victim, by constantly nursing their wounds. Others are aggressively trying to get what they want with little regard for how they are affecting those around them.

What about us? Everything in us (not inspired by the Holy Spirit) wants to deny that we too are blinded by this deeply rooted self-centeredness and pride, which compels us to overcome our vulnerability with aggression or passive self-protection.

Think about how we responded in the past or respond currently when someone hurts us-. Do we pay attention to the emotional impact of these experiences and vulnerably work through these hurts with Christ?

Or are we more prone to react, either aggressively- with dominating anger, or passively- by finding comfort in our victim identity and punishing others by withdrawal?

Aggressive narcissism involves a grasping to meet our own needs. The seven deadly sins (vices) are various manifestations of the aggressive narcissist.

Rather than trust the Father to provide for our needs, we instead take life into our own hands. We try to overcome our helplessness by exerting power and control.

Similarly, the seven deadly wounds (abandonment, rejection, fear, powerlessness, hopelessness, shame, and confusion) can easily become the building blocks of our passive narcissism. Each of the identity-lies becomes part of our victim mentality.

Rather than trusting the Father to comfort us in our wounds (see 2 Co. 1), we too easily look to our addictions to medicate our pain.

Do you see how much our life has been overtaken by narcissism? Spending a week to reflect on this gives each of us many opportunities for self-discovery, and with it greater humility. It is placed after the Whole-Life Confession to give us the confidence to approach Christ who loves us and wants to free us from what binds.

These are some of the insights from your brother priests:

✠ *I realized how subtle the aggressive and passive narcissism can be. It's not always obvious.*

✠ *It can be difficult to distinguish between the two because most of us can have both passive tendencies in life and a drive to win.*

✠ *I found the distinction between Aggressive and Passive Narcissism helpful. I see the three-fold nature of: losing power and control of the people/events in one's world; disconnection from authentic self; and false identity.*

✠ *Because of sin, we all have the tendency to make everything about us and to put ourselves at the center of everything. It may not mean that we like to be the center of attention or try to bully people into doing what we want, but the truth is that the tendency is still there. Things like wallowing in self-pity and playing the victim card are just as self-centered.*

Immaculate Heart of Mary pray for us so that our hearts may be fully aligned with the Sacred Heart of your son Jesus.

ဢ

NOTES

Week 16

FIRST

I continue to ask for patience to start each day with renewed commitment. I will not be discouraged by the times I have missed prayer but will instead ask God for help to be more faithful. I will bring my notebook to prayer and resolve to spend no more and no less than fifteen minutes in each prayer period. I will always use my personal name for God.

SECOND

This week, I am invited to learn the components of Sacred Story daily practice. My fidelity to the linked practice of these daily exercises will produce sustained spiritual growth and enlightenment. Ignatius was a strategist, and he understood that spiritual exercises must be regular, focused, and open to grace. It is up to me to ask God for help in using these resources for my healing and spiritual growth.

THIRD

I will continue to draw consolation from my letter to Jesus/whole-life confession.

I will awaken to the present moment.

I will awaken to my spiritual nature.

I will not make any decisions based on fear.

I will practice sacramental Reconciliation monthly.

This week, I will say this affirmation aloud once daily:
The pathway to God's peace and healing runs through my heart's
brokenness, sin, fear, anger, and grief.

ᚥ

Read this page at the beginning of the week:

The most important activity in any day is the time I take to direct my conscious attention—my mind and heart—to God in a prayer relationship. Not only is my relationship with God the most important dimension of life, it is also a relationship that takes time—a lifetime—to build! The depth of the relationship I desire will be evident in my fidelity to my prayer and sacramental life. As Scripture says, where your treasure is, so will your heart be (Mt 6:21).

Sacred Story Daily Practice

The Sacred Story prayer routine is a time-proven and highly effective discipline for waking up to God's life in you, and your life in God. Practiced daily, you learn to surrender to God. You will find interior freedom and peace so that your life's labor produces fruit that endures to eternity. Ignatius and the early Jesuits used similar prayers in conjunction with frequent sacramental Reconciliation as primary spiritual tools in their pastoral ministries in Europe and the New World.

The combined practice of regular prayer and sacramental Reconciliation has produced tremendous spiritual growth for countless thousands of souls and still does so today. Sacred Story prayer can bring this dual spiritual practice into your Christian life to help you encounter Christ daily. It would be hard to find a more effective prayer discipline for this purpose. This week's lesson teaches the prayer disciplines that serve as a

206

support structure for Sacred Story prayer, which you will start next week. It will be a tremendous benefit for you to learn these habits of thought and introduce them into your daily life.

One of the chief victories of human nature's enemy in modern times is the violence of hyperactivity and a loss of interior silence. The prayer disciplines you learn about this week, the Sacred Story prayer you start next week, and a regular practice of Reconciliation will help you counter this unique modern form of violence and open your heart to the voice of God. These practices are simple, take little time, and if done faithfully, will move you forward on the path of holiness and integration with your sacred story. They are valuable spiritual practices for your life.

Bookmark This Section

You will need this week's reference materials throughout the rest of the forty weeks and beyond. Use this week's prayer periods to become familiar with them, and bookmark them so you can reference them often. Remember that you are not expected to implement these exercises this week. We will begin implementing them next week.

☙

Prayer Exercise for Monday

Reflect on the instructions below for the "Prayer upon Waking," and use your fifteen-minute prayer period(s) today to understand this discipline. Note briefly in your journal what you consider significant. When you begin to incorporate this exercise into your day, you should be spending no more than fifteen to thirty seconds with it.

Prayer upon Waking (fifteen to thirty seconds)

Before arising from your bed, consciously awaken to Creation, Presence,

Memory, Mercy, and Eternity (these concepts are explained more later this week). Note any significant movements in your heart and mind that come from your dreams. Note the state of your heart regarding any planned events of the day. Pay particular attention to feelings of peace or anxiety that stir in you. Anticipate any challenges that might confront you today, especially those linked to your wounded human nature that might stir fear, anger, or grief in you. With gratitude, offer the thoughts, words, and deeds of your day to God.

C8

Prayer Exercise for Tuesday

Reflect on the instructions below for the "During-the-Day Awakening" prayer, and take your fifteen-minute quiet period(s) today to understand this discipline. Note briefly in your journal what you consider significant. This exercise is linked to the exercises on sin, addiction, vices, Commandments, narcissism, and people in your life narrative.

During-the-Day Awakening
to Sins, Addictions, and Compulsions (fifteen to thirty seconds)

Prepare your heart to watch and listen to your day as it unfolds. Be attentive to the events and circumstances that evoke temptation and incite your attraction to things low and earthly. These are easily recognized, because they trigger your angers or addictions. They hook into your vices and the fault lines in your mind and heart. You are, in short, seeking to "wake up" to what makes living the gospel of Christ Jesus difficult. Discipline yourself to not react to these things outwardly.

Be curious about why you are tempted or angry. Remain open to the links between the events that spark your temptations, angers, addictions, narcissism, and attractions to things low and earthly. Be conscious of the theme and the fact of the temptation. Wake up, and watch the process with Christ so He can teach you how to grow in grace.

When you are tempted or when you fail in the course of your day, Jesus is the Divine Physician who desires to help you. He judges you, but with compassion. He desires you to awaken to patterns of addiction, anger, narcissism, and chronic failures that rob you of freedom and peace, so they can be healed, you can be forgiven, and hope and peace can return to your life. Establish this ritual each time you are tempted and each time you fail by giving in to your core sins, wounds, addictions, angers, and narcissism:

✠ **DECLARE** the specific sin, addiction, narcissistic habit, or destructive compulsion as a false lover.

✠ **DESCRIBE** the specific sin, addiction, narcissistic habit, or destructive compulsion as coming from the enemy of your human nature.

✠ **DESCEND** with Christ into your memory, to see and feel your first experience of this specific sin, addiction, narcissistic habit, or destructive compulsion, asking Him to compassionately reveal the stress fractures, loneliness, and wounds in your heart that it promised to satisfy. (Once you have identified the first experience of various issues, you need only access the memory and then move to the next step).

✠ **DENOUNCE** the specific sin, addiction, narcissistic habit, or destructive compulsion for its ruinous effect in your life.

✠ **DECIDE** for Christ to heal this wound, defuse the stress, anxiety, and fear feeding it, and transform its damaging effects on your life into sacred story.

Your goal in this short exercise is to invite God's grace to be present in your most difficult issues. Do the exercise two or three times a day on the most obvious sins, angers, and failures. And then move on. Your awakening and healing is on God's schedule, not yours. Over time, this will become a spiritual exercise that comes naturally. It takes people varying amounts of time to make it a habit. But it will become a positive spiritual habit that decreases your fears, reveals your truest self, and deepens your trust in Jesus as your protector and healer. It will also open you to Christ constantly at the most critical moments during your day, reminding you that He is Lord and Savior of your life. Remember, you are not doing this exercise to learn how to save yourself. You are doing it to turn to the Savior who forgives, loves, and heals the sins, addictions, angers, and compulsions from which you cannot save yourself!

Cঙ

Prayer Exercise for Wednesday and Thursday

Reflect on the instructions on this page and the next for "Sacred Story Prayer at Midday and at Evening," and take your fifteen-minute prayer period(s) to understand the purpose of this discipline. The content for this main Sacred Story prayer will be given to you over the next ten weeks. It will take that long to learn the five meditations of Creation, Presence, Memory, Mercy, and Eternity and how to combine them into a single fifteen-minute prayer exercise. While we use the Creation, Presence, Memory, Mercy, and Eternity elements below to explain aspects of Sacred Story discipline, you will only fully understand these pieces once you have been introduced into their full practice over the next ten weeks. Consider this a preview, and do not be anxious if you "don't get it."

Sacred Story Prayer at Midday and at Evening (fifteen minutes)

Find a quiet place apart where you will not be disturbed. Bring with you the particular issues that surfaced in your day related to any specific annoyances or strong emotional events you experienced. Bring also your particular graces and inspirations.

During this time, you may kneel or sit, whichever is better suited to your prayer style and more conducive to contemplative reflection, prayer, and devotion. Keep your eyes closed or, if opened, in a fixed position, not allowing them to roam.

Take a full fifteen minutes for this exercise—no more and no less. You can consciously enter Sacred Story prayer for these fifteen-minute periods in one of two ways. Try both, and determine which best suits your character and personality. No matter which way you choose, at the beginning and at the end of the prayer time, in your imagination, see your whole life in God's hands, and say this antiphon inwardly, while breathing slowly and deeply:

"Creation...Presence... Memory...Mercy...Eternity."

First Way

Say "Creation," and continue meditating upon this word as long as you find meaning, connections, delight, and inspirations in considering it and some positive fruit in the graces you seek. The same method of reflection should be followed for each meditation in Sacred Story (Presence, Memory, Mercy, Eternity).

Second Way

With each breath you take, say interiorly, "Creation." And from one breath to another, ponder the graces and inspirations you seek. For this space of time, direct your attention mainly to the meaning of the word and graces you seek, the Person who is addressed, and why you need those graces. Follow this method with the other words (Presence, Memory, Mercy, Eternity) until you finish all the meditations in Sacred Story prayer.

For the body of the fifteen-minute prayer, after the opening antiphon and before the closing antiphon, you can be flexible. On some days, you may spend equal amounts of time on each meditation. On other days, you may spend most of your time on one meditation. Let your heart lead you, based on the events of the day and the images and emotions that emerge in your reflections.

As the lessons progress and you learn each meditation in Sacred Story prayer, only say the word[s] of the specific lesson for each week. Some weeks you will have only one word. Other weeks you will be combining two or more until you finally combine all five into your completed prayer.

After your closing litany, end the fifteen-minute Sacred Story Prayer at Midday and at Evening with one or the other of these two vocal prayers:

Our Father
This is the prayer favored by Ignatius for this discipline
Our Father, who art in heaven, hallowed be Thy name. Thy Kingdom come, Thy will be done, on earth, as it is in heaven. Give us this day our daily bread, and forgive us our trespasses, as we forgive those who trespass against us. Lead us not into temptation, but deliver us from evil.
Amen.

Suscipe
This is the prayer of St. Ignatius that concludes his Spiritual Exercises

Take Lord, receive, my liberty, my memory, my understanding, my entire will. Whatsoever I have or hold, You have given to me. I surrender it all back to you to be governed by your will. Give me only Your love and grace. This is enough for me, and I ask for nothing more.
Amen.

CB

Prayer Exercise for Friday

Reflect on the instructions below for "Daily Journaling" and "Prayer upon Retiring," and take your fifteen-minute quiet period(s) today to understand these disciplines. Note briefly in your notebook what you consider significant.

Daily Journaling (no more than two minutes)

Write in your journal daily, after you end your evening Sacred Story prayer session. It is not a diary but a logbook (of jottings, most accurately). What you write should be only single words or short phrases. The goal is to track the most significant events from your days. You are looking, first and foremost, for destructive patterns and trends in your life: patterns of fear, anger, and grief, and patterns of sin, compulsion, and addiction. In both of these patterns, you are also looking for links to persons, events, and issues. On the graced end of the scale, you are looking for gratitude, hope, and peace linked to your sacred story and the daydreams and fantasies coming from the Divine Inspirer.

The patterns and trends that are most relevant to Sacred Story in awakening to your life as a whole, and growing in interior freedom, are those that help you identify damaging, addictive, sinful habits at their roots. (This is the principal goal of the Particular Examen of St. Ignatius, which helps individuals name and target their core sins.) So be aware of patterns and trends that reveal triggering mechanisms that make you easy prey to habits, sins, angers, addictions, and vices. Pay attention in order to source the origins and "roots" of those habits from your early life. Remember that day's During-the-Day Awakening exercises, and ask for the grace to be aware of the importance of any significant events that open you to anger, fear, and grief or temptations, failures, and sins. Ask for God's grace to see your life integrated and holistic, as God does. God longs for your freedom, forgiveness, peace, and healing.

To help you in your journaling exercises, write the ideas discussed above by focusing your short entries within the following framework:

✠ Desolation from the Day: Write no more than two sentences on what decreased your faith, your hope, and your love for God and neighbor today.

✠ Consolation from the Day: Write no more than two sentences on what increased your faith, your hope, and your love for God and neighbor today.

People who engaged the journal exercise gained much more from the entire Sacred Story method than those who did not write in their journal. Those who persevered in the journal practice are the ones who learned to be brief and to do as instructed: write no more than a few words or a short phrase. You will not succeed in the journal practice if you take more than two minutes a day to accomplish it. Be brief but specific. (You can download a daily logbook for this purpose for free from the "Members" section of sacredstory.net.)

Prayer upon Retiring (fifteen seconds)

At day's end, listen to your heart for its state of spirit—peaceful or anxious—and what person or event inspires one or the other emotion. Speak a few words to God appropriate to your heart's peace or anxiety, and then invite God into your dreams.

 C3

Prayer Exercise for Saturday

Reflect on the instructions below for the "Journal at Week's End" and "Journal at Month's End," and take your fifteen-minute quiet period(s) today to understand these disciplines. Note briefly in your notebook what you consider significant as you come to understand the purpose of this exercise.

Journal at Week's End

On Sunday (or Saturday, if that is your "weekend"), in place of the daily journal exercise, review the words and phrases from your journaling of that week. Ponder the words and phrases, and ask to see the story of your whole life (Creation, Presence, Memory, Mercy, and Eternity). Notice what particular insights or inspirations arise in you. Do not try to force insights. Most likely, you will awaken gradually to patterns and trends.

After you read over your journal entries from the week, write a brief entry of a few sentences that captures any insights you have gained about your life over the course of the week's prayer and reflection process. Be attentive for any connections between persons, events, temptations, sins, fear, anger, grief, and strong emotions.

Pay particular attention to insights that can help you unravel the manifest and root spiritual and psychological stresses (sinful habits, psychological stresses, addictions, and vices) that might be linked to significant events from your past history. Write these insights in a new section of your notes (perhaps entitled "Insights and Integration.") Date these reflections so you can watch your progressive growth and awakening.

Journal at Month's End

At the end of a month, in place of the journal at week's end, review your summary insights from these end-of-week exercises, and look for any patterns that are emerging in your life story, especially those linked to the matrix of spiritual and psychological stresses highlighted by these insights. In your "Insights and Integration" section, write several sentences (such as "I think...." "I believe...." "I discovered....") that reveal any changes you have experienced in your life as a result of grace, healing, forgiveness, or the insights you receive.

It is highly recommended that you initiate a monthly ritual of receiving the sacrament of Reconciliation. This discipline of grace and sacramental accountability will give you energy to engage the Sacred Story daily practice and will provide a clear focus for your journal exercises. Those who engage this discipline of monthly Reconciliation, accompanied with Sacred Story prayer, advance immeasurably more than those who forgo the graces of this great sacrament of insight and healing. Your journal practice is excellent preparation for sacramental Reconciliation.

When you receive monthly Reconciliation, consider following the same pattern as when you made your whole-life confession. Write your confession and speak directly to Christ and talk about the events of your life and where you need healing and peace. Do not tire of repeating the same issues, sins, and failures. Rely on and ask for the grace to see more and more clearly the roots and origins of the challenges in your life. St. Ignatius even suggested that his followers make a life confession every six months! He said it would help them make a new book of their lives. However, monthly Reconciliation is sufficient for measured spiritual, psychological, and emotional growth and enlightenment—unless you have grave matter that begs immediate attention.[14]

SACRED STORY DAILY PRACTICE AT A GLANCE

✠ **Prayer upon Waking**

Attune to the day ahead, and invite God's help.

✠ **During-the-Day Awakening**

Awaken to sins, addictions, habits, and compulsions.

Declare the false lover.

Describe it as coming from the enemy of your human nature.

Descend with Christ into your memory.

Denounce the false lover for its ruinous effect.

Decide to allow Christ to heal you.

✠ **Sacred Story Prayer at Midday**

Opening antiphon

Meditation on

Creation, Presence, Memory, Mercy, and Eternity

Closing antiphon

Closing vocal prayer

✠ **During-the-Day Awakening**

✠ **Sacred Story Prayer at Evening**

✠ **Daily Journaling**

Note significant event(s) of the day that increased and/or decreased your faith, hope, and love.

✠ **Prayer upon Retiring**

Attune to your heart; invite God into your dreams.

✠ **Journal at Week's End**

Review daily journals; listen for and note trends, patterns, links.

✠ **Journal at Month's End**

Review weekly journals; listen for and note trends, patterns, links; compose statements expressing growth and change.

✠ **Monthly Sacramental Reconciliation**

You will be renewed and powerfully graced.

✠ **Consult the Affirmations Frequently**

These are your thumbnail discernment aids.

ଔ

Lord, you have been our refuge
through all generations.
Before the mountains were born,
the earth and the world brought forth,
from eternity to eternity you are God
(Ps 90:1–2)

ଯ

Dr. Schuchts' Reflection ~ Week Sixteen

The Examen Prayer

This 16th week is focused on different aspects of the Examen Prayer. This centuries-old prayer discipline stands at the Center of Ignatian Spirituality.

The particular prayer exercises you are studying this week will serve as the foundation for your prayer life throughout the rest of the Forty Weeks, and hopefully for the rest of your life.

Practiced with humility and faith, these simple prayers will transform your anti-story into a Sacred Story.

As you continue to practice, you will have the knowledge and experience to pass these spiritual disciplines to those you serve in your priestly ministry.

Day I

The exercises for Monday are intended to raise your awareness of how you wake up in the morning. What are the movements of your heart that come from your dreams? What stirs anxiety at the beginning of each day? What brings peace?

As you become more adept at paying attention to these movements of your heart, you will grow in greater awareness of the counter inspirations of the enemy, the unmet longings of your human nature, and the grace-filled inspirations from the Holy Spirit.

This fine-tuning of awareness is critical to your own personal spiritual growth as well as an invaluable aide in helping others in confession, spiritual direction, and pastoral counseling.

As you practice these five movements of Sacred Story--Creation,

Presence, Memory, Mercy and Eternity-- you are cultivating a more acute awareness of the movements of the Holy Spirit in your life.

Furthermore, this prayer activity will train you to turn your mind away from the bombardments of the world and the enemy of your human nature, while being renewed with "the mind of Christ" (1 Co. 2:16).

Day II

On the second day of week 16, you are awakening to your conscious thoughts throughout your day. The particular focus of attention is on those events and circumstances that evoke temptation or trigger vices.

I found this activity easy to apply, and helpful beyond what I anticipated. By naming, describing, and denouncing my sin or temptation as soon as I became aware of it, I found myself much freer to live in the present moment.

I was able to catch myself from the downward spiral of indulging in the temptation and/or in condemning myself for the sin. Inviting God's grace into those moments of awareness was freeing and brought peace.

I also found it extremely helpful to pay attention, when tempted, to the fractures of my heart that gave access to these counter-inspirations.

Days III-IV

During the middle days of this week you are given tools to practice Sacred Story prayer, by meditating on the issues that surfaced earlier in the day, to bring them into the light of Creation, Presence, Memory, Mercy, and Eternity.

This "meditation" is fully Christian in its focus. Rather than emptying the mind it is filling the mind with the truths of our Christian faith.

Breathing, a fundamental part of Creation, is a human way of "inspiring" and opening yourself to the inspirations of the Holy Spirit. The "mantra" is simply focusing on these very Christian understandings of the gospel message condensed into five simple words.

Days V-VI

The last two days of this week are designed to preview how to keep a logbook, using simple words and phrases, to capture the two kinds of movements of your heart-counter-inspirations and divine inspirations. These are for day's end, week's end and month's end.

Can you see how all this fits together in helping you allow Christ to transform your mind and heart.

The following observations from your brother priests show how this week's activity can strengthen your prayer life:

✠ There truly are times of day that are "most critical" to open our hearts to Christ --the times we are most likely to be worn down or caught off guard, and then fail to love as we should. Vigilance there is key.

✠ Movements of the heart are important to pay attention to. They can help us to identify our struggles and our aches and the way we try to satisfy them.

✠ The prayer templates - especially the prayers around rebuking evil & lies - offer a useful way to interiorly face the struggles & conflicts ministry involves.

✠ Reviewing the prayer template reminded me of the necessity to pray always. The more attentive we are to God's grace and the movements of our hearts, the better we will be able to respond to Him throughout the day.

Immaculate Heart of Mary pray for us so that our hearts
may be fully aligned with the Sacred Heart of your son Jesus.

ℰ

NOTES

Week 17

FIRST

I will ask for patience to start each day with renewed commitment. I will have my notebook at hand for each prayer period and resolve to spend no more and no less than fifteen minutes in each formal prayer session. I will always use my personal name for God.

SECOND

I will continue to draw consolation and insight from my letter to Jesus/whole-life confession.

THIRD

This week I am invited to learn the first meditation in Sacred Story prayer: Creation. My fidelity to the linked practice of these daily exercises will produce life-long sustained spiritual growth and enlightenment.

I will awaken to the present moment.
I will awaken to my spiritual nature.
I will not make any decisions based on fear.
I will practice sacramental Reconciliation monthly.

This week, I will say this affirmation aloud once daily:
God resolves all my problems with time and patience.

Sacred Story Prayer—Creation

Every day, consciously enter Sacred Story prayer during your set time(s). For these next weeks, we are building the five meditations of Sacred Story prayer. Set aside the other meditations, and focus on Creation for your fifteen-minute prayer sessions this week.

Remember the structure of the fifteen-minute Sacred Story prayer sessions you were introduced to last week. Be faithful to the structure. Ignatius was wise in developing the ritual, and rituals are very important. The ritual itself detailed below does not save you. Yet the ritual, faithfully practiced, makes it easier for you to open your mind and heart to the One who does save you! Rituals are good.

Remember that the complete Sacred Story daily practice has six parts:

1. Prayer upon Waking

2. During-the-Day-Awakening exercises over the course of the day

3. Sacred Story Prayer at Midday (this week, Creation prayer only)

4. Sacred Story Prayer at Evening (this week, Creation prayer only)

5. Daily Journaling immediately following Sacred Story prayer at evening

6. Prayer upon Retiring

During this week, we are only focusing on Creation for the fifteen-minute prayer period(s) so you can learn it by heart. There are four ways to learn a meditation: a single word, a single phrase, a single description ("Prelude"), and a single grace for which to pray ("Illuminative Grace").

All four elements compose a single exercise. It seems like a lot at first, but in time you will be able to understand the elements of Creation without having to refer to any text. One way to internalize the meaning of the meditation is to read through the prayer exercise text (the word, the phrase, the Prelude, and the Illuminative Grace) and then ponder those ideas while using one of the two ways to focus (letting yourself be led by the inspirations of the word or letting yourself be led by the conversation with the Lord about the graces you seek related to the word).

Remember, eventually we will be meditating on five different words but only spending significant time with those words that the Spirit is leading us to for that day. This is why it is important for us to learn both the substance for each of the words as well as the standard meditation process for the fifteen-minute periods.

Do not be anxious about learning everything at once—we are going slowly for a reason! This week, focus on internalizing the meaning of Creation and learning the rhythm of the fifteen-minute prayer period. The meditation text for Creation is below. (Remember, this is the summary of the word, which you will use as a guide during your meditation). Review the structure of the fifteen-minute prayer sessions. You will find these at the bookmark you left in week 16.

CREATION
I believe God created everything in love and for love;
I ask for heartfelt knowledge of God's love for me
and for gratitude for the general and particular graces of this day.

Prelude
God created the universe—all persons and all things—in love and for love. Every person and every thing in creation is linked in Love, through Christ, in whom and for whom everything was made. We are made to reverence God and each other and to delight in creation as both divine gift and support for our lives. The God of All knows me personally and loves me, even before I was knit in my mother's womb. So fearfully and wonderfully made am I! (Ps 139:13–14). My gratitude increases as my awakening to these truths is illuminated.

Illuminative Grace

225

Here I ask for what I desire: to know and feel God's tender and passionate love and to know myself as beloved—a treasure of God's heart in the grand symphony of creation. I pray for the grace of gratitude. In particular, I pray to know by whom I am created and why I am loved. I pray to know and believe that I am fearfully and wonderfully made.

 C3

> When I see your heavens, the work of your fingers,
> the moon and stars that you set in place—
> What is man that you are mindful of him,
> and a son of man that you care for him?
> Yet you have made him little less than a god,
> crowned him with glory and honor.
> You have given him rule over the works of your hands,
> put all things at his feet:
> O LORD, our Lord, how awesome is your name
> through all the earth!
> (Ps 8:4–6)

SO

Sacred Story Prayer—Creation

This week you are meditating on this singular aspect of the Sacred Story prayer. The goal is to be able to internalize the meaning and purpose of *Creation* and to live in continual wonder for all the gifts the Father continues to pour out every moment of every day.

The grace you are praying for this week is gratitude for the Father's tender and compassionate love and to accept your identity as His Beloved Son.

This meditation begins with our understanding of four of the most fundamental truths of our faith:

✠ "God is Love" (1 John 4:8).

✠ The Trinity is a communion of self-giving love (CCC, 221)

✠ All of creation is an expression of this boundless love (CCC, 293)

✠ We are His cherished and beloved children (1 Jn. 3:1).

Allowing those truths to penetrate our hearts inspires us to worship, wonder, and to be filled with gratitude.

The psalmist awakens us to the most obvious reality: the heavens and the earth reveal the glory of God! (Ps. 19). All we have to do is look around us at any moment to realize this truth.

Everything we see and experience in the natural order is an extravagant and purposefully wise gift from our Heavenly Father, given in communion with Jesus and the Holy Spirit.

Pause a moment to allow that reality to sink in. Our existence is pure gift. The stunning beauty which surrounds us is a lavish endowment from our generous Father, who is the source of all beauty and goodness.

Every molecule of air we breathe and the ground we walk on is a fresh donation from the One who is continuously creating everything anew. How much sky and dirt do we do we really need? Do you see the magnificence of his generosity and super-abundance?

Now consider this larger reality in pondering the gift of yourself and the rest of the human race. You and I are fearfully and wonderfully made. Every thought and word is beheld by the Father before we consider it (Ps. 139).

We are the glorious crown of His creation, made a little lower than the angels for a season, but destined to spend eternity in intimate communion with Him.

Why is this so hard to take into the depths of our being? Why do we resist? Do you see how much sin has tarnished our ability to perceive God's greatness and our own greatness as a reflection of His?

From the moment we were born into God's glorious creation, we have been blessed by his generosity, but also bombarded by the lies of the enemy of our human nature distorting our identity and diminishing our worth.

St. John Paul II once said the gravest danger is not thinking too highly of ourselves but failing to see our true dignity and inestimable worth in the eyes of Father.

This heart-felt knowledge that you are a delight to the Father is foundational for your healing. You will live in wholeness and integrity to the extent that you believe this truth about yourself and receive it deeply into your heart and spirit.

You are his *beloved son*, in whom the Father delights! You are treasured beyond measure, amazingly gifted, lavishly blessed, and eternally chosen! Why do you continue to reject yourself and believe you are worthless? That is a lie which originates from the enemy of your human nature.

At Jesus' baptism, the Father did not just speak the words that Jesus is his Beloved Son. He sent His Spirit, the Gift of Love, to confirm it. You have also received the same Spirit of Love from the Father when you were baptized.

Remember, the words of St. John Paul II at World Youth Day in Toronto: "You are not the sum of your weaknesses and failures. You *are the sum of the Father's love for you* and your real possibility of becoming the image of his Son."

As I write all this, I think of one of the priest who recently attended a conference and came away with a new acceptance of his identity as a beloved son. He said when he returned to his parish, he began to see every person differently and wanted everyone to receive this gift of knowing they were the Father's beloved.

Your brother priests had similar insights as they meditated on creation, gratitude, and identity this week:

✠ *The wonders of creation have been created in love by God for us to be happy. Creation is a poem of God's love for his people.*

✠ *I was led to receive the truth that I am wonderfully made. I feel that most people who approach us for ministry have not received that truth. Taking to heart these and other foundational truths is essential to the healing process.*

✠ *Every time I meditated on Creation, I was filled with gratitude for the awesome and wonderful gift of life and my vocation as a priest. This was especially poignant as it is Holy Week.*

✠ *Meditating on the fact that I was created in love and for love helps me feel secure in my identity and purpose in life. The creation meditation grounds me and makes my foundation clear. So, whenever I'm unsure in my work or ministry, I can always recall these truths, quickly reorient myself, and allow the Lord to reassure me of who I am - His beloved child.*

Immaculate Heart of Mary pray for us so that our hearts may be fully aligned with the Sacred Heart of your son Jesus.

☙

NOTES

Week 18

FIRST

As I engage Sacred Story prayer this week, I may find it helpful to recommit to my daily fifteen-minute sessions. I resolve to spend no more and no less than fifteen minutes in each formal prayer session. I will always use my personal name for God.

SECOND

For week 18, I am invited to open my heart to Presence, the second meditation in Sacred Story prayer. I will strive to trust St. Ignatius's wisdom and engage the prayer disciplines at least once daily as he suggested.

THIRD

Use your first prayer session to read through Presence, and then do the Sacred Story prayer exercise as suggested during your fifteen-minute prayer sessions for the rest of the week.

I will awaken to the present moment.
I will awaken to my spiritual nature.
I will not make any decisions based on fear.
I will practice sacramental Reconciliation monthly.

This week, I will say this affirmation aloud once daily:

I will always have difficulties in this life.

ⱋ

Sacred Story Prayer—Presence

Every day, consciously enter Sacred Story prayer during your set time(s). For these next weeks, we are building the five meditations of Sacred Story prayer. Set aside the other meditations, and focus on Presence for your fifteen-minute prayer sessions this week.

Remember the structure of the fifteen-minute sessions you were introduced to last week. Be faithful to the structure. Ignatius was wise in developing the ritual, and rituals are very important. The ritual itself detailed below does not save you. Yet the ritual, faithfully practiced, makes it easier for you to open your mind and heart to the One who does save you! Rituals are good. Review the structure of the fifteen-minute prayer sessions. You will find these at the bookmark you left in week 16.

PRESENCE

I believe God is present in each moment and event of my life,
and I ask for grace to awaken, see and feel where and how,
especially in this present moment.

Prelude

The eternal God can only be experienced in the here and now, for everything in the universe is sustained by God's love in the present moment. When I worry about the past or fret about the future, my consciousness of God, of creation, and of my deepest desires is blocked. My challenge is to anchor both heart and mind firmly in the present—in each thought, word, and deed—as the story of my life evolves, in each moment, in God's presence.

Illuminative Grace

Here I ask for what I desire: to be present and awake to every feeling, thought, word, and deed—in the present moment. I beg for the grace to wake up to God's presence in every person, experience, and event—good or ill—that I encounter in my day.

ↄ৪

How lovely your dwelling,
O Lord of hosts!
My soul yearns and pines
for the courts of the Lord.
My heart and flesh cry out
for the living God.
As the sparrow finds a home
and the swallow a nest to settle her young,
My home is by your altars,
Lord of hosts, my king and my God!
Blessed are those who dwell in your house!
They never cease to praise you.
(Ps 84:2–5)

৪ↄ

Dr. Schuchts' Reflection ~ Week Eighteen

Sacred Story Prayer: Presence

This week you are continuing your reflection on the second aspect of Sacred Story prayer: *Presence.* The goal is to become more aware of God's presence in every moment, person and event, so that you can become increasingly more aware of the movements of desolation and consolation in your own heart.

In my own personal reflections this week, the Holy Spirit led me to contemplate God's presence as it continuously emanates throughout all of creation. Realizing in a deeper way that creation is held together at every moment by God's sustaining love, I grew in appreciation for the wonder of all that is "seen and unseen".

The Spirit then led me to a greater awareness of how God's presence sustains me personally in every moment of every day. I realize that I could not think, feel or breathe apart from God. Whether or not I am consciously aware of His presence in and around me, my existence is living proof of His intimate presence. Even in times of doubt or distance this reality is self-evident. Coming to this awareness naturally progressed to a greater appreciation of God's manifest presence in every person that I encounter in my daily life.

When I am aware of this reality on a daily basis (that God is present in the people I encounter), I grow in reverence for every person. When I lose sight of God's presence in others, I unwittingly lose respect for them.

But then I wondered why some people seem to radiate his presence more than others. And for each one of us, I noted that there seems to be a tremendous amount of variance at different times in how present we are to God, ourselves, and others.

I have been asking myself, what keeps me from being more aware of God's presence? And what prevents me from being more present to myself and to those around me? I believe it has to do with my reluctance to face the daily suffering in my life. When I disconnect from my heart, I similarly disconnect from God and the people around me.

I have been told by those who met St. John Paul II that he had an amazing gift of presence when people encountered him. He certainly suffered, but somehow, he allowed the Holy Spirit to transform him.

I can only imagine what it must have been like to encounter Jesus in person. Living in full awareness of the Father's presence, He was able to manifest that presence with others. Remember His words to Philip: "Whoever has seen me has seen the Father!" (Jn. 14:9).

This train of thought led me to reflect on my experiences with Jesus' Real Presence in the Eucharist. My faith tells me He is visibly and manifestly present. But I wonder how present I am, when I receive Him in Holy Communion and adore Him in the Blessed Sacrament.

Too often, that same detachment of heart, perpetuated by my sin and addictions, keeps me half asleep and minimally conscious of His Presence. Yet there have also been many experiences where I have intensely experienced His Presence. Those peak spiritual experiences give me a glimpse of heaven and a taste of what it means to be fully awake and alive.

As I reflect on all these things, I am reminded of the Psalm 16:11: "You make known to me the path of life. In your presence there is fullness of joy." I long for this fullness of joy, don't you?

Can you envision how Christ's priestly ministry through you will be transformed as you grow in greater awareness both of His presence and your own attentiveness to your interior states of consolation and desolation? Can you see yourself impacting the people you encounter, the way that St. John Paul did?

Here are some reflections from your brother priests as they reflected on Presence this week:

✠ Presence is another way to sense and experience God whose name is I AM. Being strong in faith means the awareness of the Father's presence with us no matter what the influence (good or bad) of people, events, and circumstances we experience. Therefore, the awakening to God's presence will lead to success.

✠ Being aware of the presence of God completely changes my perspective on events, feelings, prayer.

✠ It is very difficult to be present in the moment, to focus on God with me now, and not to worry about the past or future. This shows me how important it is to continually make time for God and create space for Him. Otherwise, I will quickly be swept away in work, anxieties, and plans.

✠ This really does work - telling myself that I will remember that God's grace is experienced in the PRESENT kept me more anchored there.

Immaculate Heart of Mary pray for us so that our hearts
may be fully aligned with the Sacred Heart of your son Jesus.

℘

NOTES

Week 19

FIRST

As I engage the Sacred Story prayer this week, I will make a point of reviewing my prayer discipline and make any necessary changes to be more faithful to the daily disciplines I have committed to. I also resolve to spend no more and no less than fifteen minutes in each formal prayer period. I will always use my personal name for God.

SECOND

For week nineteen, I am combining meditations one and two in the Sacred Story prayer: Creation and Presence. I will enter my prayer at least once daily as St. Ignatius suggested.

THIRD

I will commit to reviewing the prayer structures from week 16.

I will awaken to the present moment.
I will awaken to my spiritual nature.
I will not make any decisions based on fear.
I will practice sacramental Reconciliation monthly.

This week, I will say this affirmation aloud once daily:
There are just two ways to cope with my difficulties.

One leads to life; one to death. I will choose life.

൦ჳ

Review the structure of the fifteen-minute prayer sessions. You will find these at the bookmark you left in week 16. For this week, you are combining the first two meditations in Sacred Story prayer: Creation and Presence. Use your fifteen-minute prayer sessions this week to pray these two meditations together, following the wisdom you learned in week 16 for this practice.

CREATION

I believe God created everything in love and for love;
I ask for heartfelt knowledge of God's love for me
and for gratitude for the general and particular graces of this day.

Prelude

God created the universe—all persons and all things—in love and for love. Every thing and every person in creation is linked in Love, through Christ, in whom and for whom everything was made. We are made to reverence God and each other and to delight in creation as both divine gift and support for our lives. The God of All knows me personally and loves me, even before I was knit in my mother's womb. So fearfully and wonderfully made am I! (Ps 139:13–14). My gratitude increases as my awakening to these truths is illuminated.

Illuminative Grace

Here I ask for what I desire: to know and feel God's tender and passionate love, and to know myself as beloved—a treasure of God's heart in the grand symphony of creation. I pray for the grace of gratitude. In particular, I pray to know by whom I am created and why I am loved. I pray to know and believe that I am fearfully and wonderfully made.

PRESENCE

I believe God is present in each moment and event of my life, and I ask for grace to awaken, see and feel where and how, especially in this present moment.

Prelude

The eternal God can only be experienced in the here and now, for everything in the universe is sustained by God's love in the present moment. When I worry about the past or fret about the future, my consciousness of God, of creation, and of my deepest desires, is blocked. My challenge is to anchor both heart and mind firmly in the present—in each thought, word, and deed—as the story of my life evolves, in each moment, in God's presence.

Illuminative Grace

Here I ask for what I desire: to be present and awake to every feeling, thought, word, and deed—in the present moment. I beg for the grace to wake up to God's presence in every person, experience, and event—good or ill—that I encounter in my day.

03

୬

LORD, who may abide in your tent?
Who may dwell on your holy mountain?
Whoever walks without blame,
doing what is right,
speaking truth from the heart;
Who does not slander with his tongue,
does no harm to a friend,
never defames a neighbor;
Who disdains the wicked,
but honors those who fear the LORD;
Who keeps an oath despite the cost,
lends no money at interest,
accepts no bribe against the innocent.
Whoever acts like this
shall never be shaken.
(Ps 15)

୬

Dr. Schuchts' Reflection ~ Week Nineteen

Sacred Story Prayer: Creation and Presence

This week we are combining the first two meditations of Sacred Story Prayer: *Creation* and *Presence*. In this reflection, you are praying to awaken your spiritual and physical senses to recognize God's presence in every moment of your life and throughout creation. The goal is so that you can both grow in gratitude and deepen your identity as a beloved son.

This heightened awareness, made possible only by a gift of God's grace, includes awakening to every thought, word, and deed, as well as to the manifestation of God's presence in every person, experience, and event in your life.

This week's meditation brings to mind a modern-day proverb (attributed to many different sources) that awakens us to the power of our thoughts, words, and actions and how these bear fruit in our habits, character and ultimately our destiny:

> *Plant a thought and reap a word;*
> *plant a word and reap an action;*
> *plant an action and reap a habit;*
> *plant a habit and reap a character;*
> *plant a character and reap a destiny.*

This process of sowing and reaping works both ways-for good or for evil. Jesus spoke often about the seed of God's life-giving word vs. the seed planted by the enemy of our human nature. Both find roots in our hearts and bear fruit in our lives (see Mathew 12 and 13).

Notice the different fruit that is produced by each. Good habits (virtues) are cultivated through an entire life-time of acting on Holy Spirit inspired thoughts, producing the fruit of the Spirit in our lives (Godly character).

Likewise, our vices and addictions did not just pop up out of nowhere. They too, were formed and reinforced over time by our repeated thoughts, words, and actions. St. Paul calls these thoughts and actions inspired by our lower nature "the works of the flesh" (Gal. 5:19).

Neuro-science has demonstrated that our good thoughts and actions really do produce what appear on brain scans to be healthy little "trees" in our brains, whereas our chronic patterns of bad thinking and acting produce what look like dark thorn bushes. (See *Switch on Your Brain*, by Dr. Caroline Leaf, pg. 21)

Long before brain scans could verify this reality, St. Ignatius was inspired by the Holy Spirit to develop the Examen prayer, to distinguish between those interior movements of the mind and heart which are live-giving and those which produce death in our spirits and souls.

This is summed up well in the Affirmation for this 19th week that you were encouraged to recite aloud daily: *"There are just two ways to cope with my difficulties. One leads to life, one to death. I will choose life."*

Meditating on God's presence in all we encounter is one way of choosing life. We choose to see the goodness in every person (including ourselves) and become aware of God's abiding presence in every situation. Through this habit of meditation, we learn to live with more gratitude and can begin to see everything as a gift from the Father.

As participants in the priesthood of Jesus Christ, you have been granted the seed of life to plant in the hearts of all God's children through your preaching and teaching. You have also been given the gift of uprooting the weeds through the sacraments.

The more you sow good seed in the garden of your own heart-the more you will be able to proclaim the word of God in your words and actions, with the authority of Christ. The more you allow God to uproot the weeds through your own practice of prayer and reception of the sacraments, the more you will be able to minister to those trapped in spiritual darkness.

As your brother priests testify, this is the grace of meditating on Creation and Presence:

✠ *One of the helpful points for meditation is the reality that God is present even in the dark times. We may tend to think that when we sin God leaves us or could get disgusted with us. There is great comfort in knowing that God is present always. It is only we who can distance ourselves from Him.*

✠ *Praying at specific times on God's presence helps me to be more aware of His presence and movements throughout the day. If I am not taking time to reflect on the fact that God is here now in the moment, it will be difficult to see Him at other times and to respond effectively to Him in my ministry.*

✠ *Considering the physical impact that meditation can have on my brain was very helpful. It takes time, consistency, and practice and if I persevere, I will see the fruit of a healthy tree planted in my soul and body.*

✠ *The affirmation about the 2 choices we have for dealing with our difficulties reminds me that I am not trapped by sin, but always free to choose the good. The reflection on the reality that vices and addictions don't pop out of nowhere is a good reminder. It makes me remember the importance of uprooting those things and of not allowing new "weeds" to take root.*

Immaculate Heart of Mary pray for us so that our hearts may be fully aligned with the Sacred Heart of your son Jesus.

℘

NOTES

Week 20

FIRST

I resolve to ask God for help to be faithful to my prayer disciplines. I also resolve to spend no more and no less than fifteen minutes for these times of prayer. I will always use my personal name for God.

SECOND

For week 20, I am invited to enter the third meditation of Memory. As St. Ignatius suggested, I will engage my formal prayer at least once daily.

THIRD

Use your first prayer session to read through Memory, and then do the Sacred Story prayer exercise as suggested during your fifteen-minute prayer sessions for the rest of the week.

I will awaken to the present moment.
I will awaken to my spiritual nature.
I will not make any decisions based on fear.
I will practice sacramental Reconciliation monthly.

This week, I will say this affirmation aloud once daily:
"Impossible" is not a word in God's vocabulary.

℅

Every day, consciously enter Sacred Story prayer during your set time(s). For these next weeks, we are building the five meditations of Sacred Story prayer. Set aside the other meditations, and focus on Memory for your fifteen-minute prayer sessions this week.

Be faithful to the structure. Ignatius was wise in developing the ritual, and rituals are very important. The ritual itself detailed below does not save you. Yet the ritual, faithfully practiced, makes it easier for you to open your mind and heart to the One who does save you! Rituals are good. Review the structure of the fifteen-minute prayer sessions. You will find these at the bookmark you left in week 16.

MEMORY
I believe every violation of love committed by me and against me
is in my memory, and I ask God to reveal them to me,
especially those that have manifested themselves today,
so I can be healed.

Prelude
I hold in my heart, by the power of God's grace, the memory of every action—of every thought, word, and deed—done to me and done by me, that has eroded my innocence. I affirm that these unloving thoughts, words, and deeds have spiritual, physical, and emotional consequences that wound me, others, and creation and for which Christ had to suffer for my redemption. I believe all these unloving actions have both generational and evolutionary consequences. At the root of my own narcissism are some events that, more than others, have significantly distorted my heart and mind. These events cripple my desire and my ability to love selflessly and to freely forgive others.

Illuminative Grace

Here I ask for what I desire: to become conscious of my lost innocence; to have the grace to see and the power to touch the Original Sins and wounds, especially the most vital ones, which shape in me an anti-story instead of a sacred story. I ask for the grace of an illumined conscience to know intimately how these wounds and sins connect to everything I do that makes life burdensome; to know how and why these wounds so often compel me to violate God's life in myself, others, and creation. I ask God for the grace to wake up so I can see, feel, and name these thoughts, words, and deeds and bring them to the light of day, to be healed by the Divine Physician.

ଔ

Oh, that today you would hear his voice:
"Harden not your hearts as at Meribah,
as in the day of Massah in the desert,
Where your fathers tempted me;
they tested me though they had seen my works."
If today you hear his voice,
harden not your hearts.
(Ps 95:8–9)

ଜ

Dr. Schuchts' Reflection ~ Week Twenty

Sacred Story Prayer: Memory

We are now at the midway point of the *Forty Weeks* reflections-- and how fitting that we are focused on Memory.

If you were asked to list all the topics of the first 20 weeks, how many of them would you be able to name? That is no easy feat for any of us to remember back 20 weeks, let alone remember things from 20 or more years ago.

However, scientific research has validated that every experience in our life is stored in our brains. That means we have the capacity to remember everything that has ever happened to us. Yet, most of these memories are not in our conscious awareness.

Our conscious memories are much more selective. We tend to consciously remember those things that are most important to us or that have left a lasting impression.

We also tend to remember those events, people and experiences that impact us personally, such as the violations of love committed by us and against us.

Some of these memories are in our conscious awareness, while many of them are not. That is why we need to ask the Holy Spirit to reveal them to us as we engage in this process of healing.

In the past couple of years, I have become much more aware of how central memory is in all of our lives. As I age, I find myself less sharp in my ability to remember things, such as people's names.

I am also watching my dad's decline in memory as he ages. He was recently diagnosed with dementia. We were not surprised by the diagnosis. We have been watching his gradual loss of short-term memory over the past few years.

But an amazing thing is also happening in the midst of his short-term memory loss—it seems he is even more attentive to those things in his long-term memory that are still unresolved.

It's as if the Holy Spirit is working even more powerfully at this stage in his life to reveal to him those violations of love that he has committed and that have been committed against him.

In the abundance of his kindness and mercy, Jesus is healing my dad through these memories. His grace is operating powerfully through my dad's weakness (2 Co. 12:90).

This week we too are inviting God's grace into our weaknesses to see where our innocence has been compromised by our personal sin and the wounds of others sins.

These unresolved wounds against love are not just in the past. Many of them, unforgiven and unhealed, continue to burden us in the present in our daily activities and relationships.

Have you noticed how frequently your present struggles are rooted in unhealed memories? This is Fr. Watson's point that we want to remember on two levels: what happened in the last day and how it might be connected to something that happened long-ago in your past. This is Holy Spirit work!

This week is a tremendous opportunity to be attentive to those sins and wounds of the past that continue to hinder your joy and freedom in the present.

I want to share two ways to go about this process of inviting God to heal your memories this week. Choose whichever one suits you best, or you may be inspired in a completely different way.

1) Ask the Holy Spirit to help you be attentive to the things that distress

you during each day of the week. As you become aware of the distress, ask the Holy Spirit to reveal if this has a deeper root in your life. That root can be a wound or your personal sin or both. Write down in your journal what you discover in your 15-minute prayer time.

2) As an alternative, you can choose one of the deadly sins and one of the deadly wounds each day and ask the Holy Spirit to reveal where these are rooted in your memory, how the wounds and sins are interrelated, and how they play out in your present circumstances.

As an illustration, this is the pairing I used for each day of this Week Twenty:

WEEKDAY	**DEADLY SIN**	**DEADLY WOUND**
Sunday	Lust	Shame
Monday	Greed	Fear
Tuesday	Sloth	Hopelessness
Wednesday	Anger	Powerlessness
Thursday	Envy	Rejection
Friday	Gluttony	Abandonment
Saturday	Pride	Confusion

If you decide to approach this week's activity in this way, pray for the particular way you would pair these sins and wounds in your life. For me it was illuminating to see how my current circumstances were being influenced by these sins and wounds.

These are only suggestions. Feel free to approach this week as the Spirit leads you. However, he leads you will also be part of your formation in ministering to the memories of those you serve.

Your brother priests offered these insights from their reflections on *memory* for Week 20.

✠ *Memories are very much a part of who we are. It is how they affect us that can be changed or healed. We have much to learn and gain from memories.*

✠ *I was particularly struck by the reflection upon long-term memory. It is amazing to think about the power of events in our lives (good or bad) and how they stick with us. Our roots are very important.*

✠ *I have learned that God has blessed us with the faculty to remember every thought, word, and deed done to me or done by me. The memory of these actions has made me lose innocence or has wounded myself, others, and creation.*

✠ *Looking at my memories allows the Holy Spirit to heal them and bring new life and peace into my heart.*

Immaculate Heart of Mary pray for us so that our hearts may be fully aligned with the Sacred Heart of your son Jesus.

℅

NOTES

Week 21

FIRST

As I engage the Sacred Story prayer this week, I will continue to ask God's help to be faithful to my commitment. I will also resolve to spend no more and no less than fifteen minutes in each formal prayer session, as St. Ignatius suggested. I will always use my personal name for God.

SECOND

For week 21, I am invited to pray with the first three meditations in the Sacred Story prayer. As St. Ignatius suggested, I will commit to entering my prayer at least once daily.

THIRD

Use your first prayer session to read the reflection, and then do the Sacred Story prayer exercise as suggested during your fifteen-minute prayer sessions for the rest of the week.

I will awaken to the present moment.
I will awaken to my spiritual nature.
I will not make any decisions based on fear.
I will practice sacramental Reconciliation monthly.

This week, I will say this affirmation aloud once daily:

Sacred Story practice leads to my freedom and authenticity,
but does not always make me feel happy.

೦೩

Review the structure of the fifteen-minute prayer sessions. You will find these at the bookmark you left in week 16. For this week, you are combining the first three meditations in Sacred Story prayer: Creation, Presence, and Memory.

Use your fifteen-minute prayer sessions this week to pray these three meditations together, following the wisdom you learned in week 16 for this practice. You can also refresh your memory on the Preludes and Illuminative Graces of these three meditations if you find it helpful.

CREATION
I believe God created everything in love and for love;
I ask for heartfelt knowledge of God's love for me
and for gratitude for the general and particular graces of this day.

PRESENCE
I believe God is present in each moment and event of my life,
and I ask for grace to awaken, see and feel where and how,
especially in this present moment.

MEMORY
I believe every violation of love committed by me and against me
is in my memory, and I ask God to reveal them to me,
especially those that have manifested themselves today,
so I can be healed.

ॐ

Come, let us sing joyfully to the Lord;
cry out to the rock of our salvation.
Let us come before him with a song of praise,
joyfully sing out our psalms.
For the Lord is the great God,
the great king over all gods,
Whose hand holds the depths of the earth;
who owns the tops of the mountains.
The sea and dry land belong to God,
who made them, formed them by hand.
(Ps 95:1–5).

ॐ

Sacred Story Prayer: Creation, Presence and Memory

During this 21ST week, we are bringing together the first three elements of Sacred Story Prayer: Creation, Presence and Memory.

We are praying for a deeper *heart-felt* knowledge of God's love, an increased *awareness* of His presence in each moment of our lives, and the *healing* of memories in those situations where love has been violated.

As I reflect on these three elements of Sacred Story Prayer, I am struck by the similarity between this process and the prayer for healing of memories, which is also a foundational part of St. Ignatius' Spiritual Exercises.

In praying for the healing of memories, we ask the Holy Spirit to reveal those times in our life where we have been wounded by our own sin and the sin of others.

These areas of spiritual and emotional wounding can greatly hinder our ability to *receive* God's tenderhearted and merciful love for us.

Our wounds and sins can also effectively *blind* us to an awareness of God's intimate presence, both in our past or current day-to-day circumstances.

When these *impediments* are removed through healing prayer, our capacity to give and receive love increases dramatically. Our hearts then become increasingly more open to recognize God's presence in all the people, events and circumstances of our lives.

This healing process is an amazing thing to witness! Jesus is ever waiting to perform this miracle in our souls and the souls of those to whom we minister. Jesus came for this reason: to heal our broken-hearts, to release us in places where we are bound, and to replace our shame with his glory (See Isa. 61:1-4; Luke 4:18).

Isn't this the miracle that happens, in a slightly different way, every time you celebrate the Sacrament of Reconciliation? Representing Jesus' eternal priesthood, you are healing memories and replacing shame with God's merciful love in administering every good confession.

Where sin has violated the nature of God's love, and blocked the flow of grace, you, through the power of the Holy Spirit, are releasing the blocked areas of the heart, so love can pour in again. You are representing God's presence and his love in a very tangible way.

No amount of psychological or theological insights, by themselves, can heal these wounds caused by our sin or the sins of others. Jesus' loving presence is the only healing remedy. He is the Physician of our souls and bodies (CCC, 1509). As we will see in the next reflection-his mercy is the healing remedy!

Many of your brother priests have discovered that the healing of memories is a great complement to the sacrament of reconciliation. At times, this process can be exercised within the Sacrament itself, or as an augment through spiritual direction, or in pastoral counseling and prayer.

That is why it is so important for you to walk through this process yourself. Only as you experience Jesus' healing love and presence in those areas where you are bound by deadly sins and wounds, can you have the insight and the hope to help others walk through it.
This process of praying through the healing of memories is simple and yet tremendously powerful. Here are the basic elements:

Begin by quieting your mind and acknowledging the Lord's presence with you.

1) Remember you are the Father's beloved son in whom he delights
2) Ask the Holy Spirit to show you the specific sin or wound that needs to be healed
3) Pray for insight into the nature of the sin or wound (one of deadly sins or deadly wounds)
4) Ask Jesus to reveal His presence in the memory that needs healing.
5) Test the revelation by these measures: love, truth, freedom, and fruit of the Spirit.

The prayer process is the same, whether the injury to our heart and soul occurred long ago or happened that same day.

Can you see how practicing the Sacred Story prayer daily is a way to keep cleansing your heart of the things that build up-so that you can experience his love and presence with you moment by moment?

The following insights were offered by your brother priests as they reflected on Week 21: Creation, Presence, and Memory:

✠ *I am beginning to experience the integration of the three (and in the future the five) in a seamless way in my 15-minute period of prayer. I am experiencing the Spirit lead me from one to another, so as to follow the lead of the Spirit.*

✠ *It's amazing to be aware of all the connections in our heart, memories, and events. Without the light of the Holy Spirit it's impossible to be aware of this.*

✠ *Just reflecting upon the healing (clearing/cleansing) aspect of the Sacrament of Reconciliation is a great help. It is truly a blessed experience.*

✠ *The healing of memories is a life changing grace!*

Immaculate Heart of Mary pray for us so that our hearts may be fully aligned with the Sacred Heart of your son Jesus.

⟡

NOTES

Week 22

FIRST

I will preview my week and visualize the places and times for my prayer. They will be places apart—technology-free zones. I also resolve to spend no more and no less than fifteen minutes in each formal prayer session, as St. Ignatius suggested. I will always use my personal name for God.

SECOND

For week 22, I am invited to pray the fourth meditation in Sacred Story prayer: Mercy. Read through Mercy, and then do the Sacred Story prayer exercise as suggested during your fifteen-minute prayer sessions for the rest of the week.

THIRD

I will begin my week reviewing the prayer structure from week 16.

I will awaken to the present moment.
I will awaken to my spiritual nature.
I will not make any decisions based on fear.
I will practice sacramental Reconciliation monthly.

This week, I will say this affirmation aloud once daily:

My life's greatest tragedies can be transformed
into my life's major blessings.

ಝ

Sacred Story Prayer—Mercy

Every day, consciously enter Sacred Story prayer during your set time(s).
For these next weeks, we are building the five meditations of Sacred Story
prayer. Set aside the other meditations, and focus on Mercy for your
fifteen-minute prayer sessions this week.

Be faithful to the structure. Ignatius was wise in developing the ritual, and
rituals are very important. The ritual itself detailed below does not save
you. Yet the ritual, faithfully practiced, makes it easier for you to open
your mind and heart to the One who does save you! Rituals are good.
Review the structure of the fifteen-minute prayer sessions. You will find
these at the bookmark you left in week 16.

MERCY

I believe that forgiveness is the only path to healing and illumination.
I beg for the grace of forgiveness and the grace to forgive,
especially for the general and particular failures of this day, and from my
past.

Prelude

The path to Christian holiness and an illumined consciousness runs
through the darkest memories and deeds of your life, strangely enough.
These memories and deeds corrupt your innocence and blind your vision
to the sacredness of all life. These memories and deeds can, by choice,
act as a wall blocking the peace that leads to holiness and highest
consciousness, or as a gate opening to them. The gate is unlocked by
forgiveness and compassion, both received from God and then extended
to all those entwined with the lost innocence that broke your heart. This
includes those who hurt you, those whom you hurt, and the gifts of

creation that you abused or misused as a result. This miracle of peace and enlightenment is attainable through Christ, who bore in love the wounds of every sin and dark deed since time immemorial. Christ has the power to transform darkness, sin, and death into grace for the salvation of the world.

Illuminative Grace

Here I ask for what I desire: the grace to forgive any person who wounded my innocence or broke my heart. I pray to not only forgive them, but to have compassion and mercy on them. I ask for the grace of mercy and forgiveness for those whose hearts I have broken, those whose innocence I have wounded, and the gifts of creation that I have misused. I beg to know personally the One who absorbed in His heart and body every wound and every sin of this dark evolution across the millennia. I beg for the dual knowledge of sin and mercy as it affects my life story. I beg for patience, knowing that accepting and offering mercy and forgiveness leads me to holiness. This awakening to highest consciousness takes a lifetime.

☙

Fill us at daybreak with your mercy,
that all our days we may sing for joy.
Make us glad as many days as you humbled us,
for as many years as we have seen trouble.
Show your deeds to your servants,
your glory to their children.
(Ps 90:14–16)

☙

Dr. Schuchts' Reflection ~ Week Twenty-Two

Sacred Story Prayer: Mercy

This week we are focusing our attention on the fourth meditation of Sacred Story Prayer-*Mercy*. In Latin, the primary word for mercy is "Misericordia", which is a combination of two root words: "miseria" (misery) and "cordia" (heart).

This meditation draws our attention to the tender heart of our heavenly Father who is moved with compassion for each one of us in all the areas of our personal misery.

Pope Francis refers to Jesus as "The Face of the Father's Mercy" because he fully reveals the Father's compassionate and forgiving heart.

Throughout the Gospels we see Jesus repeatedly "moved with compassion" for those who are suffering. He unconditionally offers forgiveness for the sins of humanity that lie at the root of our misery.

Acting in *Persona Christi*, you too have been commissioned in your priesthood to reveal the face of the Father, manifesting his mercy not only through the Sacraments, but in every thought, word, and deed in your personal life.

This is an enormous responsibility, one that can only be accomplished by God's gracious intervention in your personal history.

Each one of us has lost innocence as a result of our own sins and the sins of others. This loss of innocence is the source of our shame and hardness of heart.

We all have shame in our lives where we have compromised our innocence. Similarly, all of us have areas where our hearts have become hardened through the deceitfulness of sin (see Heb. 3:13).

But thanks be to God, Jesus takes our sin and absorbs our suffering into the depths of his heart and body, so that we, in turn, may release our guilt and misery, offering it to back to him.

His forgiveness gradually restores our innocence in the places where shame has kept us bound. His compassion softens our hearts and allows us to become tender-hearted towards ourselves and others.

You have been praying this week for the grace to forgive any person who has wounded your innocence or broken your heart, and for compassion for any whose hearts you have broken.

The Holy Spirit is fully capable of accomplishing this in and through you, as you give your consent. But without your surrender to the Spirit, this will continue to be an insurmountable challenge.

Oftentimes, the person we have the most difficulty forgiving and feeling compassion for is ourselves. This is why we need to receive compassion first, from Jesus.

If we believe that Jesus forgives us for our sins and has compassion for our misery, then we too can forgive ourselves and have compassion for ourselves in the areas of our suffering.

As we receive this gift from Jesus, we are enabled to give it freely to those around us. This is how we become, with Jesus, "The Face of the Father's mercy."

Jesus calls us to "Be merciful as your heavenly Father is merciful" (Lk 6:36). This mercy must begin with ourselves and extend out to every person we encounter, most especially those who have hurt us the most.

Can you see why Fr. Watson says that forgiveness is the only path to healing and illumination? Through forgiveness our life's greatest tragedies can be turned into life's greatest blessings.

The following outline is the process we use in our "Healing the Whole Person" conferences to help people walk through the process of forgiveness:

Prayer of Forgiveness

1. Ask the Holy Spirit to show you who you need to forgive (could be family, friend, abuser, God, yourself)

2. Picture the person in front of you and pay attention to what you feel.

3. Make an account of the debt they owe you (what did they take from you, how did they hurt you? It is okay to feel angry.

4. Imagine yourself telling them what they did to hurt you and how it has affected you.

5. Ask the Holy Spirit to reveal to you what you believe about yourself based on that incident (identity lie);

6. Renounce the identity lie. (For example: "I renounce the lie that I am not loved or cared for, etc.")

7. Ask the Holy Spirit to reveal the judgments you hold towards that person who hurt you.

8. Renounce the judgments.

9. Ask Jesus to forgive the person.

10. Forgive the person and ask for the grace of compassion for them.

11. Pray a prayer of blessing over that person-ask God to bless them in the opposite way that they hurt you.

12. Ask Jesus to seal this forgiveness and heal the wounds of both you and them.

13. Thank the Father for his healing.

Here are a few insights from your brother priests for Week 22:

✠ *God is gracious and merciful which encourages us to seek his mercy and forgiveness every time. At the same time God gives us an example to follow for those who live with us, particularly those who have hurt us. Mercy is meant to be received and given.*

✠ *The power of forgiveness, for me and others, is a source of healing and renewal.*

✠ *Openness to forgiveness is really the first and biggest step of healing.*

✠ *I learned a very practical way to show mercy to those who have hurt me.*

Immaculate Heart of Mary pray for us so that our hearts may be fully aligned with the Sacred Heart of your son Jesus.

℁

NOTES

Week 23

FIRST

I will assess my fidelity to the fifteen-minute prayer periods and make the adjustments necessary to be more faithful. I resolve to spend no more and no less than fifteen minutes in each formal prayer session. I will always use my personal name for God.

SECOND

For week 23, I am invited to combine meditations one through four in the Sacred Story prayer. I will enter my prayer at least once daily, as St. Ignatius suggested.

THIRD

I will use my first prayer session to review the daily prayer structure and then use my fifteen-minute prayer periods for the rest of the week for the combined prayer.

I will awaken to the present moment.
I will awaken to my spiritual nature.
I will not make any decisions based on fear.
I will practice sacramental Reconciliation monthly.

This week, I will say this affirmation aloud once daily:

Times of peace and hope always give way
to times of difficulty and stress.

℅

Review the structure of the fifteen-minute prayer sessions. You will find these at the bookmark you left in week 16. For this week, you are combining the first four meditations in Sacred Story Prayer: Creation, Presence, Memory, and Mercy. Use your fifteen-minute prayer sessions this week to pray these four meditations together, following the wisdom you learned in week 16 for this practice. You can also refresh your memory on the Preludes and Illuminative Graces of these three meditations if you find it helpful.

CREATION
I believe God created everything in love and for love;
I ask for heartfelt knowledge of God's love for me
and for gratitude for the general and particular graces of this day.

PRESENCE
I believe God is present in each moment and event of my life,
and I ask for grace to awaken, see and feel where and how,
especially in this present moment.

MEMORY
I believe every violation of love committed by me and against me
is in my memory, and I ask God to reveal them to me,
especially those that have manifested themselves today,
so I can be healed.

MERCY
I believe that forgiveness is the only path to healing and illumination.

I beg for the grace of forgiveness and the grace to forgive,
especially for the general and particular failures
of this day, and from my past.

 C3

My heart is steadfast, God;
my heart is steadfast.
Let me sing and chant praise.
Awake, lyre and harp!
I will wake the dawn.

I will praise you among the peoples, Lord;
I will chant your praise among the nations.
For your mercy is greater than the heavens;
your faithfulness, to the skies.

Appear on high over the heavens, God;
your glory above all the earth.
Help with your right hand and answer us
that your loved ones may escape.
(Ps 108:2–7)

&

Sacred Story Prayer: Creation, Presence, Memory and Mercy

This week we are combining the first four meditations of Sacred Story Prayer: *Creation, Presence, Memory and Mercy.* Do you notice the pattern in each of these meditations? Each one begins with a *Prelude,* affirming a specific aspect of our faith in God. This is followed by asking for a particular *Illuminative Grace.*

Fr. Watson mirrors St Ignatius in the *Spiritual Exercises* where as part of all his meditations and contemplations he incorporates the discipline of asking God for graces: "I ask for what I want: here I ask for interior knowledge of the Lord who became human for me so that I may better love and follow him."[15]

Our beliefs embolden us to ask God for these graces. The illuminative graces, in turn, flow from our convictions. The firmer our convictions, the more confidence we have in asking for the graces. Let us take *Creation* as a way of applying this process. We assert the truth that "God created everything in love and for love."

The more we believe this and meditate on this reality with the aid of the Holy Spirit, the more we will cultivate "gratitude" and "a heart-felt knowledge of God's love for me". We will grow in our capacity to see everything, including ourselves, as a gift of love from the Father.

St. Thomas Aquinas said that love is "willing the good of another." Everything created, seen and unseen, comes from this singular motivation of God. He wills everything for our good.

The implication of this truth is that we can begin to see that everything around us is a gift of love from the Father. The Father gives only good gifts. The challenge, and invitation, is for us to open our eyes, ears, and heart to recognize His manifest presence and loving kindness.

When we wake up every day and hear the birds chirp, feel the sun's warmth, and watch the trees sway, we can grow in our awareness that all of this is a gift from the Father.

When you breathe in the fresh air, do you stop and thank God for the gift of oxygen, your lungs, and your circulatory system keeping you alive at every moment?

I never thought of thanking God for these simple things, until I went to Africa many years ago. When I greeted the people in the small village where I was staying, they would say: "Praise God for my life today. I thank him that he has given me good air to breathe."

I was overwhelmed by their simple faith which sprang forth in joyful gratitude. They did not take these basic things of creation for granted. They appeared to be grateful for everything.

They also saw one another as gift and honored my presence with a gratitude that was foreign to me. They seemed to reverence every part of Gods' good creation, including one another.

In addition to seeing God's love in all of creation, they also seemed to have a keen awareness of God's presence and mercy and allowed His mercy and presence to permeate and heal their memories.

I doubt they learned Sacred Story prayer in any formal way, but they seemed to live it naturally. They were awake and aware, and turned regularly to God's mercy to heal the distortions of love. Forgiveness became a way of life in that village among those Christians I met.

For those of us living in the West, where we take so much for granted, we need to consciously awaken to these realities. This is the purpose of Sacred Story prayer--to awaken us to see God's love, presence, and mercy in every moment of our lives, past and present.

The more we see with this new awareness, the more our memories are healed. The distortions of love in our life are met with the transforming love, presence and of mercy of our heavenly Father.

We are all walking through this journey in our own way, at our own pace. Notice the varying experiences this 23rd week among your brother priests:

✠ The grace of the Holy Spirit is allowing the prayer to be seamless....one leads to another in a natural progression.

✠ I have to confess that I once again did not do as well in my commitment to my time of prayer, but there is value in simply keeping these themes rattling through one's thoughts and prayers. Sometimes perhaps it is not always as essential to do things exactly as hoped or planned as it is to be reminded and conscious of the bigger picture.

✠ Ending on mercy was actually as difficult to me as ending on memory; I could tell that something in me - likely a wound, perhaps unrepentance – is resisting letting mercy penetrate. It was a somewhat painful week, but I am still trusting.

✠ Forgiveness heals the memory of the present and past violations of love, which violations have ignored God's investment of love in creation, including human beings. That is why Forgiveness is the only path to healing and illumination. Mercy is gratitude par excellence toward the Creator.

Immaculate Heart of Mary pray for us so that our hearts may be fully aligned with the Sacred Heart of your son Jesus.

℘

NOTES

Week 24

FIRST

As I engage the last meditation in Sacred Story prayer this week, I will review my commitment to develop a rhythm that will carry me the rest of my life. To help me with that commitment, I resolve to spend no more and no less than fifteen minutes in each formal prayer session. I will always use my personal name for God.

SECOND

For week 24, I am invited to pray meditation five in the Sacred Story prayer: Eternity. Read through Eternity, and then do the Sacred Story prayer exercise as suggested during your fifteen-minute prayer sessions for the rest of the week.

THIRD

I will use my first prayer session to review the daily prayer structure from week 16.

I will awaken to the present moment.
I will awaken to my spiritual nature.
I will not make any decisions based on fear.

I will practice sacramental Reconciliation monthly.
This week, I will say this affirmation aloud once daily:
Times of difficulty and stress always give way to
times of peace and hope.

⊗

Sacred Story Prayer—Eternity

Every day, consciously enter Sacred Story prayer during your set time(s). For these next weeks, we are building the five meditations of Sacred Story prayer. Set aside the other meditations, and focus on Eternity for your fifteen-minute prayer sessions this week.

Be faithful to the structure. Ignatius was wise in developing the ritual, and rituals are very important. The ritual itself detailed below does not save you. Yet the ritual, faithfully practiced, makes it easier for you to open your mind and heart to the One who does save you! Rituals are good. Review the structure of the fifteen-minute prayer sessions. You will find these at the bookmark you left in week 16.

ETERNITY

I believe the grace of forgiveness opens my heart,
making my every thought, word and deed bear fruit
that endures to eternity.
I ask that everything in my life serve
Christ's Great Work of Reconciliation.

Prelude
The sacred story of all history, revealed on the last day, will show that the lost innocence and the broken hearts of humankind inaugurated the Great Work of Reconciliation. Because of Christ's mercy, each of us is now being invited to take our part in this work. The grace of mercy and forgiveness, received and offered, is the reconciling work that brings true

progress to the world; it is the only work that brings fulfillment and bears fruit that endures to eternity. A holy life and the highest consciousness attainable come in personally knowing the One who both reconciles my life and reconciles all creation. In this reconciling Love, I daily discern how to direct each thought, word, and deed to eternal glory—to the divine work of reconciliation.

Illuminative Grace

Here I ask for what I desire: to be graced daily with a profound consciousness of Christ Jesus's healing love, personally experienced, that will so enlighten my heart and mind that my every thought, word, and deed can serve His Great Work of Universal Reconciliation.

I will listen for what God, the Lord, has to say;
    surely he will speak of peace
    To his people and to his faithful.
    May they not turn to foolishness!

Near indeed is his salvation for those who fear him;
    glory will dwell in our land.
    Love and truth will meet;
    justice and peace will kiss.
    Truth will spring from the earth;
    justice will look down from heaven.

Yes, the Lord will grant his bounty;
    our land will yield its produce.
    Justice will march before him,
    and make a way for his footsteps.
    (Ps 85:9–14)

                   80

Dr. Schuchts' Reflection ~ Week Twenty-Four

Sacred Story Prayer: Eternity

This week our meditation is concentrated on *Eternity.* We are praying for the grace of a *daily consciousness of Jesus' healing love* and allowing that awareness to shape our thoughts, words and deeds in the present moment. Personally, I had to overcome a bit of a hurdle in this meditation, because without realizing it, I had a negative emotional connection with the whole concept of *Eternity.*

Just saying the word "Eternity" triggered a painful memory for me. It brought me back to a time when I was 13 after my dad left during the months following my parents' separation (and subsequent divorce).

During this wintery season, I would lie in bed at night in a state of nearly constant desolation, wondering if I would ever see my dad again. I missed him terribly and felt completely cut off from him. After months of no contact with my father, I began to wonder if he was dead. This thought of his death naturally led me to reflect on eternity, but not in a way that brought any consolation.

I was in an emotionally disconnected and desolate state of mind. The thought of eternity frightened me. The possibility of being eternally separated from my dad was horrifying. I tried to imagine how it was possible for there to be no ending. Everything in life has an ending, but I couldn't wrap my mind around the whole idea that eternity does not end.

While this bedrock hope of our faith is meant to be deeply consoling, at the time the concept of eternity only increased my desolation. The enemy of my human nature had planted seeds of hopelessness in my soul, related to everlasting life.

As the years passed my concept of *Eternity* has become much more positive. Many experiences of Jesus' healing love and reconciliations with my dad and others have re-defined eternity.

One of those moments, my brother Dave's death, epitomizes the illuminative grace of this week: a consciousness of Jesus' healing love and an understanding of our call to be ministers of reconciliation. As my brother was dying, my dad, my wife and I shared the precious moment together. It was a time of deepening the reconciliations which had been going on for years. Jesus' healing love was fully manifested as the presence of the Holy Spirit filled the room.

In that moment Eternity was a great comfort and a reality. We were living in eternity in the moment, enjoying a profound spiritual communion with one another, with Jesus and with my brother Dave.

Since his death, I have a real sense of the communion of persons that spans time and eternity. I am connected to him still and at the same time connected to the whole communion of Saints.

Through all this, my heart has come to realize what my mind already knew: that *Eternity* is a state of constant consolation, living in communion with the Father, Jesus, the Holy Spirit, Mary, and all the Saints.

What could be more consoling than constantly beholding God's beauty and goodness, while being fully immersed and fully able to receive the Father's all-embracing love, intimacy, and wholeness? Yet, despite many similar healing experiences and reconciliations over the years, this part of my heart as a 13-year old had remained hidden.

During this week's meditation, I discovered that I still associate *Eternity* with mind-boggling confusion, hopelessness and endless separation from my father.

The two competing concepts of *Eternity* clashed this week. I have been asking for the grace to live the awareness of connectedness and healing in my 13-year old heart, so that it can become a greater part of my daily consciousness.

These are a few of the reflections from your brother priests this week:

✠ *Eternity is about the reconciliation of everything in Christ. This reconciliation takes place in my life through forgiveness. The grace of forgiveness enables each of my thoughts, words, and deeds to bear fruits that endure forever. That is why we need the grace of forgiveness always in order to be one with Christ.*

✠ *Eternity is not just something that happens to us but something that we participate in by working with God in His plan of reconciling the world to Himself.*

✠ *It's incredible to see how big an impact forgiveness has in our eternity.*

✠ *By creating us body and soul intimately united, God wanted us to be eternal. The purification of our memories through the mercy of God enlightens us in order to embrace eternity.*

Immaculate Heart of Mary pray for us so that our hearts may be fully aligned with the Sacred Heart of your son Jesus.

ℰↄ

NOTES

Week 25

FIRST

As I combine all five meditations in Sacred Story prayer this week for the first time, I will review my commitment and imagine a rhythm that will carry me for the rest of my life. To help me with that commitment, I again resolve to spend no more and no less than fifteen minutes in each formal prayer session. I will always use my personal name for God.

SECOND

For week 25, I am praying meditations one through five in the Sacred Story prayer. I will enter my prayer at least once daily, as St. Ignatius suggested.

THIRD

I will use my first prayer session to review the daily prayer disciplines from week 16. I will use the remainder of the week's fifteen-minute prayer periods for the combined prayer exercise.

I will awaken to the present moment.
I will awaken to my spiritual nature.
I will not make any decisions based on fear.
I will practice sacramental Reconciliation monthly.
This week, I will say this affirmation aloud once daily:

I will not tire of asking God for help, because God delights in my asking.

ᚖ

Review the structure of the fifteen-minute prayer sessions. You will find these at the bookmark you left in week 16. For this week, you are combining the five meditations in Sacred Story prayer: Creation, Presence, Memory, Mercy, and Eternity.

Use your fifteen-minute prayer sessions this week to pray these five meditations together, following the wisdom you learned in week 16 for this practice. You can also refresh your memory on the Preludes and Illuminative Graces of these five meditations if you find it helpful.

ᚖ

CREATION

I believe God created everything in love and for love;
I ask for heartfelt knowledge of God's love for me
and for gratitude for the general and particular graces of this day.

PRESENCE

I believe God is present in each moment and event of my life,
and I ask for grace to awaken, see and feel where and how,
especially in this present moment.

MEMORY

I believe every violation of love committed by me and against me
is in my memory, and I ask God to reveal them to me,
especially those that have manifested themselves today,
so I can be healed.

MERCY

I believe that forgiveness is the only path to healing and illumination.
I beg for the grace of forgiveness and the grace to forgive,
especially for the general and particular failures of this day,
and from my past.

ETERNITY

I believe the grace of forgiveness opens my heart,
making my every thought, word and deed bear fruit
that endures to eternity.
I ask that everything in my life serve
Christ's Great Work of Reconciliation.

CB

May God be gracious to us and bless us;
may his face shine upon us.
So shall your way be known upon the earth,
your victory among all the nations.
May the peoples praise you, God;
may all the peoples praise you!
The earth has yielded its harvest;
God, our God, blesses us.
May God bless us still;
that the ends of the earth may revere him.
(Ps 67:2–4, 7–8)

BO

Dr. Schuchts' Reflection ~ Week Twenty-Five

Sacred Story Prayer: Creation, Presence, Memory, Mercy and Eternity

During this twenty fifth week, we are now ready to pray with all five meditations of Sacred Story Prayer: *Creation, Presence, Memory, Mercy & Eternity.*

As I have been personally meditating on these five words during Eucharistic adoration, I am struck by how these meditations illuminate the essence of the Eucharist, and by extension the Holy Sacrifice of the Mass. Essentially when we pray with the five meditations of Sacred Story, we are living the reality of the Eucharist in our lives every hour of the day. Each of the five meditations represents what we celebrate and offer in the Mass.

The elements of the Eucharist, bread and wine, represent the most basic essentials of **Creation.** God graciously gives what he has made for our good- to nourish and sustain us. In the Holy Sacrifice of the Mass, every priest stands representing Jesus and the entirety of *Creation*, offering back to the Father everything he has graciously provided out of love for us.

In the Eucharist, we give thanks to God for all he has given us. Jesus fully expresses our *gratitude* and our identity as the *Beloved Son*.

We offer ourselves, our food, our labors, our resources, our time, our worship. Everything that the Father has given to us in *Creation* is given back to Him in gratitude. During the Consecration, as we all know, the elements of *creation* are transformed into the Body and Blood of Jesus Christ, who himself took on our human nature and entered into the *Creation*.

In Jesus Incarnation, God's **Presence** is fully revealed. In the Mass, that *Presence* is made manifest in a most profound way-through the priest, the congregation, the Word of God, and most especially in the Eucharist. All who receive His Sacred Body and Blood become carriers of His *Presence*. We are to be witnesses to the world around us as living tabernacles, *consciously aware of His presence* in and around us.

The Eucharist involves our **Memory,** from beginning to end. We begin Mass, by bringing to the Father all of the violations of love which we carry with us in our memories. Mass is also a bringing forth in the present, the *memory* of Christ's death and Resurrection as a way of restoring our unhealed memories. Throughout the Mass, we also remember all who have gone before us and the whole world that surrounds us.

We take every violation of love and bring it humbly before God to receive His **Mercy**. More than anything else the Mass is a celebration and participation in the *Mercy* of God. We begin Mass by asking Jesus to apply his *mercy* for our sins. The readings are filled with reminders of God's *forgiveness and compassion*, and the intercessory prayers call us to extend that compassion to our brothers and sisters.

Before receiving the Eucharist, we pray specifically again, asking for the Father's forgiveness for the ways we have violated his love. Similarly, we ask for the grace to forgive those who have violated us in any way.

All of this brings us into a deeper and greater participation in **Eternity,** where we open our hearts to receive *reconciliation and healing*. In turn, we are invited to participate in Christ's ongoing work of reconciliation as our mission. The entire Mass is a participation in *Eternity*, a celebration with the angels and Saints, worshipping "Holy, Holy, Holy" to the One who stands outside of time.

Do you see how your participation in Christ's priesthood is a Sacred

Story, restoring all things in Christ as you yourself are being restored?

The greatest act of Christ's priesthood--the celebration of Holy Eucharist--must become an ongoing prayer occurring every moment of your life. By practicing Sacred Story Prayer, you are reminding yourself to live the Mass in every thought, word and deed throughout each day.

These are a few reflections from your brother priests as they prayed with Sacred Story prayer for Week 25:

✠ *Sacred Story prayer awakens me to truth, grounds me in my identity as a priest, and helps me be more effective in my ministry. When I pray in this way I am more sensitive to God's inspirations and movements and am comforted by the fact that I do not have to rely on myself as much to complete each day's necessary tasks.*

✠ *I have learned that the five meditations- creation -presence - memory- mercy - and eternity-give me the way to read my Sacred Story. They help me write my Sacred Story.*

✠ *At Mass creation is represented by the persons and the gifts of bread and wine which will be transformed in the Holy Body and Blood of Christ and offered back to the creator in a spirit of reconciliation and thanksgiving by the priest who represents Jesus. The memorial of Jesus' love on the Cross is celebrated while the violations against love are confessed and the harmony between God and his people restored. We taste a glimpse of eternity at Mass.*

*Immaculate Heart of Mary pray for us so that our hearts
may be fully aligned with the Sacred Heart of your son Jesus.*

℘

NOTES

Week 26

FIRST

I visualize the week ahead and plan how I will engage my fifteen-minute prayer times. I resolve in my heart to allow God to help me be faithful to these set times of prayer. To increase my fidelity, I also resolve to spend no more and no less than fifteen minutes in any formal prayer period. I will always use my personal name for God.

SECOND

For week 26, I am invited to continue a life-long process of praying the five meditations of Sacred Story prayer. I will enter this prayer at least once daily, as St. Ignatius suggested.

THIRD

I will personalize meditations one, two, three, four and five: Creation, Presence, Memory, Mercy and Eternity.

I will awaken to the present moment.
I will awaken to my spiritual nature.
I will not make any decisions based on fear.
I will practice sacramental Reconciliation monthly.

This week, I will say this affirmation aloud once daily:
The urge to stop Sacred Story practice
always comes before my greatest breakthroughs.

ભ

Ongoing Awakening to Sacred Story Prayer

A very significant exercise for us in the first weeks of learning Sacred Story prayer was finding the personal name for God that touches our hearts. Praying to God by saying this name often continues to be a powerful spiritual experience. Personalizing prayer and our relationship with God is an essential step in deepening our understanding of, and belief in, the God who is lovingly present to us each day of our lives.

Take what you are learning from praying with your personal name for God to understand why it is important to personalize the five meditations of Sacred Story. This week, you are invited to write your own single sentence for each of the meditations in Sacred Story. You are invited to continue working on this exercise until you know each of your sentences by heart. In this exercise, you are personalizing the Sacred Story of creation, the Fall, and our redemption in Christ to your own life story.

Engage all the other disciplines associated with Sacred Story prayer as part of your daily practice: Prayer upon Waking, During-the-Day Awakening exercise, daily journaling, and Prayer upon Retiring. Personalize Creation, Presence, Memory, Mercy, and Eternity during your fifteen-minute sessions this week. Use the blank spaces provided on the next page, or write the sentences in your personal journal.

CREATION

PRESENCE

MEMORY

MERCY

ETERNITY

Come, children, listen to me;
I will teach you fear of the LORD.
Who is the man who delights in life,
who loves to see the good days?
Keep your tongue from evil,
your lips from speaking lies.
Turn from evil and do good;
seek peace and pursue it.

The eyes of the Lord are directed toward the righteous
and his ears toward their cry.
The Lord's face is against evildoers
to wipe out their memory from the earth.

The righteous cry out, the Lord hears
and he rescues them from all their afflictions.
The Lord is close to the brokenhearted,
And saves those whose spirit is crushed.
(Ps 34:12–19)

SO

Dr. Schuchts' Reflection ~ Week Twenty-Six

Personalizing the Five Meditations of Sacred Story Prayer

During this twenty sixth week, you are invited to personalize the five meditations of Sacred Story Prayer. This practice of personalizing prayer is vital for making it life-giving and applicable to your day- to-day experience. The Catechism of the Catholic Church speaks to the importance of personalizing prayer in its insightful description on meditation. The following is from Catechism 2723:

Meditation is a prayerful quest engaging thought, imagination, emotion and desire. Its object is to make our own in faith the object considered, by confronting it with the reality of our own life.

When we personalize the five meditations, we actively engage our thoughts and imaginations, which then awaken our emotions and desires. Think for a moment about each of the Five Meditations and ask the Holy Spirit to guide you in the process of imagining, feeling and desiring.

When you think about *Creation*, what images come to your mind? Spend time reflecting on those images and allow your imagination to daydream. As you daydream, pay attention to the emotions that are evoked by these images. What desires are stirred in you as you meditate on the images? These desires are the essence of your prayer. Bring them confidently to the Father.

Now walk through the same process with *Presence, Memory, Mercy,* and *Eternity*. Pay attention to what you are thinking and feeling as you meditate on each one of these words. What images come to mind and what desires are stirred in you? Submit these images to the light of Christ and bring your desires to the Father, who longs to fulfill these desires of your heart.

As you enter into meditation in this way with each of the five words, you will notice how easy it is to write out your personal one-sentence version for each one. You will also find that your heart is more fully engaged in the process of Sacred Story Prayer.

This is how we overcome the monotony and dryness that too easily interferes with our meditation. As we rely on the Holy Spirit, the divine inspirer invites our humanity to fully participate in the prayer.

We all know from experience what repetitive prayer can be like when neither the Holy Spirit nor our own humanity is active in the process. This so-called "prayer" can become lifeless and boring.

This is the danger with repetitive prayer. We too easily tend to go through the motions, without allowing the words and images to become personal and heart-felt. We then develop an aversion to prayer, giving room for the enemy of our human nature to pull us away from intimacy with God.

Are you becoming more attentive to the movements of your thoughts, feelings and desires as you enter into this daily form of prayer? If you are having difficulty, it could be that you are avoiding intimacy with God or running away from an area of sin or wounding. Or it could just be a seasonal dryness that happens for all of us from time to time, as the Holy Spirit is bringing us deeper into a dark night.

In either case, remind yourself of the Affirmation you are reciting aloud each day of this 26th week: "The urge to stop Sacred Story practice always comes before my greatest breakthroughs."

Keep pressing in and you will see the fruits in your personal life and in your priestly ministry.

Here are comments from your brother priests after personalizing these meditations during this 26th week:

✠ *The personalization of the statements is a work of mine in union with the Father*

✠ *Personalizing the Examen statements is helpful. I am nearly satisfied with them.*

✠ *It is certainly true that personalizing things helps to break the monotony in which I seem so tempted to leave my prayer.*

✠ *I am discovering a common theme of integration among all five; how they fit and "work" together, and how the Father guides me through the meditation.*

Immaculate Heart of Mary pray for us so that our hearts
may be fully aligned with the Sacred Heart of your son Jesus.

৪০

NOTES

Week 27

FIRST
I will visualize my prayer times this week and resolve to spend no more and no less than fifteen minutes in each formal prayer session. I will always use my personal name for God.

SECOND
For week 27, I am invited to continue developing a life-long process of praying the five meditations of Sacred Story prayer. As St. Ignatius suggested, I will enter my prayer at least once daily.

THIRD
I will continue my process of writing a personalized version of the five meditations.

I will awaken to the present moment.
I will awaken to my spiritual nature.
I will not make any decisions based on fear.
I will practice sacramental Reconciliation monthly.

This week, I will say this affirmation aloud once daily:
God gives me insights, not because I am better than others,
but because I am loved.

Ongoing Awakening to Sacred Story Prayer

Sacred Story prayer is designed to carry us through our Christian journey to our heavenly home. It is also designed to open us to grace so that our story is shaped more and more by Christ's Sacred Story. Living our story in Christ is a labor of love, accomplished as we awaken to the truths of Creation, Presence, Memory, Mercy, and Eternity.

Let us resolve this week to continue our journey by praying with Creation, Presence, Memory, Mercy, and Eternity. By our openness and God's grace, our history and the history of the Church and world are changing. Make an act of faith this week that this is indeed true.

We also engage all the other disciplines associated with Sacred Story prayer as part of our daily practice. You can review these in week 16. Continue to use your personalized prayers of Creation, Presence, Memory, Mercy, and Eternity for the fifteen-minute sessions this week. Review the template from last week for this exercise.

ॐ

Many are the troubles of the just one,
but out of them all the Lord delivers him;
he watches over all his bones;
not one of them shall be broken.
Taste and see the goodness of the Lord.
(Ps 34:20–21)

ॐ

Dr. Schuchts' Reflection ~ Week Twenty-Seven

Daily Disciplines of Sacred Story Prayer

During this 27th week, you are continuing to develop the habit of *Sacred Story Prayer*, including the personalized five meditations, as well as the following daily disciplines: *On Waking, During the Day Consciousness Exercise, Journal* and *On Retiring Exercise.*

Since it has been a while since we have discussed the daily disciplines, I would like to focus there this week. I want to remind you why we are engaging in these disciplines. (The daily disciplines are all listed in Week 16).

Sometimes when we lose focus of our "why", we also lose our passion and desire for the "what". Gradually, our disciplines become outward duties without an investment of our hearts. Before we know it, we find ourselves going through the motions rather than growing in love. Our "rote" prayer leads to "ruts."

The purpose of spiritual *disciplines,* as you know, is to continuously bring about our transformation as *disciples* of Jesus Christ. We are not just engaging in an exercise, for the sake of exercise. We are exercising spiritually so that we can grow stronger in the life of the Holy Spirit.

The ultimate purpose of these spiritual disciplines is to bring about a deeper encounter with Jesus Christ and in doing so to transform our minds and hearts, so that like St. Paul we can say: "It is not I who lives, but Christ who lives in me."

This is the work of the Holy Spirit in our lives. The Catechism says: "The desire and work of the Holy Spirit in the heart of the Church is that we may live the life of the Risen Christ." (CCC, 1099).

Your participation in Christ's priestly ministry represents the heart of the Church. Do you desire what the Holy Spirit desires? Do you really want to be transformed so that you are of one mind and one heart with Jesus?

Do you desire to think with the mind of Christ and to love with the heart of Christ, with the passionate fire of the Holy Spirit?

I was recently inspired and humbled by reading an excellent biography of St. John Paul II: *St. John Paul the Great: His Five Loves*, by Jason Evert. If you haven't read it, I highly recommend it.

John Paul II exemplified this burning desire to live Christ in every moment of his life. Reading his life story inspired me to want to emulate his example of holiness, but it also humbled me realizing how far I am from actually living it.

This passage in particular spoke to me, perhaps because of our meditations on *Presence* in Sacred Story Prayer:

"John Paul viewed each encounter as a divine appointment, and those who conversed with him sensed this... 'Despite his killing schedule, he never rushes things. He focuses his whole attention on me. He has ears only for me. I'm chosen. Raised up. Unique. The most important one.'"

John Paul II carried the presence of Christ, and each person who encountered him encountered the love of God in and through him. The secret to John Paul's gift of personal presence is no doubt attributable to his prayer life. He went to prayer expecting to encounter Jesus and to be transformed by him.

His waking and his retiring, and all the hours in between throughout the day, were dedicated to practicing the Presence of Christ in every aspect of his life.

This is the purpose of the daily disciplines of Sacred Story Prayer. The *On*

Waking and *On Retiring Exercises* are like bookends to the day. The *During the Day Consciousness Exercise* and *Journaling* are meant to help us become aware of Christ's Presence throughout the Day. The *Five Meditations* give us a daily reminder to live by.

You are not alone in this process. Your brother priests are journeying with you. Here are their insights for Week Twenty-Seven:

✠ *Sacred Story prayer helps me situate myself consciously within the big picture of God's economy. I am able to refocus every morning on who God is, who I am, where I come from, and where I need to be going; and to seek the healing that I need from the hurts I pick up through life.*

✠ *The grace of God's mercy and forgiveness received and given to others enables me to enjoy a healed and purified memory that allows me to live in the consciousness of everlasting life at each moment.*

✠ *Combining the 5 meditations and the 5 daily disciplines is the best way to increase permanent prayer. This is a good way to live permanently in the presence of the Lord.*

✠ *It was good to reflect upon Pope John Paul II and his holy influence. There was just something different about him!*

Immaculate Heart of Mary pray for us so that our hearts may be fully aligned with the Sacred Heart of your son Jesus.

℘

305

NOTES

Part Three
Entering the
School of Discernment

"Beloved, do not trust every spirit
but test the spirits to see whether they
belong to God, because many false prophets
have gone out into the world."
1 Jn 4:1

The Spiritual World

Spiritual discernment is challenging for a reason. Due to Original Sin, we have lost our capacity to readily distinguish truth from falsehood. To enter the path of discernment, we need to understand God and the universe God created. It is a universe that is both physical and spiritual. To help you enter the "school of discernment," Sacred Story prayer proposes a relational model (or paradigm) for God, human persons, and the created universe. Let us take a few moments to explore this relational paradigm.

First, we affirm a simple truth: God is Love. The essence of God as Love is God as Perfect Relationship. God is a Trinity of perfect, loving relationship. The Trinity—Father, Son, and Spirit—are three totally distinct, unique persons with no boundaries to their giving and receiving love. God is Love. It is a Love without beginning or end. God is Perfect Relationship. Love is always about relationship; the loss of love is always about the breaking of relationship. So everything not of God is anti-relationship, what Scripture calls the spirit of anti-Christ, "which is to come, but is already in the world" (1 Jn 4:3).

Second, God "created mankind in his image; in the image of God He created them; male and female he created them" (Gen 1:27). God willed human nature's form, freely creating persons as a perfect relationship of body and spirit.[16] The human nature God willed is the person as an embodied spirit. Human nature as embodied spirit is fashioned in God's own image. Consequently, persons are made to share in the Love that the Trinity enjoys—unique beings created to freely give and receive love with no boundaries.

For the human person, perfect love is the experience of being a completely unique individual and in that uniqueness, being completely transparent to one's beloved, who is also completely unique, perfectly transparent in the giving and receiving of love, perfectly giving, perfectly accepted, perfectly loved, perfectly loving, and eternally cherished! This giving and receiving of love, with no boundaries, was intended in God's plan to be realized between the persons and their Creator, and among the persons themselves. The relational paradigm of the Trinity is enriched immeasurably by God's free act of creation.

Third, the story of paradise in the book of Genesis reveals the state of perfect relationship between our first parents and God. This state of intimacy with God enabled a state of perfect justice and righteousness— a paradise! As long as our first parents remained in this state of spiritual intimacy with the Divine—as long as the state of perfect justice held— they were free from sickness and death.[17] This state of immortality was possible as long as they allowed God to be the very center of their lives— as long as they stayed in perfect, intimate relationship with God. In this state of perfect intimacy—their hearts undivided—they knew themselves. They had perfect interior harmony between their body and spirit.

Because they were innocent and radically transparent to their Creator, they cherished each other as sacred in God's eyes. As incarnate spirits they shared intimate knowledge, respect, trust, complementarity, uniqueness, separateness, and transcendent love. And they understood the creation. They had perfect relationship with creation, because they understood it as God's gift. God gifts the human persons with the power to name the plants and animals. We understand that this gift of "naming" includes the knowledge of creation's rhythms. They would understand how creation works to their benefit and their delight. The gift of Love freely given to our first parents by God was to expand in cosmic harmony.

The tragedy of Original Sin severs the perfect relationship between the incarnate spirits and the Creator:

> "When they heard the sound of the Lord God walking about in the garden at the breezy time of the day, the man and his wife hid themselves from the Lord God among the trees of the garden." (Gen 3:8)

The perfect relationship they had enjoyed now becomes filled with blame and grief. They will fight each other, and their offspring will fight them. Their perfect relationship with creation is now also cursed (Gen 3:17–19), and they lose immortality. They are vulnerable to sickness and disease. Free will, essential for love, also allows persons to sever their relationship with Love, with God. Relationship violated and severed is the true face of sin.

This is why abandonment and loneliness are the heart's deepest fears. As the most profound misery caused by sin, it is what Christ suffered on the cross, for all of humanity for all time, to a degree unimaginable: "My God, my God, why have you abandoned me?" Love itself suffered love's complete absence (Ps 22:1; Mt 27:45–46).

But God's work in creation cannot be undone by sin. The original unity is lost forever, but out of this tragedy, God creates an even more astonishing good. God would not create such beauty without a way to rectify even this tragedy with something more glorious. We are now invited to accept the mission of participating with Christ in His Grand Work of Reconciliation. We do this by opening to life as sacred story. We allow God to work His miracle of healing and forgiveness for the hope that we, as brothers and sisters of Christ and children of God, are destined to share:

> "I consider that the sufferings of this present time are as nothing compared with the glory to be revealed for us. For creation awaits with eager expectation the revelation of the children of God; for creation was made subject to futility, not of its own accord but because of the one who subjected it, in hope that creation itself would be set free from slavery to corruption and share in the glorious freedom of the children of God. We know that all creation is groaning in labor pains even until now; and not only that, but we ourselves, who have the first fruits of the Spirit, we also groan within ourselves as we wait for adoption, the redemption of our bodies. For in hope we were saved. Now hope that sees for itself is not hope. For who hopes for what one sees? But if we hope for what we do not see, we wait with endurance. In the same way, the Spirit too comes to the aid of our weakness; for we do not know how to pray as we ought, but the Spirit itself intercedes with inexpressible groanings. And the one who searches hearts knows what is the intention of the Spirit, because it intercedes for the holy ones according to God's will." (Rm 8:18–27)

Your discernment is made easier if you can see everything in light of the paradigm of perfect relationship—given, lost, and being restored in Christ:

✠ Perfect relationship of incarnate spirits in our unity of body and spirit

✠ Perfect relationship of created, incarnate spirits with our Creator God

✠ Perfect relationship of incarnate spirits with each other as unique individuals

✠ Perfect relationship between incarnate spirits as male and female, called to fruitful, respectful, loving, and joyful reverence

✠ Perfect relationship between created, incarnate spirits and the earth, which is given for our delight, refreshment, and sustenance

✠ Perfect relationship with the Church, the Body of Christ, as the community formed by Him for the work of Reconciliation, leading to a new heaven and a new earth

Every thought, word, and deed that seeks to affirm the meaning of perfect relationship and the human nature willed by God, everything that is working to heal damaged relationships, is a work of the Divine Inspirer—God the Creator.

Every thought, word, and deed that moves to alter the meaning of perfect relationship and the human nature willed by God, everything that is further undermining damaged relationships, is a work of the counter-inspirer—the enemy of human nature, who is from the beginning a murderer and a liar, the "father of lies" (Jn 8:43–45).

As you enter the school of spiritual discernment, keep your heart and mind focused on the relational paradigm. You are seeking the knowledge of your identity as a child of God, but informed by the truth of perfect relationship. Your authentic identity is a human nature, willed by God, as unity of body and spirit. You seek also the knowledge of your authentic God-given human nature as it has been violated and broken by Original Sin. And you seek this knowledge in light of what Christ is offering: by His life, death, and resurrection, you are offered the beginning of the full healing that will be completed in the world and the life to come.

In short, you are seeking the knowledge of perfect relationship and how in your own life and the world, that perfection has been broken but can also be restored, healed, and redeemed by the Divine Physician. You are also seeking knowledge of the thief and the robber—the enemy of human nature—who seeks to distort what authentic relationship is and to hide from you the truth of God and your authentic human nature. You are seeking to discern the two plotlines in your story: the one that leads to curse and death, and the one that leads to life and blessings. Ultimately, you are seeking to know truth from falsehood in all of your thoughts, words, and deeds.

❧

So Jesus said again,
"Amen, amen, I say to you,
I am the gate for the sheep.
All who came [before me] are thieves and robbers,
but the sheep did not listen to them.
I am the gate.
Whoever enters through me will be saved,
and will come in and go out and find pasture.
A thief comes only to steal and slaughter and destroy;
I came so that they might have life
and have it more abundantly.
I am the good shepherd.
A good shepherd lays down his life for the sheep."
(Jn 10:7–11)

☙

NOTES

Week 28

FIRST
I will visualize the week ahead and imagine where and when I will find a technology-free zone for my time(s) of prayer. As before, I resolve to spend no more and no less than fifteen minutes in each formal prayer session. I will always use my personal name for God.

SECOND
I realize I am developing a deep, personal relationship with Christ. My lifelong process of praying Sacred Story prayer is a commitment to my relationship with Christ. As St. Ignatius found so fruitful, I will enter my prayer at least once daily.

THIRD
This week I enter the twelve-week school of spiritual discernment. It is essential for my progress to understand how the spiritual world works. My goal is to lay a foundation to understand Ignatius's guidelines for discerning the difference between the "voice" of God and the "voice" of the enemy of human nature. I will resolve not to become discouraged. The school of discernment requires spiritual exercise. Learning to distinguish the difference between the voice of God and the voice of the enemy of human nature takes practice. Most importantly, it requires listening, time, trial and error, prayer, patience, and God's grace.

I will awaken to the present moment.
I will awaken to my spiritual nature.
I will not make any decisions based on fear.
I will practice sacramental Reconciliation monthly.

This week, I will say this affirmation aloud once daily:
The insights and graces I need to move forward in life's journey
unfold at the right time.

�೮೩

Cultivate the interior freedom to continue pondering the discernment reflections as they link to your own life. Understand them as an essential component to living your Sacred Story prayer.

Beginning in the School of Spiritual Discernment

As we begin discernment, continue with your daily prayer disciplines and the five meditations of Sacred Story. The materials for this third part of Forty Weeks are not new elements to integrate into the prayer discipline you are practicing. The discernment lessons are designed for you to learn more about how the spiritual world works. They are also an invitation for you to comprehend more fully the spiritual influences that are shaping your sacred story. Resist the temptation to incorporate these lessons on spiritual discernment into the structure of your fifteen-minute prayer periods. See them more as essential guidelines that will help you enter more fully into the daily disciplines of Sacred Story prayer

If you are praying the Sacred Story prayer faithfully, you will naturally encounter the dynamics taught in these guidelines on spiritual discernment. There is a reason for this. If you think and pray about Creation, Presence, Memory, Mercy, and Eternity in your Sacred Story prayer every day, the spiritual world awakens to you. The God of Grace who seeks to support you with divine inspirations, and the enemy of your human nature who seeks to disrupt your life with counter-inspirations, will both become apparent. If you seek daily to grow in faith, you will consciously encounter the spiritual world that supports your growth and the spiritual world that wants to disrupt your growth. While both forces have always been present in your life's story, you may have never before consciously noticed their activity.

These lessons on discernment will help you navigate these two spiritual currents so you can more readily move forward in your sacred story. If you do not now understand everything you are reading, you will one day, if you remain faithful to your prayer disciplines in the context of practicing your faith.

The first lesson examines God's intentional creation of human nature as a unity of spirit and body. We also examine why God willed the form of our human nature and created us as embodied spirits. Read the lesson several times this week and reflect on it. These truths need to be rediscovered and consciously reflected upon to help bring clarity to our lives. We are all influenced by the secularism of our age, to a greater or lesser degree, and need to wake up to what is real, because what is real may seem like spiritual fairy tales. But the principles of discernment we present here are the time-tested doctrines of our faith. If you do not believe or accept these fundamental Christian truths, Ignatius's discernment guidelines will make no sense whatsoever.

Church Tradition affirms that human nature, as a unity of spirit and body, was willed by God. We are human because our physical body is animated by an immortal, rational soul. No other creature is gifted with a rational soul to animate its physical body. Why did God will our human nature as a unity of physical body and rational soul? So God could be intimate with us. God communicates with our human nature by means of our spiritual soul. Complete intimacy with God is our destiny, our glory, and the purpose of our creation. Only a being with a spirit can know and love. A spirit's two chief faculties are the intellect (which knows) and the will or

317

heart (which loves). Human beings are spiritual since humans both know and love.

Church Tradition also affirms that God created human beings as immortal beings. This is known as the condition of original holiness or original justice. The state of original justice means that the physical body and spiritual soul of our first parents were in complete harmony. The state afforded our first parents complete self-mastery. That state of sinlessness allowed all our thoughts, words, and deeds to be in complete harmony with the Divine.

We were without sin and thus without suffering, disease, or death. Immortality was the result of the total intimacy our first parents shared with God. Without complete spiritual intimacy with God, immortality would not be possible. Our first parents were at one in themselves, at one with each other and creation, and at one with God. Our spiritual nature, completely intimate with God, perfectly guided the lower nature of our material body. We call this period of history "paradise."

Our first parents were knowing beings (Homo sapiens). They knew themselves, God, and the purpose of creation's gift. They were the apex of God's creation and were given dominion to act as co-creators with God. To be co-creators means they were given power to cultivate and care for the earth and to name all living creatures (Gen 2:15–20). As woman and man, they had the power to give birth to other beings that would have an eternal destiny. Their role as co-creators could be accomplished with total integrity and justice because of their complete self-mastery. The triple corruption (1 Jn 2:16) of human nature "that subjugates us to the pleasures of the senses, covetousness for earthly goods, and self-assertion, contrary to the dictates of reason" had not yet poisoned God's plan for humanity and creation.

The Fall

The Tradition affirms that sin entered into creation originally from a spiritual entity, Lucifer, and the other spirits who irrevocably rejected God. Thus, sin first enters into God's creation in the spiritual realm, through a spiritual act of the will. It was an act of disobedience. Lucifer is the embodiment of sin, which is hatred of God and God's creation. Lucifer's hate, pride, and envy seek to destroy everything God creates. Lucifer operates through a gateway from his spiritual realm to the material realm so as to infect creation and activate its destruction. His gateway is the spiritual nature of our first parents. The perfect expression of hatred toward God is to destroy the beautiful, innocent immortals created to share in God's life.

Why Did God Allow Us to Disobey and Suffer?

God is love. Love always offers a choice to accept or reject divine love. If the woman and man cannot freely reject God's offer of life and love, God violates the freedom of the beings made in the divine image. Yet God would not have allowed this freedom if it would undo his plan for humankind. Our promise is that Jesus's Redemption will open a new heaven and a new earth with more blessing and glory than the first creation.

Lucifer's malevolent design starts by sabotaging the unity of human nature as a perfect relationship of body and spirit. His seduction begins by inviting persons to worship themselves instead of God. From this perversion of God's design, all other relationships will shatter. Lucifer's hope is that the virus of self-love—of narcissism—and the rejection of God's love that it manifests, will eventually evolve to destroy humanity and creation itself.

The time of paradise was real, and the plan to destroy paradise was also real. The plan to destroy creation required separating our first parents from their total intimacy with God. Here is the allegorical description in Genesis of the Original Sin that describes this heartrending primordial event:

> Now the snake was the most cunning of all the wild animals that the LORD God had made. He asked the woman, "Did God really say, 'You shall not eat from any of the trees in the garden?'" The woman answered the snake: "We may eat of the fruit of the trees in the garden; it is only about the fruit of the tree in the middle of the garden that God said, 'You shall not eat it or even touch it, or else you will die.' " But the snake said to the woman: "You certainly will not die! God knows well that when you eat of it your eyes will be opened and you will be like gods, who know good and evil." The woman saw that the tree was good for food and pleasing to the eyes, and the tree was desirable for gaining wisdom. So she took some of its fruit and ate it; and she also gave some to her husband, who was with her, and he ate it. (Gen 3:1–6)

This account is an allegory, a symbolic description of a real event that Tradition calls the Original Sin. We will never know the exact context for the Original Sin that ruptured God's plan for humanity and creation itself. And we cannot know the way the enemy of human nature insinuated itself into the consciousness of our first parents to get them to reject God and to make themselves gods, "masters" of the universe.

Yet the Genesis account provides valuable spiritual and theological material for reflection about the nature of temptation and the horrifying fall from grace that has evolved over time because of God's displacement from the center of human hearts. We see it in insatiable greed and grinding poverty; personal hatred and fratricidal war; the violation of the innocent in abuse and human trafficking; the legal murdering of children in the womb; the discarding of the weak, the vulnerable, and the aged; the lonely and despairing exploited by predators of all sorts; intellectual and scientific arrogance that subverts human nature and the created order; and self-serving political and financial collectives whose power is destabilizing and destroying families, nations, and creation itself.

Dissecting the story, we can imaginatively enter into this frightening and grief-filled catastrophe and see it with new eyes, through the relational paradigm: the plan of human nature's enemy to destroy the perfect ordering in love of all relationships, and to destroy God's creation.[18]

Stages of Original Sin Violation of Obedience and the Birth of a Divided Conscience: In the state of original justice, the woman and the man were completely intimate with God. Their spiritual nature was ordered solely to the Divine, and this gave them self-mastery over their lower physical nature. They also had the gift of immortality, because they listened only to God. The Latin root for obey means "to listen deeply." Lucifer inserts himself between our first parents and God. He did this by engaging them in seemingly innocent conversation. They violated obedience to God by elevating the voice of Lucifer to a status equal to God. This foreshadowed

---

What is Sin?

Every sin, in its essence, is a perversion and erosion of the perfect love and relationship that God gave to human persons as gift, life, and truth. And every sin in evil's evolution mimics the Original Sin. Each sin—whether it be a thought, word, or deed—spreads the virus of anti-Christ—anti-relationship as narcissism—to destroy human nature made in the divine image. Creation's perversion and destruction is the goal of evil's architect—the one St. Ignatius calls "the enemy of human nature."

---

unspeakable tragedy and loss. Turning from God to listen and speak to Lucifer constitutes the first stage of Original Sin.

Stages of Original Sin

1.   Violation of Obedience and the Birth of a Divided Conscience: In the state of original justice, the woman and the man were completely intimate with God. Their spiritual nature was ordered solely to the Divine, and this gave them self-mastery over their lower physical nature. They also had the gift of immortality, because they listened only to God. The Latin root for obey means "to listen deeply." Lucifer inserts himself between our first parents and God. He did this by engaging them in seemingly innocent conversation. They violated obedience to God by elevating the voice of Lucifer to a status equal to God. This foreshadowed unspeakable tragedy and loss. Turning from God to listen and speak to Lucifer constitutes the first stage of Original Sin.

2.   Violation of Chastity and the Birth of **Illegitimate Desires:** In a state of original justice and with trusting innocence, the man and woman obeyed God, knowing the truth of their being, God, and creation. Engaged in conversation with the prince of lies, they were invited to see with new eyes what before had held no interest and incited no desire. But now, their hearts (consciences) were divided. They could not properly reason; nor could they maintain self-mastery over their physical nature. Cut off from God, their spiritual nature experienced the lust of self-assertion. They now contemplate (see with new eyes) an illegitimate desire opposed both to God and to their own human nature. All illegitimate desires are described in Tradition as appetites linked to the seven capital vices (pride, envy, anger, gluttony, greed, lust, sloth). This is the second stage of Original Sin.

3.   Violation of Poverty and the Taking of What Does Not Belong to Me: Their total intimacy with God severed, the woman and the man had new desires and contemplated an electrifying, exciting, and seemingly glamorous choice: to be like gods, knowing good and evil. God had told them that they would die if they ate this fruit. But Lucifer soothed them with lies to trick them into taking what they must have known in their

hearts was wrong. The third stage in Original Sin is this: to experiment and find out for yourself who is telling the truth. And so our first parents took what they did not need and what did not belong to them. Devastation, heartache, and unspeakable tragedies followed.

The Three Stages of Original Sin in My Life

1.   By choice and/or habit: By choice and/or habit, the heart—conscience—is distant from God. I think I am following my own plans, but I am easily and subtly influenced to choose against God and my authentic self. I disobey my conscience. This lack of obedience ("deep listening") begins with my self-assertion. I make myself the final arbiter of truth. I break relationship with God and become independent of God, serving self over God.

2.   In this self-assertion, I open myself to all manner of illegitimate desires and entertain them. All these illegitimate desires are, in their essence, perversion and erosion of authentic relationships. Illegitimate desires are deemed "objectively wrong" by the Commandments, the gospel, and Tradition, but I judge them appropriate options, because I decide what I ought and ought not do. In so doing, I violate chastity. Violations of chastity are perversions and erosions of perfect relationship.

3.   I move from considering options to experimenting and trying what I like, because "It's my life." In this I violate poverty by taking what does not rightfully belong to me. Violations of poverty are perversions and erosions of relationship, because I take what I do not need or is not mine.
Jesus Redeems the Fall

Before the incarnate God-man Jesus begins His public ministry, He confronts this triple sin of our first parents. He confronts the temptation of Lucifer to turn the stones into bread. In this He confronts the violation of poverty by refusing to take what is not offered Him by the Father: "One does not live by bread alone, but by every word that comes forth from the mouth of God" (Mt 4:4).

Next, He confronts the violation of chastity and illegitimate desires by refusing to gain attention by plunging from the temple parapet: "Again it is written, 'You shall not put the Lord, your God, to the test'" (Mt 4:7).

Finally, He confronts the violation of obedience and the divided consciences it wrought by refusing to serve Lucifer and rule on this earth: "At this, Jesus said to him, 'Get away, Satan! It is written: "The Lord, your God, shall you worship and him alone shall you serve"'" (Mt 4:10).

The Sacred Story prayer journey challenges you to awaken to the voice of God in your own unique history, calling you to the poverty, chastity, and obedience that can bring peace and repair sin's damage. To do this effectively, it is essential to learn the language of discernment. The Discernment Guidelines presented in the coming weeks are modeled on St. Ignatius's classic Rules for spiritual discernment. For thirty years, Ignatius had made decisions based on self-assertion, with little thought of God. Both the desire and the choice to advance spiritually were totally new for him.

Ignatius's awakening forced him into uncharted terrain where he did not know how to navigate. He was not spiritually literate. He did not know himself—his authentic self—because he had lived controlled by sensual lusts and the desires of riches, honors of the world, and pride. All are values readily celebrated by our culture today.

God instructed Ignatius in discernment during his conversion journey. In his awakening process, he writes, "What is the new life we are living?" In this phrase he was discovering what Nicodemus was told by Jesus: "Amen, amen, I say to you, no one can see the kingdom of God without being born from above" (Jn 3:3).

Ignatius, in being born from above, was reconnected by grace to his spiritual nature and to God. He was awakening to realities he could not have known previously. He was learning that there were two "voices" and learning how to distinguish between them. By understanding the discernment guidelines that God revealed to Ignatius, we can awaken more easily to our authentic human nature.

To prepare ourselves, we will learn a new language of discernment and discover in our own life history the two voices "inspiring" us—one voice working to help us unite our spiritual and physical nature, and one voice working to keep us separated from God and divided within ourselves. You will learn how to distinguish in your thoughts, words, and deeds the voice of God from the voice of the enemy of human nature.

But they soon forgot all he had done;
they had no patience for his plan.
In the desert they gave in to their cravings,
tempted God in the wasteland.
They exchanged their glory
for the image of a grass-eating bull.
They forgot the God who had saved them,
who had done great deeds in Egypt,
They sacrificed to demons their own sons and daughters,
Shedding innocent blood,
the blood of their own sons and daughters,
Whom they sacrificed to the idols of Canaan,
desecrating the land with bloodshed.
They defiled themselves by their actions,
became adulterers by their conduct.
Save us, Lord, our God;
gather us from among the nations
That we may give thanks to your holy name
and glory in praising you.
(Ps 13–14, 20–21, 38–39, 47)

ဆ

The School of Spiritual Discernment

With the foundation of the Whole-Life Confession and the Sacred Story Examen Prayer, we are now ready for "Entering the School of Spiritual Discernment."

Fr. Watson summarizes this section with great clarity and simplicity in his final paragraph of Week 28. I want to repeat his words to add emphasis to them:

> "You will learn how to distinguish the *voice of God*
> from the *voice of the enemy* of human nature
> in your *thoughts*, *words* and *deeds*."

This, in all its simplicity, is what spiritual discernment is all about. But we all know from experience this is not as easy as it sounds. In our weakened spiritual state, we are all vulnerable to deception from the enemy of our human nature working in all our "thoughts, words and deeds."

Fr. Watson goes on to describe the tell-tale signs of these competing voices:

God's voice: "working to help us *unite* our spiritual and
physical nature",
Enemy's voice: "working to keep us *separated* from God
and *divided* within ourselves."

The Holy Spirit is the bond of unity and charity. The enemy separates and divides. So, let's apply this to your thoughts, words, and deeds. As you become more aware of your thoughts, you will notice, like St. Ignatius, that they evoke very diverse emotions and spiritual states, depending on the source of inspirations. These in turn, motivate your words and actions.

Typically, Holy Spirit inspired thoughts, words and deeds manifest the characteristics of love and bear the fruit of the Spirit, which are listed by St. Paul in the well-known passages of Scripture-- 1 Co. 13 and Gal. 5:22-23.

We can use these criteria among others to "test the Spirits" (1 Jn. 4:1). The following is a simple way to test your thoughts, words and deeds, based on these passages 1 Co. 13 and Gal. 5:21-22:

1)   **Love**: Are your thoughts, words and deeds loving or narcissistic? Are you desiring and acting for your true good and the good of others? Or are your thoughts, words and deeds self-centered and destructive in their origin and effects.

2)   **Kindness**: Are your thoughts towards yourself and others kind and compassionate? Do your words and actions speak the heart-warming language of kindness and consideration? Or do you think harsh and critical thoughts, and speak harsh and critical words towards yourself and others?

3)   **Patience**: When you have someone slowing you down or interfering with your goals, do you get frustrated and irritable? Or are you able to wait patiently? When you are stuck in traffic or God is not answering your prayers, how do you react?

4)   **Joy**: Are your thoughts filled with gratitude? Do people see you light up in their presence when you relate to them? When you worship is joy manifested in your spirit? Or in all of these areas of your life do you seem listless and lifeless? What are the thoughts which bring joy to your heart, and which thoughts snuff it out?

5) **Peace**: Are you aware of the difference inside of you when your thoughts produce peace, vs. those that produce anxiety and distress? How about when you speak and act--do your words and deeds bring peace to others or do they cause anxiety to those on the receiving end?

We could keep going with these examples covering each of the characteristics of love and the various fruits of the Spirit. But I think this illustrates the difference between the two voices in spiritual discernment.

Notice how the Holy Spirit-inspired thoughts, words, and deeds bring us into greater communion with God, ourselves, and others. In contrast, the counter-inspirations of the enemy increase division and disconnection in all these relationships.

This movement towards unity or division is happening every day in every moment of time, in our thoughts, words and deeds. We are either moving with Christ or partnering with the enemy to sow seeds of discord and disintegration. Which will we choose?

These are summary thoughts from your brother priests after reflecting on this material from Week 28:

✠ *God created us spiritual beings-- body and soul-- intimately united for an immortal life. But because of the ongoing effects of the original sin, human beings have been living with an interior separation between body and soul. Therefore, we have to learn how to distinguish the voice of God from the voice of the enemy of human nature in our thoughts, words and deeds.*

✠ *Everything goes back to relationships - salvation, sanctification, mission, etc. And so, making sure that I have right relationships with God and others will play a big role in helping me know what I'm supposed to do in my day to day ministry.*

✠ When our thoughts, words, and deeds make me feel love, joy, peace, kindness, and patience at the same time, others enjoy these feelings as such. We are to be sure that God's voice leads us because it inspires us to unity. Otherwise, if we bring separation and division around us, then this is an inspiration coming from the evil one.

✠ The reflection on love, kindness, patience, joy, and peace was most helpful. The questions helped me to reflect on the ways that I lack joy or fail to express joy ...probably because I am self-concerned.

*Immaculate Heart of Mary pray for us so that our hearts
may be fully aligned with the Sacred Heart of your son Jesus.*

☙

NOTES

Week 29

FIRST

I will visualize the week ahead to imagine where and when I can find a place apart—a technology-free zone—for my fifteen-minute periods of formal prayer. I will always use my personal name for God.

SECOND

This week, I continue the life-long process of praying meditations one through five in the Sacred Story prayer. I resolve to enter my prayer at least once daily, as St. Ignatius suggested.

THIRD

I continue my lessons in spiritual discernment. This week, I will come to understand how the world changed by the rupture of sin, and I will study God's plan to help us find our way home.

I will awaken to the present moment.
I will awaken to my spiritual nature.
I will not make any decisions based on fear.
I will practice sacramental Reconciliation monthly.

This week, I will say this affirmation aloud once daily:
My personal engagement with Sacred Story accomplishes, through Christ, a work of eternal significance.

ℭ

Continuing in the School of Discernment

Take time, at your convenience outside of your prayer periods, to read and reflect on this second lesson in discernment. The lesson will examine two elements: first, the consequences of our first parents' decision to violate the freedom bestowed upon them by displacing God from the center of their lives; second, God's rescue plan to redeem us.

God desired that we be free and that we use that freedom to remain linked to God, our source of life. The complete unity of our higher spiritual nature with God is what made us human. This complete spiritual unity with God also bestowed balance and control over our lower physical nature. We controlled our bodily appetites. This complete unity of our higher spiritual nature with God also made us, body and soul, immortal. It was paradise.

The woman and the man silenced God's voice as the center of their consciences and replaced it with their opinions. In silencing God's voice, they cut the lifeline of God's grace. As a result, human nature, as an integrated unity of spirit and body, was shattered. The higher spiritual nature no longer guided the lower physical nature. The immortality of human nature as body and soul is lost. With their appetites cut off from the Divine spiritual compass, paradise was lost.

Before our first parents used free choice to make themselves the center of their own universe—to make themselves gods—spiritual discernment was not necessary. They knew the true God, they knew who they were, and they knew instinctively how to act with integrity and holiness. Truth was instinctive, based on the complete harmony they shared with God: discernment was automatic.

We cannot determine at what point in the two-hundred-thousand-year history of modern humans this rupture took place, but we affirm that it did occur. As a result, God's plan to save humankind and creation began. Our Judeo-Christian faith is a revealed religion. This means that God reveals it to us; we do not create it. In the rupture caused by Original Sin, we lost the ability to instinctively know the truth about God, our human nature, and creation. God must reveal the idea of truth, good and evil, to His beloved creatures, which are now subject to corruption, disease, and death. It is no wonder that the first Commandment states: "I am the Lord your God; you shall not have strange gods before me."

Covering Their Nakedness

In Genesis 3:7, Adam and Eve "see" their nakedness and "cover" themselves. Their seeing and covering demonstrates that their separation from God awakens them to know and feel that they no longer have control over their physical nature. They can objectify each other—use each other—and in their loss of innocence, are shamed by this discovery. Now begins the history of psychological and physical exploitation linked to the very gift God created to give life: human sexuality. The enemy of human nature knew this tragedy would result and relishes the agony it causes. The perfect complementarity of human nature created in the divine image, male and female, is shattered by narcissism. But God has a plan to rescue us and make all things new. It begins with the miracle of the wine at the wedding at Cana, which signifies the superabundance of grace that God pours out upon the covenant of marriage through Christ's life (Jn 2:1–12).

The Ten Commandments reveal the moral truths—about God, about woman and man's proper relationship to God, and about their relationship to each other and to creation. God is revealing the knowledge of truth lost in paradise. God chose the Jewish people for this mission. The whole history of Israel is preparing for the coming of the Messiah who will save us from the devastation caused by Original Sin. Sin closes hearts to the truth, and so even the chosen people rejected God's messengers, the prophets. Christ fared no better and was executed. The Pharisees, with darkened consciences, even accused Jesus of collaborating with Satan (Mt 12:24).

What is Truth?

"'For this I was born and for this I came into the world, to testify to the truth. Everyone who belongs to the truth listens to my voice.' Pilate said to him, 'What is truth?'"
(Jn 18:37–38)

At the beginning of the third millennium, many believe truth is relative. Even before the third millennium commenced, many pointed out that the greatest threat to the faith is not atheism but relativism. Jesus tells Pilate that he was born and came into the world to testify to the truth—the truth about God, the truth about human nature, and the truth about salvation. Truth does exist, and discernment's goal is to help us distinguish truth from falsehood in our sacred story.

Your Sacred Story prayer journey links you to the entire history of salvation. In your prayer and in your discernment, you participate in the holy labor of returning body and soul to God. You join Christ's Great Work of Reconciliation by your engagement. It is a labor to be sure, as St. Ignatius learned. Recall that he had lived for thirty years with his lower appetites in near complete control of his life. His awakening was guided by God and began while recuperating from battle. Ignatius was graced to notice a difference between two sets of fantasies or daydreams.

In the first daydream/fantasy, he imagines himself successful in marrying

King Ferdinand and Queen Isabella's daughter. He describes this later as a vain fantasy. In the second daydream/fantasy, he imagines himself making a pilgrimage to Jerusalem and living like the saints.[19] Both daydream/fantasies make him feel good while he entertains them. But on deeper reflection, the afterglow of the first daydream leaves him dry and dissatisfied while the afterglow of the second daydream/fantasy leaves him feeling content and peaceful. With this awakening, he begins a lifelong practice of spiritual discernment.

<hr>

Human Nature and Authentic Identity

Films, songs, books, and newspapers often define human nature positively and solely as our lower appetites. How these lower appetites might be divided from our spiritual nature and from divine influence is usually ignored. Today, many definitions of human nature are influenced by the theories of Sigmund Freud. Freud believed that sexual drives/desires are the root of all human psychological activity, so being authentic means discerning one's identity mainly by expressing one's sensual appetites. Yet to discern one's authentic identity requires being spiritually grafted to Christ. Only then can one discern both the higher calling we have as daughters and sons of God, and our true human nature. This "being born from above" reveals the truth about God, our authentic identity, and our mission to love as Christ loved.

<hr>

What did he learn in this lesson? That the feelings associated with even imagined actions can reveal the truth about our identity. Learning to pay close attention to our feelings (our affective/emotional spiritual life) can reveal the signature of God in our authentic identity and the signature of human nature's enemy in our false identity. Ignatius was utterly amazed at this discovery. Never before had he noticed this subtle difference in his spiritual experiences.

As his Christian conversion deepened, St. Ignatius learned that there are three ways the human person can be "inspired." Inspirations can come from God, from the enemy of human nature, and from oneself. Next week, we will look at these three sources in more depth.

The first goal of spiritual discernment is to learn truth vs. falsehood about your human nature, about your identity as a child of God, and about God and His creation. The second goal of spiritual discernment is to choose thoughts, words and deeds that express your authentic identity as a child of God. You are called to surrender self-assertion in favor of humility so that your life's labor—your sacred story—produces fruit that endures to eternity.

Awaken this week to the truth that you are both body and spirit. You have a higher spiritual nature and a lower bodily nature. At one point, they were an integrated unity but now, they are divided (Jer 17:9). God desires to heal you spiritually ("Lord, I am not worthy to have you enter under my roof; only say the word and my servant will be healed" [Mt 8:8].) so that you can be at peace and gain eternal life. The enemy of human nature seeks to keep you spiritually distant from God so that your lower nature (your base appetites) guide your thoughts, words, and deeds, robbing you of peace and eternal life.

Both God and the enemy of human nature are working to achieve these very different ends. This is nothing to be afraid of, because you have given your heart to Christ. Christ will guide you to safety and holiness just like He did St. Ignatius. All the great teachers of the Church reinforce these central spiritual truths.[20]

ଔ

"And the Word became flesh and made his dwelling among us,
and we saw his glory, the glory as of the Father's only Son,
full of grace and truth." (Jn 1:14)

"God is Spirit, and those who worship him
must worship in Spirit and truth." (Jn 4:24)

"If you remain in my word, you will truly be my disciples, and you
will know the truth, and the truth will set you free." (Jn 8:31–32)

Jesus said to him, "I am the way and the truth and the life.
No one comes to the Father except through me."

(Jn 14:6)

ଞ

Dr. Schuchts' Reflection ~ Week Twenty-Nine

Discernment Guidelines

In this 29th week we are continuing to understand and apply the principles underlying spiritual discernment. These discernment guidelines serve as the basis for our Sacred Story prayer.

These principles, rooted in a Judeo-Christian understanding of reality, help us to see our own story in light of salvation history (Creation, Sin, Redemption, and Glorification).

In describing our fall from grace, Fr. Watson notes five key elements in understanding the roots of our brokenness and how we come to realize it in our personal story:

✠ **Broken Communion**: "[Adam and Eve's] *separation from God*"

✠ **Self-Awareness**: "awakens them to *know and feel*"

✠ **Loss of Integrity**: "that they *no longer have control* over their physical nature."

✠ **Objectification**: "They can *objectify each other--use each other-*"

✠ **Shame**: "and in their *loss of innocence* are *shamed* by this discovery"

These insights bring us to the heart of spiritual discernment and are reminiscent of the profound insights of St. John Paul II in several of his works.

Before becoming pope, Karol Wojtyla wrote three prominent books illuminating these realities by integrating philosophy with Christian Theology. These are:

1) The Acting Person;

2) Love and Responsibility; and

3) Man and Woman He Created Them: A Theology of the Body.

The third and most well-known of these three (*A Theology of the Body*) was not published until after Cardinal Wojtyla became Pope. Its impact in the Church and in the world is without measure.

In *the Acting Person*, Wojtyla develops an understanding of consciousness—which includes our ability to self-reflect. Like Adam and Eve, each of us has an inner awareness of our relationship with God. Like Adam and Eve, we intuitively *know and feel* our spiritual condition. We are able to experience innocence, and we can tell when we have lost innocence and cover ourselves as a result of shame.

In *Love and Responsibility*, Wojtyla provides a more comprehensive vision of relationships and sexuality. In this brilliant work, he develops the concept of respecting the dignity of the person.

Objectification—*using* another for our own selfish purposes—diminishes the dignity of both the one used and the one objectifying the other. Shame is the awareness of dis-grace that comes for both persons in this process.

All of the deadly sins are ways of using creation in a disordered way, filling the ache which comes as a result of our *separation from God*. In each of these disordered desires, we end up losing more control over our physical nature and give greater control to the enemy of our human nature. This is how addictions develop.

Sexual compulsion (lust) is the ongoing objectification of another person, putting them in the place of God and using them for selfish purposes. We all know the feeling of being used and the experience of using another—in our thoughts, words, and deeds. We also know the shame that comes from this kind of objectification.

In *Man and Woman He Created Them: A Theology of the Body*, Pope John

Paul II provides a comprehensive view of our human condition and spiritual journey. Early in this masterpiece, he speaks of Original Innocence and Original Unity, as the original gifts of creation. He goes on to show how sin breaks this Holy Communion with God and one another, leaving us with an inner awareness of shame.

So, you may be asking how this framework for spiritual discernment applies to your daily Examen and Sacred Story prayer? It is the foundation of it. When you reflect on Creation you will have an awareness of these two realities: love and sin.

With love you experience a taste of original innocence and unity, seeing all of creation as gift from God manifesting his Presence. You are able to see yourself as the Father's beloved and relate to every other person as a beloved son or daughter of God.

With sin, you become aware of shame, seeing how love was distorted by disordered desires resulting in objectification. You realize when and how you have misused creation for selfish purposes.

As you reflect on your memories, you know and feel innocence and shame. In all the acts of love and presence you grow in gratitude. In all thoughts, words, and deeds that bring up a consciousness of shame, you are invited into the Merciful love and compassion of our Heavenly Father and prepared for Eternity. This is Sacred Story Prayer.

Your brother priests offered these insights as they reflected on this material from Week Twenty Nine:

✠ *The reality of the desire to be in control is a great challenge. If only I was more able to conform my desires to Christ and to surrender my life and ministry to God completely!*

✠ *Adam and Eve lost intimacy with God in the garden by their disobedience to the word of God. Jesus, the son of God, is the truth that helps us to live again in the unity of body and spirit. With Jesus we are* able to discern our true human nature and our calling to be sons and daughters of God.

✠ Legitimate needs (for example to eat, to love and to be loved, to protect oneself) can be satisfied in a way in which you feel ashamed afterward. Our broken communion with God leads to self-awareness of objectification and losing control of physical nature, and the subsequent shame of disordered relationship.

Immaculate Heart of Mary pray for us so that our hearts may be fully aligned with the Sacred Heart of your son Jesus.

ℰℭ

NOTES

Week 30

FIRST

I resolve to spend no more and no less than fifteen minutes in each formal prayer session. As before, I will visualize the week ahead and imagine where I can find a technology-free zone for my prayer. I will always use my personal name for God.

SECOND

I continue the process of praying meditations one through five in the Sacred Story prayer and, as St. Ignatius suggested, I will enter my prayer at least once daily. This prayer, like the rosary, will never grow old. It will take on more and more meaning, helping me deepen my faith and my wisdom and awaken me to God's truth and love.

THIRD

I will continue to open my heart to the lessons on discernment as I try to understand the three different sources of inspiration that can influence my thoughts, words, and deeds.

I will awaken to the present moment.
I will awaken to my spiritual nature.
I will not make any decisions based on fear.
I will practice sacramental Reconciliation monthly.

I will ask Jesus for help when I am troubled.
I will thank Jesus daily for life's gifts.

This week, I will say this affirmation aloud once daily:
Inspirations can have a divine or a demonic source. I pray for the grace
to remember how to discern one from the other.

CB

Continuing in the School of Discernment:
Guidelines for Foundational Healing and Spiritual Growth

Take time, at your convenience outside of your prayer periods, to read and reflect on this third lesson in discernment. We will examine the three distinct sources of inspiration that can guide our thoughts, words, and deeds.

Inspirations affecting your human nature (spirit-body) can originate from three different sources, according to St. Ignatius.[21]

1. Can originate with yourself
2. Can originate from a Divine Source: the Divine Inspirer
3. Can originate from a demonic source: the enemy of human nature, the counter-inspirer

There are three sources of spiritual inspiration, but only two spiritual states. St. Ignatius names the two states consolation and desolation. Next week, we will explore these two spiritual states in more depth.

Spiritual consolation is when one experiences, to a greater or lesser degree, an increase in faith, hope, and love.

Spiritual desolation is when one experiences, to a greater or lesser degree, a loss of faith, hope, and love.

Sources of Inspiration

- ✠ ✦ Human nature as spirit/body
- ✠ ✦ The Divine Inspirer
- ✠ ✦ The counter-inspirer

Types of Inspiration

- ✠ ✦ Consolation—increase of faith, hope, and love
- ✠ ✦ Desolation—loss of faith, hope, and love

Sources of Inspiration

To affirm that our human nature can be the source of inspirations makes perfect sense. We have our own thoughts and convictions and act on them. Such thoughts originate from within our being in several ways.

First, we can let our body make decisions. We can be led by our sensual appetites and give into them with little or no conscious thought about the consequences. Sometimes that giving in is due to sickness or addictions, but it is still the appetites doing our "thinking" and inspiring our actions.

Second, we can be inspired by what we might call embedded strengths/ gifts in human nature from our Creator or by embedded diseases/weaknesses in human nature marred by Original Sin. Consolation from an embedded strength/ gift could be a bodily feeling that "life is good" after an excellent workout. It might also be a spiritual feeling of being happy to be alive, that "life is beautiful" when looking at a baby or a beautiful sunset.

Desolation from an embedded disease/weakness might be a bodily feeling that "life is miserable" when you have the flu, a chronic illness, or some type of bodily injury. It might also be a spiritual feeling that "life is difficult, burdensome, and not fair" if you are hurting in a relationship or suffering due to early life events.

If you are inspired spiritually by either the Divine Inspirer or the counter-inspirer, the inspiration will be communicated to you through your higher spiritual nature which was willed by God to guide your lower physical nature. We will look at this reality in coming weeks.[22]

You may continue your reflections on these spiritual realities by reading a homily by St. Bernard of Clairvaux and a short section from Vatican II's Gaudium et Spes: The Pastoral Constitution on the Church in the Modern World.[23]

Evil's Work is More Hidden than Sensational

Don't go looking for Exorcist-movie drama in your spiritual discernment. The counter-inspirer accomplished his greatest damage in the Original Sin when human nature was crippled. He knew you would be subject to disease and death and that the anger, cynicism, sickness, war, poverty, and injustice in human society would chip away at belief. A loss of faith, hope, and love would result, and belief in a "God of love" would diminish. Kindness avoided, forgiveness withheld, and self-centered behavior work to diminish faith, hope, and love. All have conspired to create the evolution of darkness present in our history. Exorcist-style evil does exist but serves the counter-inspirer's work mostly by making us blind to evil's greatest work: crushing the human spirit and making us believe that evil is more powerful than God and love. Yet the enemy of human nature— the counter-inspirer—has already lost his battle in Christ's victory. Be not afraid!

CB

My eyes long to see your salvation
and the promise of your righteousness.
Act with mercy toward your servant;
teach me your statutes.
I am your servant; give me discernment
that I may know your testimonies.
(Ps 119:123–125)

EO

Dr. Schuchts' Reflection ~ Week Thirty

Sources and Types of Inspiration

We are now in the fourth quarter of our *Forty Weeks* journey into wholeness. During this thirtieth week we are seeking a better understanding of three *sources* and two *types of inspiration*.

These sources and types of inspiration can be most easily detected as we pay attention to our desires, discerning where they come from and where they are leading us.

Do they come from God and lead us to God? Or do they come from another source and lead us away from God? These simple questions are at the heart of discernment. Understanding our desires provides valuable insight into discerning the source and direction of our inspirations.

The root word for *desire* has its origins in the Latin and French languages. If you break down the meaning of the word, you will see that it is comprised of two parts: "de" (of) and "sire" (father). Thus, the word "desire" literally means "of the Father." As we seek to understand the sources of inspiration, we only need to ask: "Who is the father of this particular desire?" Where does this desire originate? And where is it leading me?

The ultimate source and end of every authentic desire is our "Heavenly Father" He is the Divine Inspirer, and the true object of our desires. He has created everything as an expression of His love for us in order to bring us into our ultimate fulfillment in Christ (John 10:10).

St. James tells us: "All good giving and every perfect gift is from above coming down from the Father of Lights." (James 1:18). St. Thomas Aquinas interpreted this to mean that every good thing we desire is an expression of God in some way.

But this does not mean that *every* desire comes directly from the Father or leads us to Him. There are two other sources (i.e. fathers) that may be inspiring our urges and longings.

"Adam" is the second "father" inspiring our desires. He is the father of our human nature. Our natural yearnings are expressions of our human needs and created nature. In essence these desires are good.

But these natural desires become disordered by our sins, wounds and identity lies. The "father of lies" is the origin behind these disordered desires (Jn. 8:44). He is the enemy of our human nature and deceives us into believing that our human needs and desires can be satisfied through his seductions.

The "father of lies" first attacks our identity, leading us to believe lies about our self and about God. These lies effectively separate us from God and threaten our integrity, leaving us vulnerable to temptation and sin. As St. James notes, these disordered desires are not from the Father but from the enemy of our human nature playing on our weaknesses:

> "No one experiencing temptation should say, "I am being tempted by God"; for God is not subject to temptation to evil, and he himself tempts no one. Rather, each person is tempted when he is lured and enticed by his own desire. [15] Then desire conceives and brings forth sin, and when sin reaches maturity it gives birth to death. (Ja. 1:13-15)

The enemy of our human nature attacks us in the place of our unmet needs. He offers a quick fix and false comfort to our human suffering. But even these disordered desires can lead us to God if we will stop and pay attention to the unmet needs and the good things for which we yearn. Underlying every disordered desire there remains a good and holy desire that has not yet been fulfilled.

Spiritual discernment involves the unmasking of the lies and deceptions that seduce us, so that we can perceive the true needs and the holy desires behind them.

Paying attention to our unmet human needs and desires is the first step in the process. Then it is essential that we turn toward the Father for all of these needs to be satisfied. When we fail to do this, we open ourselves to the enemy's deceptions. In your participation in Christ's priesthood, this process of discernment is essential for you in your personal journey to holiness and wholeness. You cannot give what you do not have.

As the leader of the community, your deceptions become multiplied into the lives of thousands. On the other hand, rightly ordered desires allow you to lead many others in the same path of holiness and wholeness, to find ultimate fulfillment in God and in his divine inspirations.

The following comments from your brother priests reflect their insights during Week 30:

✠ *I was not particularly aware of the possible sources of inspirations and had not thought about a human higher or lower spiritual nature. As this all sorts out, the key is to be mindful and inquisitive about the possible sources as lived out on a day-to-day basis.*

✠ *I was able to reflect more deeply on the source of my inspirations and to apply a greater degree of discernment to them.*

✠ *Discernment concerns the fulfillment of my desires. If the way I satisfy my legitimate desires leads me closer to God I will be able to know that I am on the way of healing and spiritual growth; otherwise I will be the victim of the enemy of human nature.*

✠ *Disordered desires can be the means of deeper healing if we unmask them, bring them to the Almighty Father, and allow Him to satisfy our deepest needs..*

Immaculate Heart of Mary pray for us so that our hearts may be fully aligned with the Sacred Heart of your son Jesus.

ॐ

NOTES

Week 31

FIRST

I will visualize my week to imagine where I can find a technology-free zone to spend my fifteen-minutes prayer sessions. I will always use my personal name for God.

SECOND

I continue the lifelong process of praying meditations one through five in the Sacred Story prayer. I commit to enter my prayer at least once daily as St. Ignatius suggested. This prayer will carry me for life. It will deepen my faith and my wisdom and awaken me to God's truth and love.

THIRD

This week I will continue to seek knowledge of spiritual discernment by examining two benchmark rules: spiritual consolation and spiritual desolation.

I will awaken to the present moment.
I will awaken to my spiritual nature.
I will not make any decisions based on fear.
I will practice sacramental Reconciliation monthly.
I will ask Jesus for help when I am troubled.
I will thank Jesus daily for life's gifts.

This week, I will say this affirmation aloud once daily:
Christ, who has walked before me, shares my every burden.
Christ, who has walked before me,
will help me resolve every crisis.
Christ, who has walked before me, knows my every hope.

ଓ

Continuing in the School of Discernment:
Guidelines for Foundational Healing and Spiritual Growth

Take some time this week to read and reflect on this fourth lesson in discernment. We will examine the two types of inspiration that can guide our thoughts, words, and deeds. First, let's briefly review the past three weeks. God willed that human nature be a perfect unity of body and soul. The gift of this blessed unity of human nature in paradise made us immortal. The turning from God, which we call Original Sin, broke the perfect unity of human nature: body and soul. Lust for power and dominance and the unbridled physical desires of our bodily nature (concupiscence) battled with our spiritual nature. In this battle, our authentic identity was distorted.

Our conscience was clouded, and we lost sight of right and wrong. Disease, strife, suffering, and death resulted. Original Sin broke our perfect unity with God's loving will. Also broken was the unity between male and female and their harmony with creation. Paradise was an ecstasy of harmonious relationships. Original Sin broke all relationships. Most tragically, it broke our hearts.

The revelation of the Ten Commandments to the people of Israel was one of the most significant gifts from God to help us relearn "right relationship." In the New Covenant, Christ is the ultimate revelation of God. Christ's life and message are the most perfect expression of how each of us is called to live. This is why we call our Judeo-Christian faith a

354

revealed religion. We did not come to the truth by our own reasoning processes. It had to be revealed to us.

The teaching Church has been entrusted with interpreting, passing on, and holding secure for all people the authentic message of Christ and the revealed Truths of God. It is the same Church that Ignatius served and

loved. His discernment rules are spiritual guidelines that help us understand the revealed truth of "right relationship" in our own lives, according to the revealed truths entrusted to the teaching Church.

God Is Healing Our Broken Human Nature

Original Sin crippled our human nature. None of us will achieve perfection this side of eternity. Yet knowing that human nature was perfect once and will be perfect again informs the Church's interpretation of holiness. God's grace fosters healing in our souls, enabling us to gain a measure of mastery over the lusts and desires of our bodily nature. It also enables us to grow in forgiveness, selflessness, and charity. All of us are called to cooperate with God's grace for this healing and holiness. We are all encouraged by Christ not to be afraid but to be patient, as the process of healing and sanctification takes a lifetime.

Ignatius's discernment wisdom, in his rules, is discovered when individuals begin to pay close attention to inspirations that we identify through affective awareness. We are inspired in thoughts, words, and deeds from three sources: our own human nature (body and soul); the Divine Inspirer; and human nature's enemy, the counter-inspirer. These inspirations have one of two effects on us: they create either spiritual consolation or spiritual desolation. This week we begin looking at these two types of inspiration.

Two Benchmark Guidelines for Spiritual Discernment

To help your awakening and initiation into spiritual discernment, two benchmark guidelines will be beneficial in many life situations. It is important to understand that divine inspiration, or consolation, does not always feel good. Equally important is to realize that an unholy inspiration, or spiritual desolation, does not always feel bad. We will explore this seeming paradox in a later lesson. For now, it is sufficient to absorb the two benchmark guidelines and to understand that each is intended to influence the direction of our life in every thought, word, and deed either toward or away from God.

Benchmark One

Authentic Divine Inspirations, called Consolations, will:

1. Increase the heart's love for God and others,

2. Increase the virtues of docility, humility, and self-generosity, and

3. Not oppose the truths and teachings of Scripture, the Tradition, and the teaching Church.[24]

Consolation can be the consequence of the Divine Physician's Spirit working in you. This form of consolation helps strengthen your heart and soul, encouraging you to turn to God. Consolation helps you to choose thoughts, words, and deeds that express your authentic human nature made in the divine image.

Consolation can also be the consequence of the body/spirit aspect of your divinely shaped human nature. God created your human nature as a gift in the divine image and likeness. In spite of Original Sin's impact, cooperating with God's grace activates embedded life forces of your divinely shaped human nature, helping to heal biochemical, physiological, and emotional imbalances; energizing you; and enabling thoughts, words, and deeds that express your authentic human nature. Benchmark Two

Authentic Counter-inspirations, called Desolations, will:

1. Increase narcissism, displacing God and others,

2. Decrease docility and humility and increase pride and self-satisfaction, and

3. Arouse hungers and desires that, although they feel good, will typically contradict the truths and teachings proposed by the Scripture, Tradition, and the teaching Church. This is because the author of counter-inspirations is opposed to Christ and will lead you away from life and truth.

Counter-inspirations will produce desires that feel authentic because they are linked to fallen human nature's physical lusts and spiritual pride. They are the familiar default drives of a broken heart and a broken human nature.

Desolation can be the consequence of the enemy of human nature working in you. This form of desolation helps weaken your heart and soul, encouraging you to turn from God. Desolation helps you choose thoughts, words, and deeds that are opposed to your divinely shaped human nature.

Desolation can also be the consequence of your own fallen human nature. God created your human nature as a gift in the divine image and likeness. Yet because of Original Sin's impact, not cooperating with God's grace erodes the embedded life forces of your divinely shaped human nature, helping to destroy biochemical, physiological, and emotional balance; de-energizing you; and increasing thoughts, words, and deeds that are in opposition to your authentic human nature.

೫

It is time for the Lord to act;
they have disobeyed your law.
Truly I love your commandments
more than gold, more than the finest gold.
Thus, I follow all your precepts;
every wrong way I hate.
(Ps 119:126–128)

೫

Dr. Schuchts' Reflection ~ Week Thirty-One

Consolation and Desolation

Let's change things up a bit for this thirty-first week. This reflection will be brief. I hope it will make a lasting impact on the way you understand consolation and desolation in your life.

This was the Affirmation for Week Thirty-One, which you were invited to say aloud each day:

"Christ, who walked before me, *shares my every burden.*"

"Christ, who has walked before me, *will help me to resolve every crisis.*"

"Christ, who has walked before me, *knows my every hope.*"

At a heart level, do you believe these Affirmations? Do you believe that Jesus shares every burden in your life? If so, how does that affect the way you receive consolations? Stop and ask yourself how.

Do you believe that with every crisis situation in your life, you can trust Jesus to help you resolve it? How might that change your desolations if you lived in this trust? Stop and ask yourself how.

Do you believe that Jesus knows your every hope? How does this influence you when you are in desolation? Stop and ask yourself how. Remember that not every divine inspiration (consolation) feels good. And also remember that not every counter-inspiration (desolation) feels bad.

Applying the three benchmarks of consolation and desolation, how would you answer these different scenarios:

--When Jesus hung on the Cross, was he in consolation or desolation?

--At the foot of the Cross, was Mary experiencing consolation or desolation?

--When Peter denied Jesus was he experiencing consolation or desolation?

--St. Teresa of Calcutta experienced the long darkness- was this consolation or desolation?

--When St. Teresa of Avila was in ecstasy, was this an example of consolation or desolation?

-- St. John of the Cross experienced and wrote about the Dark Night of the Soul. Is that an example of spiritual consolation or spiritual desolation?

--When St. Ignatius wanted to die because he couldn't conquer his sins-- was that consolation or desolation?

--At the end of his life, when St. Ignatius wanted to die to be with Jesus, would you consider this consolation or desolation?

--When you are going through a crisis, what determines whether it is consolation or desolation?

--How can you tell when you are in spiritual consolation vs. spiritual desolation?

These are comments from your brother priests for the thirty-first week:

✠ *It was eye opening to see the descriptions of the two benchmarks and reflect upon my own concrete experiences of each.*

✠ *The fruits of consolations and desolations are helpful. Ultimately, I have to remember to ask if this is helping me and/or others grow closer to God. Am I really on the right track (not based on feelings alone?*

✠ *Consolation doesn't always feel good and desolation doesn't always feel bad.*

✠ *To discern consolation and desolation can be confusing if you rely on* the feeling you have, because the Divine inspiration of consolation can make you feel bad while the counter inspiration of desolation can make you feel good. What is best is to focus on God's will, which brings you back to your authentic human nature.

Immaculate Heart of Mary pray for us so that our hearts may be fully aligned with the Sacred Heart of your son Jesus.

৪৩

NOTES

Week 32

FIRST

I resolve to spend no more than fifteen minutes in each formal prayer session and to do so in some place apart – a technology free zone. I will always use my personal name for God.

SECOND

For the sake of God's greater glory, I continue a lifelong process of praying with meditations one through five in Sacred Story prayer. I enter my prayer at least once daily, as St. Ignatius suggested. This prayer will carry me for life. It will deepen my faith and my wisdom and awaken me to God's truth and love.

THIRD

By God's grace, I continue opening my heart to learn spiritual discernment. This week, I explore definitions of spiritual consolation and spiritual desolation as divine inspiration and counter-inspiration.

I will awaken to the present moment.
I will awaken to my spiritual nature.
I will not make any decisions based on fear.
I will practice sacramental Reconciliation monthly.
I will ask Jesus for help when I am troubled.
I will thank Jesus daily for life's gifts.

This week, I will say this affirmation aloud once daily:
Christ, who has walked before me, knows everything I suffer.
Christ, who walks before me, will always lead me home to safety.

∞

Continuing in the School of Discernment:
Guidelines for Foundational Healing and Spiritual Growth

Take some time this week to read and reflect on this fifth lesson in discernment. We will examine the divine inspiration of spiritual consolation and the counter-inspiration of spiritual desolation. Start paying attention to your affective moods to feel the states of consolation and desolation in your story. This process requires a graced awakening, so ask God for the "eyes to see" your story through the lens of these spiritual lessons. Be patient as you slowly learn this way of understanding your story.

The practice of Sacred Story prayer makes one aware of the spiritual forces at work in one's life and in the world. Ignatius became a master at discerning these spiritual movements. He left guidelines for understanding how they work. You have learned already that there are three distinct sources influencing your thoughts, words, and deeds:

1. Your own emotional, psychological, and intellectual makeup, shaped by concupiscence and your unique history.

2. The divine inspiration of consolation, working to draw your thoughts, words, and deeds in the direction of your authentic human nature.

3. The counter-inspirations of the enemy of your true human nature, seeking to pull you away from your authentic self.

God (Divine Inspirer) and the enemy of human nature (counter-inspirer)

364

each seek ultimate influence over how your history unfolds: God for eternal love and life, the enemy of human nature for eternal despair and death; God for eternal relationships, the enemy of human nature for eternal loneliness.

Is Prayer Helping or Hurting?

Some might say, "Until I started this prayer, I never felt bad, but now I do. I wonder if it is hurting instead of helping." If you find yourself asking the same question, you probably were feeling bad before you started the prayer discipline. You just were not aware of the pain or of your true feelings. There are many ways for us to "self-medicate" our pain, whether that pain is spiritual, emotional, or physical. The process of spiritual awakening brings to the light preexisting spiritual conditions that previously, we were simply not conscious of. Now that you are becoming more aware and actually feeling what is happening, you can ask for God's help, and God can help you. Sometimes the presence of discomfort and pain is the first step to healing. Welcome it, and invite Christ Jesus to heal your life and heart!

Both God and the enemy of human nature are aware of your strengths, weaknesses, wounded memories, hopes, dreams, and fears. God desires to stir your conscience towards freedom and light and bring you healing and hope.

God will build on your strengths, inflaming your holy desires and healing what is hurt and broken. The enemy of human nature seeks to silence your conscience and hide it in shadows. He will work to magnify your problems, diminish your holy desires, and inspire hopelessness.

We identify and distinguish divine inspirations from counter-inspirations by their intellectual and affective traits, or signature characteristics. Ignatius defines two distinct types of inspiration. The first type, caused by divine inspiration of the Spirit, he calls consolation. The second type, caused by the counter-inspiration of the enemy of your human nature, he calls desolation.

Divine Inspiration: Consolation defines the feelings and thoughts of a healing heart returning to God and/or residing in God. God always inspires movement towards reconciliation and union. The signature characteristics of divine inspiration include being passionate for God and loving all things in God, and tears of remorse and sadness when you fail—yet feeling loved by God despite your failures.

Spiritual Pleasure and Success

Illicit pleasures of our higher spiritual nature often reside in our attitudes like one's personal definition of success. I can be comforted by my own self-righteousness and contemptuous of others.

"The Pharisee took up his position and spoke this prayer to himself, 'O God, I thank you that I am not like the rest of humanity—greedy, dishonest, adulterous—or even like this tax collector. I fast twice a week, and I pay tithes on my whole income'" (Lk 18:11–12).

The Pharisee, while fulfilling the rule of law, was trapped in a false identity. Spiritual attitudes (world views and our definitions of success) need discernment to determine whether or not they are of God. Just because they are legal, does not mean they are of God!

You may experience tears of love for Christ who suffered the consequences of all sin, including your own. It is every increase in love, hope, and faith that magnetizes your heart towards holy things, and all experiences of peace and quiet in the presence of your Creator. The divine inspiration of consolation is manifest in humility that views eternal life, lasting love, and faith in God as the hope of the single-hearted and the ultimate goal of those willing to risk seeing reality as it truly is.

Counter-inspiration: Desolation defines feelings and thoughts that are the direct opposite of consolation's divine inspiration. The signature characteristics of counter-inspiration are darkness and confusion of a broken and wounded heart, soul, and spirit; magnetic and compulsive attractions to sensual and base appetites; restlessness, anger, cynicism, and temptations that make all things geared toward faith, hope, and love appear dull, absurd, and even destructive to your heart. You will feel a lazy, lukewarm, and sad spirit as if separated from God. The counter-inspiration of desolation is everything that magnetizes a broken heart toward cynicism, lusts, isolation, anger, despair, and aloneness. The counter-inspiration of desolation is manifest in an unyielding pride that views eternal life, lasting love, and faith in God as illusions of the simple-minded and the result of those unwilling to risk seeing reality as truly it is.

Consolations can make you feel bad when they move you toward your authentic human nature. The bad feelings caused by movement toward authenticity are something that applies equally to both your lower physical nature and higher spiritual nature. If you are accustomed to physical pleasures or lifestyles and relationships that fall outside the boundaries of the Commandments and/or Church teaching, the inspiration to cut loose from those pleasures can make you feel distress and anxiety. Remember that Ignatius panicked and felt distress when he realized that he would have to live without the pleasures of his first thirty years for the rest of his life.

The distress you feel when moving toward authenticity in your physical nature is also true when you are moving toward authenticity in your spiritual nature. If you are accustomed to spiritual pleasures that fall outside the boundaries of the Commandments or Church teaching, such as a false definition of success that has shaped your life, you may similarly feel distress, panic, or anxiety when contemplating a change. This is because you are uncertain of what lies beyond the false definition of success. It may feel like a frightening void.

Thus the movement toward authenticity can create fear and distress for both your physical and spiritual natures. The fear aroused by the invitation to live authentically needs to be strongly confronted, because you are being invited towards life, not death. You must learn to resist the fear when moving toward authenticity as defined by the Commandments and Church teaching.

Counter-inspirations called desolations can make you feel good even if they move you away from your authentic human nature. The good feelings caused by movement away from authenticity apply equally to both your lower physical nature and higher spiritual nature. If you are accustomed to physical pleasures that fall outside the boundaries of the Commandments and/or Church teaching, the inspiration to stay committed to those pleasures can make you feel relief—feel good.

The relief you feel when moving away from authenticity in your physical nature is also true when you are moving away from authenticity in your spiritual nature. If you are accustomed to spiritual pleasures that fall outside the boundaries of the Commandments and/or Church teaching, like a false definition of success that has shaped your life, you may similarly feel relief—feel good—in remaining committed to that false identity.

The inspiration to "stay just where you are" will most likely be supported by many logical justifications for why it is best not to change course. By staying put, you have consciously or unconsciously been manipulated by your fears. The fears aroused by the invitation to live authentically need to be strongly confronted, because you are being invited toward death, not life. You must learn to resist the fear when moving toward authenticity as defined by the Commandments and Church teaching.

This is an important discernment lesson. It is critical to understand that inspirations caused by the Divine Inspirer, as well as those caused by the counter-inspirer, can feel good or feel bad, depending on your lifestyle and the corresponding state of your heart and soul.

So always pay attention to discernment principles regarding authentic human nature as defined by the Commandments and Church teaching. It is advisable to keep an eye on the direction the inspirations lead (away from authenticity or towards authenticity) more than whether inspirations make you feel good or bad.

CB

From wanton sin especially, restrain your servant;
let it not rule over me.
Then shall I be blameless and innocent of serious sin.
The precepts of the Lord give joy to the heart.
(Ps 19:14)

EO

Dr. Schuchts' Reflection ~ Week Thirty-Two

Guidelines for Fundamental Healing and Spiritual Growth

Week Thirty-Two focuses our attention on *Inspiration* and *Counter-Inspiration* and the role they play in our healing and spiritual growth.

Inspiration allows us to follow the voice of the Good Shepherd, so that we may learn to abide in Him, and become increasingly more docile to the movements of His Spirit.

In contrast, *Counter-inspiration* leads us into further brokenness and desolation, moving out of abiding and into ungodly self-reliance, effectively separating us from authentic love.

The Affirmations for Week Thirty-Two are guideposts reminding us of Christ's compassionate presence with us in our struggles:

"Christ, who walked before me, *knows everything I suffer.*"

"Christ, who walked before me, *will always lead me home safely.*"

These Affirmations, grounded in the truth of the gospel message, anchor us in Christ, strengthening our trust and hope. They remind us that we are not alone and therefore we do not need to be afraid in the midst of our trials and difficulties.

This awareness of Christ's presence with us is critical because it allows us to abide in Him when we might otherwise run from difficult circumstances as well as our painful thoughts and emotions.

Without an awareness of His abiding Presence, we tend to anxiously avoid the suffering that is endemic to our lives. In avoiding this suffering, we move away from our authentic selves and distance ourselves from the Father. We end up choosing falsehood over truth, death over life, isolation over love.

This is a primary way that the enemy of our human nature deceives us. He leads us to believe that we have to fend for ourselves in the midst of our pain and suffering. In this weakened state of isolation and anxiety we are most prone to give into the seven deadly sins and turn to addictions to numb our pain.

Even then Jesus' hand is always reaching out to help us. As we remember to turn to Him in our suffering, his presence heals our isolation and brings us "home safely" into the embrace of the Trinity, thus calming our pervasive anxiety.

These principles of discernment are eternal truths. But they can remain abstract until we see them in operation in our self-examination and in the lives of those we accompany on the path of healing and spiritual growth.

Recently, I have been in healing conversations with a woman who is being led by the Holy Spirit into these realities. To my knowledge she has never studied the Ignatian discernment of spirits guidelines, but she is a living witness to their validity.

This woman spent many years running from one unhealthy relationship to another, unconsciously looking for a salve to her early abandonment pain with her mother.

When she converted to Christ and joined the Church many years ago, she discovered the joy of purity and wholesome relationships.

After many years of walking with Christ, she is now secure enough to begin facing her deeper core wounds, especially her shame, anxiety, and early childhood abandonment and rejection.

In this healing process, the pain has become intense at times, especially as she touches the earliest abandonment pain. In those times of intense pain, she is tempted, through counter-inspirations attached to her wounds, to run back to the false loves.

But in this time of heightened temptations, the Holy Spirit is especially active, showing her the link between her shame and abandonment, and the lifestyle she chose years ago as she ran from her pain.

Now, when she turns to Christ, she realizes that He is present with her in her deepest pain. Through this process Christ is leading her "home" to find her genuine identity and security in the Father.

Throughout this process two priests have played a vital role in her healing and spiritual growth. But not everyone is able to find priests that have walked this path before them and know how to lead them "home".

This time you are investing in the Forty Weeks is preparing you to be the kind of priest who will be able to lead others in their fundamental healing and spiritual growth. The more intimately you become aware of Christ's presence in your own suffering and learn to abide with him, the more you will be able to be Christ *in persona*, present in their suffering, leading them home."

Engaging in this process is first and foremost for your own spiritual growth and healing, but the fruit of it will be felt in the lives of every person you encounter. It is worth whatever struggle you are going through!

You are not walking this path alone. Christ is walking intimately with you. And your brother priests are walking beside you. The following are some of their reflections from Week 32:

✠ The transition from counter-inspiration to Divine inspiration is a moment of struggle and hesitation which may create a feeling of fear or discomfort.

✠ Consolation leads to peace and light, although looking back will cause remorse for the journey through the space of darkness and the confusion of broken and wounded heart, soul, and spirit. Regular confession will strengthen this peace and focus on the future of light.

✠ I'm still reflecting upon the place of my own will/inspirations in the mix of it all.

✠ Our journey of spiritual growth and healing will cross the zones of turbulence which are the zone of purification. We need not to be afraid, rather we need to keep walking in the footsteps of Jesus Christ who endured the pain and suffering of all humanity before He entered in His glory.

Immaculate Heart of Mary pray for us so that our hearts
may be fully aligned with the Sacred Heart of your son Jesus.

℘

NOTES

Week 33

FIRST

As before, I will visualize the week ahead and imagine where I can find technology-free zones for my fifteen-minute period(s) of formal prayer each day. I will consider changing the number of prayer sessions each day (from one to two or from two to one). I will make a conscious choice to adjust my prayer schedule, if I judge it a wise decision that will deepen my daily commitment to Christ. I will always use my personal name for God.

SECOND

I pray for the grace to make a lifelong commitment to daily pray movements one through five in the Sacred Story prayer. I will enter my prayer at least once daily as St. Ignatius suggested. I recognize that this prayer will carry me for life, deepening my faith and wisdom, and awakening me to God's truth and love in thought, word, and deed.

THIRD

I continue to ask God's grace to understand spiritual discernment in my life. This week I will explore definitions of spiritual consolation and spiritual desolation as embedded attitudes or lifestyles that can shape my sacred story.

I will awaken to the present moment.

I will awaken to my spiritual nature.
I will not make any decisions based on fear.
I will practice sacramental Reconciliation monthly.
I will ask Jesus for help when I am troubled.
I will thank Jesus daily for life's gifts.

This week, I will say this affirmation aloud once daily:
I will strive to curb temptations to react to people and events.
I will ask myself what causes my anger and irritation at people and
events.
I will seek to identify the source of my anger and irritation.

ೞ

Continuing in the School of Discernment:

Guidelines for Foundational Healing and Spiritual Growth

Take some time this week to read and reflect on this sixth lesson in discernment. We examined the divine inspiration of spiritual consolation and the counter-inspiration of spiritual desolation last week. This week, we focus on identifying the ways in which these spiritual states manifest as lifestyles. Continue to pay attention to your affective moods to feel the states of consolation and desolation in your story. Look too for embedded lifestyle attitudes that bear the signature characteristics of consolation and desolation.

Consolation and desolation manifest as lifestyles. We can consciously or unconsciously live a life that is either aligned with life or death. The book of Deuteronomy powerfully captures this reality. God placed before the people Israel two distinct choices:

See, I have today set before you life and good, death and evil.
If you obey the commandments of the LORD, your God, which
I am giving you today, loving the LORD, your God, and walking

in his ways, and keeping his commandments, statutes and ordinances, you will live and grow numerous, and the LORD, your God, will bless you in the land you are entering to possess. If, however, your heart turns away and you do not obey, but are led astray and bow down to other gods and serve them, I tell you today that you will certainly perish; you will not have a long life on the land which you are crossing the Jordan to enter and possess. I call heaven and earth today to witness against you: I have set before you life and death, the blessing and the curse. Choose life, then, that you and your descendants may live, by loving the LORD, your God, obeying his voice, and holding fast to him. For that will mean life for you, a long life for you to live on the land which the LORD swore to your ancestors, to Abraham, Isaac, and Jacob, to give to them. (Dt 30:15–20)

If we have become insensitive to God's presence, we can be moving away from the Author of Life in our sacred story. We may not be aware of this because of a silenced conscience. If you live in a culture or a subculture that is also insensitive to the Author of Life, you can be doubly challenged to find the path back to life. If you are sensitive to the Author of life, then your sacred story is moving in the direction of producing fruit that endures to eternity. This will be true even if you live in a culture that is insensitive to life's Author. A culture oriented away from God can make choosing the good more difficult, but Christ guarantees the fruit produced. He promises:

Blessed are you when they insult you and persecute you and utter every kind of evil against you [falsely] because of me. Rejoice and be glad, for your reward will be great in heaven. Thus they persecuted the prophets who were before you (Mt 5: 11-12).

We can also choose to align ourselves with subcultures that are counter to the life proposed by the Commandments, Scripture, and the teaching Church. It is difficult to be objective about anti-gospel lifestyles when we are immersed in these subcultures simply because we become habituated to them.

These self-selected subcultures can diminish one's ability to gain objectivity or to discern effectively. These anti-gospel subcultures can be economic, political, artistic, ethnic, intellectual, sexual, athletic, addiction-based, and web-based, just to name a few. The main challenge is that we can cocoon in these cultures, allowing their definitions of happiness, success, the good, the beautiful, and the moral to isolate us from the data coming from deep in our heart or from any other source.

This process of cocooning marks the impenetrable individualism of the present age. For these reasons, consolation and desolation can be described more comprehensively as lifestyles, so one can measure the arc of one's life—one's life style—against the traditional categories Ignatius defined as the signature characteristics of human nature's Author or its enemy.

Thus your individual lifestyle can be discerned as either influenced by the Divine Inspirer or the counter-inspirer. You can identify the trajectory of your story first by reflecting on how you live. If your story and the balance of thoughts, words, and deeds are aligned with the Commandments, Scripture, and the teaching Church, then you are choosing life. If not, then it is time to pray for light.

Divine Inspiration as a Lifestyle

Are you evolving under the divine inspirations aligned to thoughts, words, and deeds harmonious with the Scripture, Commandments, and the teaching Church? If so, the Divine author of your human nature will provide "heart-verification" to alert you to thoughts, words, and deeds that can move you off the true path. The Divine Inspirer will awaken your reason and stir your conscience.

When this happens, you will feel sadness, anxiety, grief, and remorse, the result of thoughts, words, and deeds that lead away from God. God grants these feelings if you are moving toward the counter-inspirations of anti-love, anti-Christ. Such feelings can be difficult and intense. Yet they are a gift and a certain reminder that engaging the gospel values of your faith belief and practice will bring you the peace and hope you seek.

What Are Inordinate Attachments?

If we lack freedom before created things, St. Ignatius says we have an inordinate attachment. I can be inordinately attached to wealth, youth, health, people, material goods, or a definition of success for my life. An inordinate attachment can be almost anything I control (or want to control) that affects my sacred story. The goal is not to get rid of the things that are inordinate attachments. Ignatius tells us that we want to get rid of the attachment to the things. I may have $100 and be inordinately attached to it. Ignatius would advise that I neither keep nor give the money away, but pray for the spiritual freedom to either keep it or let it go. My discernment to keep or surrender is made according to whatever action advances me further along the path of my sacred story. The Foundations Prayer from week 23's E&W (available at sacredstory.net) articulates this principle of spiritual freedom from attachments.

Counter-inspiration as a Lifestyle

Are you evolving under the counter-inspirations opposed to love? Are your thoughts, words, and deeds opposed to the Commandments, Scripture, and the teaching Church? The enemy of your human nature is able to hold you in the grip of your disordered appetites by deceit and false appearances. What leads you away from God, from Love, appears pleasurable and is presented as good, life-giving, fashionable, enlightened, and sophisticated.

Leading away from the sheltering safety of God's love and your authentic human nature, these thoughts, words, and deeds, as excessive appetites, are aptly named false loves, and false loves speak powerfully to broken hearts. If you are in the grip of the counter-inspirations of these false loves, you will feel aversion to engaging the gospel values or be hostile to the Commandments and guidelines of the teaching Church. You will experience difficulty practicing and persevering in your faith.

This is an important discernment lesson. Think of divine inspiration (spiritual consolation) as a healthy lifestyle that may not feel healthy because it is not supported by the culture or subcultures in which you live. Think of counter-inspiration (spiritual desolation) as an unhealthy lifestyle that might not feel unhealthy because it is supported by the culture or subcultures in which you live. So as you learned last week, always keep an eye on the direction the inspirations lead, more than whether inspirations make you feel good or feel bad.

If you want to map some of the influences in your life, make a small chart of the various subcultures where you spend most of your time each week: corporate culture, work environments, internet, social groups and associations, exercise or athletic environments, groups aligned with arts and entertainment, political parties, and the cultures of film, television, and or radio where you spend time. Next to each subculture, write what you believe is its signature characteristic regarding its overall influence on your lifestyle. Does the subculture support divine inspiration or support counter-inspiration? In other words, is the subculture congruent with the values of Scripture, Tradition, and the teaching Church?

Some of these subcultures may be fixed parts of your life due to career, family, or region. Others may be affiliations by personal choice. Do some of the subcultures force you to conceal your religious beliefs? Do you have what St. Ignatius defines as an inordinate attachment to any of these subcultures and the values they espouse?

Does your affiliation with the subculture move you further along in your sacred story or obstruct your movement? Does your affiliation with the subculture increase the ease or difficulty of developing your authentic human nature as guided by the Commandments and Church teaching and traditions?

℺

Set a guard, Lord, before my mouth,
keep watch over the door of my lips.
Do not let my heart incline to evil,
to perform deeds in wickedness.
On the delicacies of evildoers
let me not feast.
Let a righteous person strike me;
it is mercy if he reproves me.
Do not withhold oil from my head
while my prayer opposes their evil deeds.
(Ps 141:3–5)

℻

Dr. Schuchts' Reflection ~ Week Thirty-Three

Exploring the roots of Anger and Irritation

Each week we are growing in our capacity to distinguish the voice of God from the voice of the enemy, and how both kinds of inspiration interact with our human nature.

This Thirty-Third week we are invited to acknowledge our inordinate attachments, and the influential nature of our chosen subcultures.

The Affirmation for Week Thirty-Three challenges us to examine the underlying roots of our anger and irritation.

Let's spend some time reflecting on the Affirmation for this week and then see how it applies to our inordinate attachments and relational influences from our subcultures:

"I will strive to curb temptations to react to people and events. I *will ask myself what causes my anger and irritation at people and events.* I will *seek to identify the source* of my anger and irritation."

This affirmation highlights several realities:

1) People and events do not "cause" our anger. Have you ever noticed that people get angry at different things?

2) What "causes" my anger and irritation often lies within me. My anger is influenced by my wounds, my attachments, and by my subculture(s). My reactions reveal my expectations and what I believe and value.

3) Anger is a healthy human emotion when we experience any kind of injustice against us or against others. St. Thomas Aquinas says that anger is the passion that is aroused when there is a violation against love and goodness. This is healthy anger.

4) But not all anger is this clean. Many times, our anger and irritation come from passive or aggressive narcissism and may reveal unrepented sins, un-healed wounds or people we have not forgiven.

In discerning the roots of your anger, you may investigate the source of the inspiration: "Is my anger the response of the Holy Spirit?" "Is it coming from my human nature, or is it from the evil one?"

Remember, "God is *slow to anger* and abounding in steadfast love" (Ex. 34:6). Yet, throughout Scripture we also see many examples of the Father and Jesus expressing anger, when there is idolatry and injustice.

Perhaps this justified anger is what St. Augustine meant when he said: "Hope has two beautiful daughters; their names are Anger and Courage. Anger at the way things are, and Courage to see that they do not remain as they are."

St. Paul commands us to "Be angry but do not sin" (Eph. 4:26). He seems to be saying it is normal and healthy for us to be angry at times. But we need to be attentive to how we respond when we are angry.

We can allow the enemy of our human nature to get a "foothold" in our lives when we allow bitterness, brawling, or resentment to take hold of our hearts. Not expressing our emotions truthfully and forgiving the injustices we encounter makes the enemy's foothold even stronger.

Anger can also be an inordinate attachment to power and control and to wanting to exact our own justice in a situation that colors how we perceive God ourselves and the world.

Whole subcultures are formed around these ungodly perceptions. Racism and terrorism are two examples and what would you guess are the inordinate attachments and wounds underlying these?

Two others are militant chauvinism and feminism (displaying a hatred of true masculinity and true femininity).

Awaken to how certain subcultures can form "community" around deadly sins and deadly wounds that have become infected by the inspirations of the evil one. We don't need to look beyond ourselves to see the reality of these evils. Where are these strongholds of beliefs and inordinate attachments rooted in your own life?

As a priest of Jesus Christ, part of your community mission is to uproot these ungodly beliefs and inordinate attachments which form unholy subcultures. But the work must begin first in your own mind and heart before you can liberate your communities.

It is good to walk on this journey with your brother priests--you can help each other remove the planks that block true vision.

Here is what your brother priests had to say this week about how this discernment process is influencing their priestly ministry Week 33:

✠ Lifestyle is a practical way to discern whether you are under Divine-Inspiration or under Counter -inspiration. Healthy lifestyle based on God's commandments, scriptures and the teaching church is inspired by the Holy One even if this lifestyle is not supported by the culture or sub-culture in which you live. As long as this inspiration leads me toward communion with the Lord, I will not be concerned about pain and suffering I can experience.

✠ My life-circumstances forced me to deal with some very serious counter-inspirations. Sacred Story prayer provided a context in which to allow the Lord to "chisel" away to a deeper root of a negative trait I have long struggled with.

✠ I am grateful and will thank God for those times of experiencing anger and fear to go deeper to the core of the wounds so God can be invited into the place where He needs to be the most. This was helpful in discerning the role of anger in my ministry, especially as it is directed toward 2 particular individuals in the parish. Praying for God's revealed knowledge.

Immaculate Heart of Mary pray for us so that our hearts may be fully aligned with the Sacred Heart of your son Jesus.

છૃ

NOTES

Week 34

FIRST

I will visualize my week ahead to identify places I can find technology-free zones for my fifteen-minutes prayer times each day. I am also learning that my resolution to spend no more and no less than fifteen minutes in those prayer periods increases my fidelity to the practice. I will always use my personal name for God.

SECOND

I will continue this thirty-fourth week by praying the five meditations of Sacred Story prayer. As St. Ignatius suggested, I enter my prayer at least once daily. Each time I pray, my heart opens more fully, and I am carried forward in my sacred story.

THIRD

I will ask God to help me understand the school of spiritual discernment. This week I will ponder St. Ignatius's wisdom on how I ought to act when influenced by the desolation of counter-inspiration.

I will awaken to the present moment.
I will awaken to my spiritual nature.
I will not make any decisions based on fear.
I will practice sacramental Reconciliation monthly.

I will ask Jesus for help when I am troubled.

I will thank Jesus daily for life's gifts.

This week, I will say this affirmation aloud once daily:

I will give thanks for what angers and upsets me;

identifying their source will set me free.

I will strive to listen, watch, and pray. Listen, watch, and pray.

I will listen, watch, and pray!

ॐ

Continuing in the School of Discernment:

Guidelines for Foundational Healing and Spiritual Growth

Take some time this week to read and reflect on this seventh lesson in discernment. Last week we examined the divine inspiration of spiritual consolation and the counter-inspiration of spiritual desolation as embedded in our lifestyles. This week we will consider St. Ignatius's wisdom on how we can help defuse the impact of counter-inspiration's desolation when in its grip.

Four Principles for Defusing Counter-inspirations

Personal sin, addictions, and emotional/psychological wounds make a person vulnerable to spiritual desolation. When gripped by spiritual desolation, your faith, hope, and love is diminished. Ignatius offers indispensable guidance when you are under the influence of counter-inspirations and are spiritually desolate, discouraged, hopeless, and frustrated. If you closely adhere to these guidelines and act on them, you will avoid much pain and grief in your life. Do not despair if you do not understand the guidelines now. There will come a time when this wisdom will help you.

Ignatius offers four principles for how we ought to act when tempted by the counter-inspirations of desolation.

1.Never change course when in desolation!

When spiritually desolate and experiencing a loss of faith, hope, and love, never change course away from the positive resolutions and decisions you reached while under the influence of the divine inspiration of consolation.

Human nature's enemy feeds on spiritual/emotional wounds and on broken hearts. The counter-inspirations may seem logical, but they never lead to freedom, peace, or your heart's healing. None of the choices and decisions influenced by the counter-inspirations of desolation, no matter how utterly logical they might appear, will ever increase faith, hope, or love. One must be vigilant when tempted by an urgent or compelling need to act immediately. When you feel compelled by an anxious urgency to reach a decision or engage an action, this is a clear sign of counter-inspirations at work

2. During times of desolation, redouble efforts to open and orient your heart to God.

Use prayer, examination of conscience, and perhaps some simple penance or fasting to seek God's grace (Mk 9:29).

Counter-inspirations make it difficult to see and feel authentic human nature. Amplifying positive efforts on spiritual fronts might feel incredibly difficult. Yet St. Ignatius's experience demonstrated that we need, at these times, extra exercise of spirit and body to resist desolation. A determined spirit is necessary during such times. Also, be attentive to thoughts, words, or deeds that are based on inaccurate assessments of your authentic human nature. Allow the times of desolation to instruct you!

3. Actively trust God to provide the essential support and grace necessary to withstand these times of trial and purification.

The support you need will come from your natural abilities, assisted by divine grace. You may feel completely overwhelmed by temptations or the darkness of spirit associated with disordered attractions and compulsive behaviors. Yet there is sufficient grace for salvation, even if the logic of the counter-inspiration indicates otherwise! Jesus, the Divine Physician, is very close to you during these times of purification. When you encounter the full force and darkness of counter-inspirations, be assured that God is present to you even though you may not feel God's presence.

Watch for Obsessive Thinking

You are always either in a state of consolation or desolation. These lessons are teaching you to notice these two spiritual states that have been with you all your life. If you find yourself becoming obsessive about tracking what state you are in at each moment of the day, then you have succumbed to counter-inspirations. Strive for an alert heart and mind. Pray to avoid an obsessive attitude. Being aware will serve your spiritual growth. Being obsessive will harm your spiritual growth.

Do not be deceived by the feelings, no matter how strong or mocking they might appear. This is especially true when your weaknesses, shame, and failings are painfully highlighted. Through trial and error, St. Ignatius learned that God is not absent. Trust Ignatius's wise counsel, and affirm your faith in God during times when you do not feel the Spirit. Instead, consciously thank God, who in complete faithfulness, will embrace you. Thank God aloud and affirm God's salvific role in your sacred story.

4.Intentionally strive to cultivate patience, and persevere in the religious practices of your faith when influenced by the desolation of counter-inspiration.

The divine inspiration of consolation always returns. In the interim, use the means of prayer, penance, and self-examination to resist and gain the most from these times of trial. To counter the anxiety you may experience, embrace desolations as an opportunity to deepen your maturing life with God. Be not afraid.

When to Make Decisions

Counter-inspirations are usually accompanied by anxiety, electrical excitement, and a compelling urge to act quickly and definitively. Never make decisions when you sense these emotional states.

Divine inspirations are usually accompanied by a deep and abiding peace and calm with no urge to act quickly or definitively. Only make decisions during times of divine inspiration's peace and calm.

Learning the difference between these two spiritual states of heart/mind will serve you very well. It is hard to resist the compulsive urge to act quickly when in the grip of counter-inspiration's anxieties. Resist! You will save yourself a great deal of pain the enemy of human nature desires to inflict upon you.

Considerable spiritual and human progress, as well as illumination, will result from your patience and perseverance during these trials. In time, you will discover that these times of stress, endured in faith, can produce the enlightenment, healing, peace, and hope you seek. Therefore, do not fear them.

Say aloud the one thing that makes you question God's love for you. Now hear the Lord say: "Nothing in the past or the future; no angel or demon; no height or depth; nothing in all of creation will ever separate you from my love in Christ Jesus" (Rom 8:38–39).

CB

Let your work be seen by your servants
and your glory by their children;
and may the gracious care of the Lord our God be ours;
prosper the work of our hands for us!
Prosper the work of our hands!
(Ps 90:16–17)

BO

Dr. Schuchts' Reflection ~ Week Thirty-Four

Defusing Counter Inspirations

During this Thirty-Fourth Week we are continuing to examine the guidelines for fundamental healing and spiritual growth, with a specific focus on *defusing counter inspirations*.

As Fr. Watson highlighted, adhering to these guidelines can help us avoid adding to our pain and grief and transmitting this hurt to those people closest to us. In addition, mastering these guidelines is a sure path to growing in the virtues of faith, hope and love.

The Affirmation for this Thirty-Fourth Week seems paradoxical. How many of us ordinarily stop to give thanks to God for what angers and upsets us? For most of us, becoming irritated is usually not on the top of our gratitude list.

But in light of last week's focus in which we attended to those times and situations where our anger and irritation were easily triggered, it makes a lot of sense to give thanks for the awareness of what angers and upsets us.

As we have seen throughout Forty Weeks, reactive anger and irritation are often symptoms of a deeper spiritual disease. They are also indicators that we have fallen into spiritual desolation and turned our attention away from God's presence and mercy.

We all know by experience that this turning away from God and into desolation can happen in milliseconds when some person or event touches our wounds or arouses personal sins and addictions.

If we choose to take the time to "listen, watch and pray" at these times of reactivity, the Holy Spirit will bring us into a greater awareness of those areas in our life that need healing.

This is a very practical way of shoring up our spiritual armor, including the shield of faith, breastplate of righteousness, helmet of salvation, sandals of peace, and the belt of truth, by wielding the Sword of the Spirit (see Eph. 6: 14-17).

An example from my personal life may illuminate how this process of identifying our reactions to anger and irritation can expose underlying wounds and hidden sins. The goal is of course to lead us into greater freedom.

From the very beginning of my relationship with my wife Margie, I noticed that I would become angry and irritated every time she drank alcohol. It was an immediate and irrational trigger for me and could catapult me into spiritual desolation for days.

Early on, I tried to control her behavior by forcefully convincing her how much her drinking hurt me. At the time, I had no understanding that my reaction was revealing unseen wounds and sins in my own heart.

I had not yet studied Ignatius' Guidelines for Spiritual Discernment, but the Holy Spirit led me in the process of fundamental healing and spiritual growth nonetheless.

Gradually, the Holy Spirit illuminated my sin and wounds behind my reactions. First, I began to see symptoms of pride, in my posture of self-righteousness and judgements.

Then I became aware of the deadly sin of anger, in my judgements, control, and resentful withdrawals. I discovered these were rooted in my relationships with my father and my older brother, who both had addictions to alcohol.

Finally, as I continued to listen, watch and pray, I became able to recognize my childhood wounds of fear, rejection and abandonment, and the vows I took to protect myself from these hurts. All of this awareness unfolded over months and years.

As this pattern persisted, I felt powerless, hopeless and confused, and ashamed of my emotional withdrawals. I truly wanted to love my wife as Christ loves the Church, but these wounds and sins kept me from fulfilling his command and my deeper desires. Ungodly anger simply prevents one from loving.

But once I became aware of these areas of my life, I was able to short-circuit my reactions and avoid many of the spiritual desolations I experienced. I was quicker to repent of my sins. I learned to turn towards Christ to heal my wounds. All of this led to greater freedom as the Holy Spirit had more room to operate in my heart.

Had I discovered these guidelines for fundamental and spiritual growth earlier, I might have grown more steadily in virtue, and avoided much pain and grief for me, my wife, and our children.

I am now able to look at this entire process with gratitude, realizing that my anger and irritation led me down a path of healing and spiritual growth in Christ.

In light of this example, I encourage you to examine how your sins and wounds cause rifts in the way you love your (Christ's) bride. What are the things that trigger your anger and frustration? What pulls you away from abiding in Christ?

Thank God for your growing awareness. These insights from your brother priests may further help you diffuse the counter inspirations from the enemy:

✠ *I am grateful and will thank God for those times of welcoming the experience of anger and fear to go deeper to the core of the wounds, so God can be invited in to the place where He needs to be the most.*

✠ *St Ignatius advises me not to allow the counter inspiration to make me change the decision I have made by the time of Divine inspiration. Instead, disregarding the feelings that compel me to do so, he recommends me to* cultivate patience and persevere in my practice of the faith.

✠ Do not stop praying and do not judge your prayer life merely based on how you feel. Consolation and desolation both come and go but the Lord is always there. Be faithful to Him and His Will for you.

✠ I continue to reflect on God's presence at all times. It is so easy to get off track. Yet, God is still present to us when we are weak.

*Immaculate Heart of Mary pray for us so that our hearts
may be fully aligned with the Sacred Heart of your son Jesus.*

℘

NOTES

Week 35

FIRST

I resolve to spend no more and no less than fifteen minutes in each formal prayer period. At the beginning of the week, I will visualize where each will be, in some place apart: a technology-free zone. I will always use my personal name for God.

SECOND

For this thirty-fifth week, I resolve, by God's grace, to commit for life to praying meditations one through five in the Sacred Story prayer. As St. Ignatius suggested, I will enter my prayer at least once daily. Also, I may find it necessary to recommit to the simple, daily journal exercises explained in week 16.

THIRD

I ask God's grace to deepen my knowledge of spiritual discernment as this week I consider the three sources of desolation identified by St. Ignatius.

I will awaken to the present moment.
I will awaken to my spiritual nature.
I will not make any decisions based on fear.
I will practice sacramental Reconciliation monthly.
I will ask Jesus for help when I am troubled.

I will thank Jesus daily for life's gifts.

This week, I will say this affirmation aloud once daily:
Everyone has been mortally wounded spiritually, psychologically, and
physically by Original Sin and the loss of paradise.
Journeying with Christ to the roots
of my sins and addictions
will help break their grip.

ଓଃ

Continuing in the School of Discernment

Before proceeding, it is important to revisit the indispensable practice of
the daily, weekly, and monthly journal exercises.

A Review of the Journal Exercises

Early in the Sacred Story prayer journey, you wrote two things that
surfaced in your life each day: something that brought encouragement,
and something that upset you or generated fear, anger, or grief. By briefly
focusing every day on these two categories, you will be recording the
necessary data that will help you to understand Ignatius's spiritual
discernment rules in your own story and life history.

Every day, write one experience that increases faith, hope, and love.
Write a second experience that decreases your faith, hope, and love.
Make sure you write a complete sentence. For example, "The Sunday
homily about forgiveness helped me understand God's mercy and
brought me hope." or "The Sunday homily about forgiveness upset me
and made me wonder if God can ever forgive some of the things I have
done." The first experience increases faith, hope, and love; the second
diminishes faith, hope, and love.

These short statements are different than a diary or a regular journal. The statements help to track trends in your spiritual life. Done faithfully, you will begin to identify the signature of God's grace in your particular joys and encouragements, and the signature of the enemy of human nature's presence in your particular temptations and discouragements. For this week, every day, write two experiences you noticed from each source (instead of the usual one experience from each source). This exercise ought to be no more than one minute in length, as explained in the lesson from week 16.

At the end of each week, identify the most significant consolations and desolations. Write two short sentences at week's end that capture what you observe to be the most significant statement on each side of the spiritual divide: spiritual consolation and spiritual desolation.

At month's end, create a monthly summary from your eight weekly consolations and desolations. Sort through those statements (four consolations and four desolations), and identify the two that you consider have most increased and most decreased your faith, hope, and love. These monthly summary statements, for both consolation and desolation, might be a new statement that is a composite of the four you wrote. Or it may be one of the four you wrote that stands out as the most important in each category (consolation or desolation).

An analogy from the medical world might help. Imagine I am diabetic. Daily (or perhaps hourly) I have to monitor my blood sugar. I will become quite attentive to foods and drink that increase or decrease my blood sugar.

In like fashion, this simple writing exercise, done faithfully—daily, weekly, and monthly—will provide spiritual illumination on what increases and decreases your faith, hope, and love. Graced insights will reveal how God and the enemy of your human nature work in your life history. Grace will attract you toward peace and hope, while the enemy's influence will manifest in discouragement and despair.

Guidelines for Foundational Healing and Spiritual Growth

Take some time this week to read and reflect on this eighth lesson in discernment. Last week we examined four important ways to respond during a time of counter-inspiration's spiritual desolation. This week we consider three reasons Ignatius gives for why we experience spiritual desolation.

Three Reasons for Spiritual Desolation

Personal sin, addictions, and your emotional/psychological wounds make you vulnerable to spiritual desolation. When gripped by spiritual desolation, faith, hope, and love diminish. Ignatius offers indispensable guidance to assist you through the temptations of these counter-inspirations.

Recall that when you are spiritually desolate, you will experience discouragement, hopelessness, and frustration. By paying close attention to these guidelines and applying them daily, you will avoid much pain and grief in your life. Do not despair or get frustrated if you do not understand the guidelines now. There will come a time when this wisdom will be crystal clear.

God allows us to experience desolation to orient our hearts toward genuine love and our true human nature. We experience counter-inspiration's desolation for one of three reasons:

1. Wrong Choices

Desolation can be directly related to wrong choices in thoughts, words, and deeds made under the influence of the false logic of the counter-inspirations.

God removes the divine inspiration of consolation as a holy warning that you are straying from your authentic human nature. God acts this way to stir your conscience to remind you to return to authenticity. God allows the loss of consolation so you can feel the consequences of your thoughts, words, and deeds associated with counter-inspirational choices. Such false choices will, in due course, destroy relationships, creation, human life, faith, hope, and love.

Essentially, your false choices erode and destroy the very things that God provides, so you can find fulfillment, communion, and peace in this life and eternal joy in the next. Our own choices and the consequences of those choices lead us to experience the reality of counter-inspiration's desolation.

2.Healing

God can allow desolation, which is directly linked with your human growth and spiritual progress, in order to awaken your whole being—spirit, mind and body—to its spiritual, emotional, and psychological wounds.

Desolation reveals the ways in which your destructive desires and habits have taken root in your spirit, mind, and body. Desolation is evidence of how your wounds contribute to the division of your being. Spiritual progress and forward movement in your life story is only possible when you awaken and confront this damaging pattern.

We need to be courageous. Identifying and uprooting these appetites and habits can be likened to spiritual surgery. This awakening, and the spiritual renewal and healing it initiates, can at times be painful and intense, resulting in our feeling hopeless and/or abandoned. But recall that spiritual maturity cannot be evaluated by unpleasant feelings. Take courage and walk forward, trusting in God.

It is essential that you allow these deeply rooted destructive tendencies to surface, so that a new consciousness and freedom can be born. Giving God permission to move forward with your spiritual growth is the only way these habits, grounded in counter-inspirations, can be uprooted, defused, and healed.

Ignatius taught that God supports us most especially during these times when we can feel lost. At times, we might feel condemned by the darkness in our being: heart, mind, and body. These can be present events or ones we experience through memories. St. Ignatius advised, based on his own experiences of these intense moments, that God's grace is enough to support us.

You can have feelings of desolation associated with the awareness of your disordered appetites and a human nature wounded by sin. The feelings do not indicate how God views and feels about you. Since these feelings offer a false reading of your authentic human nature, do not be fooled into believing that God does not love and cherish you because you feel and experience these periods of darkness.

You are completely distinct from the darkness or the disordered, shameful appetites that you experience. God loves you and supports your most authentic self as you suffer the stripping away of the pain, sin, narcissism, and wounds that hide your authentic human nature.

Feelings of darkness are associated with your false self: the false loves; the broken heart and dreams; the narcissism and pride; the extravagant appetites and the destructive drives associated with your spiritual and psychological wounds. With your cooperation, God is gradually uprooting these from your heart.[25]

3. Growth

Counter-inspirations of desolation may appear during times of spiritual advancement.

After a period of purification marked by desolation, your heart finds peace in the divine inspiration of consolation. During these graced rests, you may be tempted to believe the illusion that you have arrived and/or reached the end of your spiritual journey. You experience this state of calm and peace as definitive and feel that you have achieved sanctity, completion, and holiness.

During these times, and almost imperceptibly, a spirit of pride and self-sufficiency takes hold in your heart. When this happens (when, not if!) the counter-inspirations of desolation return as a warning. This happened to St. Ignatius once. He felt that he was among the just and that his spiritual growth was complete, but then, having experienced desolation, he realized that he was actually only beginning on the road to salvation.

Everything achieved up to this point has occurred through God's grace and through your cooperation with that grace. Grace has reunited you with God, and as a result the virtues of humility, trust, and dependence are beginning to develop.

God allows desolations as a warning to remind you that although you have grown in authenticity and holiness, you are still susceptible to the narcissism and destructive pride that will halt all your progress toward further union with God. Be watchful for the first signs of narcissism and pride. They usually manifest when you start to fall away from your spiritual disciplines and other practices of your faith. You might say to yourself, "I am healed." or "I don't need those practices anymore." or "At least I don't heed them as much as I used to!" You are deceiving yourself and being deceived, to believe such things.

Therefore, cultivate humility during the consoling times of the divine inspiration. Use your periods of consolation as a preparation for the times of desolation. Be aware and awake, always anticipating the return of desolation.

Plan ahead for when desolation makes its return. During your time of consolation, remember how helpless you felt during your time of desolation. This serves as a reminder that God is the only one who stabilizes your heart with the divine inspiration of consolation.

When the counter-inspiration of desolation returns, pray to understand which of Ignatius's three reasons might be its origin. When under the influence of desolation, hold steady! Nurture humility and patience, doing everything possible to orient your thoughts, words, and deeds toward an awareness of God's presence in your life. Recall Creation, Presence, Memory, Mercy, and Eternity.

Remember that God holds you fast during the divine inspirations of consolation and holds you even closer during the cleansing times of desolation. Affirm your faith in God. Hold fast to the spiritual disciplines offered here as well as the other practices of your faith. Seek stability and fidelity in times of peace and calm as well as in times of turbulence and struggle.

ଔ

Behold, the eye of the Lord is upon those who fear him,
upon those who count on his mercy,
To deliver their soul from death,
and to keep them alive through famine.
Our soul waits for the Lord, who is our help and our shield.
May your kindness, O Lord, be upon us
who have put our hope in you.
(Ps 33:18–22)

ଋ

Dr. Schuchts' Reflection ~ Week Thirty-Five

Root Issues in Spiritual Desolation

During this Thirty-Fifth Week, we are focusing on the three reasons for Spiritual Desolation: Personal Sins, Wounds, and Purifications.

The Affirmation for this week highlights the fact that we are all spiritually, psychologically, and physically wounded by Original Sin. That means each one of us is vulnerable to all three sources of spiritual desolation.

Our fundamental spiritual growth is intricately connected to the healing of these wounds, sins, and addictions.

Growth in faith, hope and love can only be accomplished as we overcome, in cooperation with God's grace, these impediments to wholeness and holiness.

If you remember my example from Week Thirty-Four, I fell into desolation each time I listened to the counter-inspirations of the enemy and became "offended" by my wife's drinking.

Drinking alcohol had very different meanings to me than it did for Margie. For me drinking became synonymous with abandonment and infidelity, as I associated my dad's unfaithfulness and abandoning our family with drinking alcohol.

For Margie, drinking alcohol had a very different connotation. During her childhood, she would cherish the time with her dad when he got home from work, opened a Budweiser, and sat under his big shade tree in the back yard before dinner. This was her favorite memory of one-on-one time with her dad. In her mind, drinking meant relaxing and being connected.

As you might imagine, I was not very sensitive to Margie's perspective during those times of spiritual desolation. Rather, I was absorbed in my own narcissistic thinking, feeling and acting.

My aggressive narcissism manifested in self-righteousness and emotional withdrawal (capital sins of pride and anger). My passive narcissism became evident in the way I took on a victim identity from my childhood wounds (of fear, abandonment, rejection, hopelessness, confusion, shame and powerlessness).

At the time, I did not realize I was in desolation, or wounded. But in retrospect all the symptoms were evident: I felt angry, agitated, and hopeless and did not turn towards God but instead became self-reliant and self-protective. Needless to say, I was not growing in faith, hope and love.

When I was in the cloudiness of desolation, none of my "solutions" actually helped the situation. They only made things worse. I ended up hurting myself and my wife. She felt rejected and judged by my attitudes and behaviors.

Over time, this unchecked desolation eroded our intimacy and even our trust in marriage. By the time I reached the age of 33, the very same age my dad was when he left, I became preoccupied with thoughts of divorce.

Thanks be to God for his great mercy and grace! It was during this period of time is when I had a life-changing encounter with his love. Motivated by the pain of these desolations, I began seeking a more intimate relationship with Jesus.

Looking back, I now recognize that the Lord worked through these desolations in a time of spiritual purification to highlight my sins and wounds.

As I became aware of my sins of pride and anger, I started going to confession regularly. Because of my encounter with the Father's love, I began to face and heal these underlying wounds of abandonment and rejection, lessening my fear and need to be in control.

Some of these wounds were very deep and painful. But working through them has also been liberating and fruitful.

The more I repented of my sins and brought my wounded identity to Jesus, the more I became my true self. I also became more aware of Margie's needs and perspectives and could see her in her wholeness. This has allowed our relationship to heal over time.

Along the way, there have been many healing breakthroughs, but overall the process of healing has been slow and progressive.

Over the years, I have become more aware of the triggers and the wounds and those familiar sins have less power to keep me stuck in desolation. When I do fall into desolation, by God's grace, I have learned how to turn towards Him for help.

I know I am not alone in the process of growing in grace through the experience of desolations. You are also on the same journey.

As you enter into the depths of your own desolations—facing your sins, wounds and addictions—you will grow in wisdom and insight as a confessor. Your preaching and pastoral direction will bear even greater fruit. Many people will be transformed through your ministry.

Below are some reflections from your brother priests as they reflected on Week Thirty-Five:

✠ *Even though desolation may not feel good and very possibly can end in committing sin, it can also help guide us to healing or be a sign that healing is already taking place. If God's love for us is always kept in mind, then it becomes much easier to understand that desolation occurs in order to lead us to faith, hope and love.*

✠ *The subtleties of the enemy of human nature become more complex as we grow spiritually. He adapts the attacks to the person's spirituality. But we can rely on the assurance that God is capable of battling our ancient enemy. Examining and tracing the trajectory of the thought and desires* will help us notice the alarm bells God rings in order to keep us on the right path.

✠ These examples are vivid & tie together healing ministry with the Sacred Story program. I am finding the same in my own story.

✠ I could see my own responses becoming more effective when confronted with triggers to desolation, as I reflected on these illustrations.

Immaculate Heart of Mary pray for us so that our hearts may be fully aligned with the Sacred Heart of your son Jesus.

℘

NOTES

Week 36

FIRST
I resolve to spend no more than fifteen minutes in each formal prayer session and to visualize my week ahead for where these will be. I will choose a place apart. I will always use my personal name for God.

SECOND
I continue praying meditations one through five in the Sacred Story prayer in this thirty-sixth week. I enter my prayer at least once daily, as St. Ignatius suggested. If I have not been faithful to my journal exercises, I will recommit to this very important discipline.

THIRD
I ask God's grace to deepen my understanding of spiritual discernment as I consider two of the three strategies the enemy of human nature employs to stall my spiritual growth.

I will awaken to the present moment.
I will awaken to my spiritual nature.
I will not make any decisions based on fear.
I will practice sacramental Reconciliation monthly.
I will ask Jesus for help when I am troubled.
I will thank Jesus daily for life's gifts.

411

This week, I will say this affirmation aloud once daily:
I will not waste time worrying about my sins and failures.
I will use my time wisely and ask God to help
me understand the source of my sins and failings.
I will trust that Christ came to heal all my wounds.

ᘉ

Continuing in the School of Discernment:
Guidelines for Foundational Healing and Spiritual Growth

Take some time this week to read and reflect on this ninth lesson in discernment. Last week, we examined the three principal reasons we experience counter-inspiration's spiritual desolation. This week we look at two of the three attack strategies used by the enemy of human nature to obstruct our spiritual progress.

All three strategies use elements of our life story as weapons against us: our unconscious fears; our psychological and spiritual vulnerabilities; and our long-standing addictive, compulsive, and/or sinful habits. These sinful habits do not make us happy. But they are familiar behaviors, and the pain of the familiar is often preferred to the fear of the unknown.

Ignatius learned these three attack strategies from his own experience of being deceived during his conversion process. Learn from his hard-earned wisdom. You might be at a place in your life where you have not yet encountered any of these tactics. If that is the case, the explanations may not make sense now, but they will in time. Notice again that fear is the common basis for all lines of attack.

Three Strategies of the Enemy of Human Nature:
Frighten, Deceive, Viciously Attack

When you engage your faith practice daily, the enemy of human nature can employ three subtle and malicious lines of attack to discourage you. He will use the weaknesses associated with your vices, your extravagant appetites, your compulsive drives, your spiritual/psychological wounds, and your broken heart. This week we will consider the first two of the three strategies:

1. Frighten: Fear and panic attacks are strategically employed to block growth.

If you stay committed to the process of uprooting vices, sins, addictions, and destructive habits from your life and heart, you may be attacked with waves of fear and panic to turn you away from the healing process. If you waver in your commitment to the healing process, the fear and panic can intensify exponentially. In the extreme, you can be paralyzed by unrelenting terror and withering dread.[26]

Directly confront the menacing fear. If you hold steadfast to the commitments associated with your spiritual and psychological growth, the panic and fear will eventually abate. If you consistently confront the fears and hold fast to the healing process, you will notice that the strategy of "fear and dread" is just that: a strategy. As a ploy, the fear and the dread are never realized. Nonetheless, it is maliciously effective if and when you surrender to it.[27]

2. Deceive: Narcissism and false values masquerade as true love and authentic values.

Those committed to allowing vices, addictions, sins, and destructive habits to be uprooted from their life and heart will also confront other tricks. The enemy can portray narcissism as authentic love and vices as positive values. These are tactics of the father of lies to deceive you. The enemy of human nature knows that every heart searches for true love.

But every heart is also divided and broken by the effects of its multiple spiritual and psychological wounds. The counter-inspiration of desolation blinds your heart's perception of what is spiritually and humanly authentic, and what leads to eternal life. Your heart can be easily fooled and tempted by false promises of love. All false loves are illicit, because they are lusts masquerading as love. False loves are like mirages for parched and anxious hearts hoping to quench their thirst and find comfort. Instead of providing lasting peace, these illicit loves—illusions really—merely intensify longings, self-deception, self-preoccupation, and narcissism, ultimately leading to spiritual and psychological death.

Be Not Afraid!

The enemy of our human nature likes to conceal himself and manipulate us with our conscious and unconscious fears. It is a carefully planned strategy. The strategy of the enemy is to play on our greatest vulnerabilities, even menace us and taunt us with them.

A part of the carefully designed strategy is to keep us bending to our fears. The more we bend to them, the stronger the fears become the next time we consider opposing them. This is why it is imperative to call fear's bluff and confront the fear—whatever fear it may be. "Be not afraid" is one of the most common phrases in the Old and New Testaments. God uses hope. The enemy uses fear. Discern the difference in their "voices."

It is easy to observe the corrosive effects of sins and addictions in other individuals and other groups. But when you are in their grip, it is difficult to imagine these sins and addictions as anything other than a precious lifeline. God clearly sees the corrosive and poisonous effects of false loves on persons, families, societies, and nature. But those in their grip are seduced into believing in false love's comforts, because all false loves can appear as good, life-giving, and natural. The deception to believe false loves as good, life-giving, and natural is complicated by evil's evolution in political and financial collectives, in educational systems and philosophies, in family structures and social networks, and in culture and entertainment. Evil's evolution in all of these can support and reward those trapped in the deception.

Sin is Missing the Mark

The most common word in Greek for sin is hamartia, meaning to miss the mark. If we define sin primarily by what it does—destroy relationships—then sin means missing the mark in both our understanding and practice of "right relationship." Let's take a recurrent song lyric theme: "How can something that feels so right be so wrong?" If the love this lyric expresses stands outside gospel values, then "what feels so right" can be an experience of love that feels better than the lifelessness one had previously experienced. Or here's a variation on this lyric: "Feels so good to be loved so bad." This expression demonstrates the "false love" of lust that has become an addiction. Both types of love might feel better than what one had previously experienced. But both loves miss the mark on the true love God wants for us. They will not ultimately bring us to the fullness of our authentic human nature. This is why they are "wrong" in God's eyes and why Jesus does not bless them. Jesus wants much more for the Father's beloved children.

The varieties of deception and seduction are as numerous as the ways a heart can be broken. God will not sanction these lusts because they issue from a violated heart and lead to your heart's further violation. Once acted upon, you will most assuredly violate the hearts of others. God is Love: the origin, the end, and the defender of the human heart. While God is infinitely merciful with our struggles, God cannot sanction anything that breaks your heart, destroys your authentic human nature,

415

or leads to your spiritual death.

Bring all false loves to full consciousness. Examine them in light of the writings of saints, doctors of the Church, and the mystical Christian traditions of West and East. Identify and name your sins, addictions, and habits truthfully as false lovers. Speak about these false loves with a spiritual guide who holds sacred the Tradition and the Gospels

You will not be convinced of these false loves' unholy origin until you are honest about them. Examine your false loves in the light of day, not by the cover of night. Here in the light of grace, they will be revealed as neither true servants of the heart nor pathways to the Divine. By exposing them, you will not lose love and life, as you fear. You will find, eventually, the path to Love itself: the Christ who is worthy of your total devotion and self-surrender.

When you are in the grip of false loves, activate Ignatius's "Truth Paradigm" (as we first learned in week 16). With Christ at your side, consciously take these steps:

✠ **Declare** to Christ the specific sin, addiction, or destructive compulsion, and name it as a false lover.

✠ **Describe** to Christ the specific sin, addiction, or destructive compulsion as coming from the enemy of your human nature.

✠ **Descend** with Christ into your memory to see and feel your first experience of this specific sin, addiction, or compulsion. Ask Christ to compassionately reveal the stress fractures, loneliness, and wounds in your heart it promised to satisfy.

✠ **Denounce**, with Christ as your witness, the sin, addiction, or destructive compulsion, for the ruinous effect in your life, others' lives, and society.

✠ **Decide** for Christ to heal this wound, defuse the stress, anxiety, and fear feeding it, and transform its damaging effects on your life into sacred story.

ଔ

For I know well the plans I have in mind for you—
plans for your welfare and not for woe,
so as to give you a future of hope.
When you call me, and come and pray to me,
I will listen to you.
When you look for me, you will find me.
Yes, when you seek me with all your heart.
(Jer 29:11–13)

ଯ

Dr. Schuchts' Reflection ~ Week Thirty-Six

The Truth Paradigm: Unmasking the Deception of Fear and Narcissism

During this Thirty-Sixth Week, we are shining a light into two areas of spiritual darkness (*Fear* and *Narcissism*) that make us vulnerable to counter-inspirations and thus desolation.

The Affirmation for this week offers great wisdom, allowing us to perceive how we become susceptible to these deceptions, while also providing the way back into the light of truth:

"I will not waste time worrying about my sins and failures. I will use my time wisely and ask God to help me *understand the source* of my sin and failings."

Understanding the source of our sins and failures enables us to find freedom from our fear and narcissism. This is a good investment of our time and energy. In contrast, it is a literal waste of time and energy to focus on self (narcissism) and to give into worry (fear).

When we get absorbed by our sins and failings, this negative inward preoccupation can entrap us in a web of spiritual oppression (fear and control).

This operates like a spiritual straightjacket--the more we try to fix the problem on our own, the more fear and narcissism tighten their grip on us. This allows the enemy of our human nature easy access to our soul.

There are many facets to narcissism: Justifying our sins and failings (self-righteousness), hating ourselves for them (self-condemnation), or trying to fix ourselves (ungodly self-sufficiency).

These may mute our fear in the short-term, but in long-term they only increase our separation from God and thus increase our fear and insecurity.

As we become self-focused, we lose sight of our need for God and his grace, slowly drifting away from the posture of abiding. Our heart then moves out of peace and into anxiety.

The Truth Paradigm is a very practical way to bring our struggles back to God, thus delivering us from narcissism and fear (and thus out of desolation).

Narcissism (pride) is the root sin of the *seven deadly sins*. The false loves are represented in the specific idolatries connected to each of the deadly sins.

The Truth Paradigm starts by naming and describing these sins and false loves, which almost always have a compulsive and addictive quality to them. Whenever you are not free in your desires, it is an indicator of a false love. In the Truth Paradigm process, declaring and describing the sin, addiction, or destructive compulsion moves you out of self-condemnation and self-reliance and into spiritual understanding. This is a movement towards freedom in the Holy Spirit.

Once you have named the sin, it is essential to ask Jesus to reveal the first experience of the sin or addiction. This is the doorway through which the spiritual darkness entered your soul.

It is even more essential to bring this awareness before Jesus, to receive his mercy and compassion. This represents the first layer of healing. But too often we stop there after receiving God's mercy for our sin.

Full healing requires that we allow God's grace to help us delve deeper, to reach the stress fractures where these sins and compulsions are rooted in the wounds of a broken heart.

Fear is the signal that leads us to these wounds since it is the linchpin of the *seven deadly wounds*. Operating in the Truth Paradigm, we can name our fears, and ask God to show us the root insecurities underlying these fears.

In doing so, we disarm their power to deceive us and to keep us bound. You are no doubt familiar with the acronym for *FEAR*--False *E*vidence *A*ppearing *R*eal. This kind of ungodly fear is based on the lies of the enemy.

As Fr. Watson notes, these lies are embedded into our broken hearts, often through traumatic memories. By descending with Christ into your memory you are reaching the place where specific fears are rooted.

These wounds embedded in your memory are the source of your false identity. Healing must reach this deeper level. Sins, addictions and compulsions (the false loves) are characteristically rooted in these wounds and identity distortions.

If we live from a distorted view of our identity, we will not know that we are Beloved Sons of the Father and will thus not trust and receive the Father's love. Without true love, we inevitably turn inward in narcissistic self-love which gives way to all the false loves—and desolation!

In all of this we must rely on the Holy Spirit rather than on ourselves. As the Catechism confirms: "only the Spirit of God can fathom the human heart and know it fully... The heart is the place of truth...the place of encounter" (CCC, 2563).

When we encounter God's love and truth in the depths of our hearts, fear and narcissism are displaced—the accuser is cast out (Rev 12:10). This is the process of fundamental healing and spiritual growth.

Below is an insight from one of your brother priests after working through Week Thirty-Six:

✠ *The enemy of human nature is jealous of our authentic nature particularly when we are committed to pursue the glory of heaven in Christ. Therefore, he uses our unconscious fears, psychological and spiritual vulnerabilities, and sinful habits to attack us.*

✠ *The enemy uses fear to prevent us from loving selflessly and reaching* higher consciousness. Fear creates defensive or aggressive thoughts, words, and deeds, which would have been avoided by the spirit of trust, gratitude, and forgiveness.

Immaculate Heart of Mary pray for us so that our hearts may be fully aligned with the Sacred Heart of your son Jesus.

જી

NOTES

Week 37

FIRST

Visualizing the week ahead, I will decide where to spend my fifteen minutes in each formal prayer period. As before, I will select a place apart, a technology-free zone. I will always use my personal name for God.

SECOND

I will continue this thirty-seventh week by praying meditations one through five in the Sacred Story prayer. I will enter my prayer at least once daily, as St. Ignatius suggested. I will make a firm commitment to the simple, daily journal exercises, because they are an invaluable part of awakening to my sacred story.

THIRD

I will ask God's grace to help me master spiritual discernment. This week, I am invited to understand the third of the three strategies the enemy of human nature employs to stall my spiritual growth.

I will awaken to the present moment.
I will awaken to my spiritual nature.
I will not make any decisions based on fear.
I will practice sacramental Reconciliation monthly.
I will ask Jesus for help when I am troubled.

I will thank Jesus daily for life's gifts.

This week, I will say this affirmation aloud once daily:
I alone control Christ's ability to transform my life into a sacred story.
The process begins when I ask for the grace
to honestly name my sins and addictions.
The process continues when I invite Christ to illuminate my narcissism.
Only God's grace and mercy can write my sacred story.

ଓ

Continuing in the School of Discernment:
Guidelines for Foundational Healing and Spiritual Growth

Take some time on the weekend or during the week to read and reflect on this tenth lesson in spiritual discernment. Last week we examined two of the three attack strategies used by the enemy of human nature to obstruct spiritual progress. All three strategies use elements of our life story as weapons against us: our unconscious fears, our psychological/spiritual vulnerabilities, and our long-standing habits. These habits do not create long-lasting happiness, but they are familiar. The boredom and/or pain of the familiar is often preferred to the fear of the unknown.

This week we examine the third attack strategy used by the enemy of human nature to obstruct our spiritual progress. Just as in the first two lines of attack, fear is the weapon used here by the enemy of human nature.

3. Viciously Attack

When you commit to uprooting sin, addictions, and vices from your body and soul, you will be assaulted by attacks directed at the spiritual and psychological wounds that make you most vulnerable.

The enemy of human nature can viciously attack where your wounds have left you most vulnerable. Those wounds might be spiritual, emotional, psychological, or moral. Core spiritual and psychological injuries to your heart and mind affect your capacity for self-transcendence. They make it difficult to love selflessly and achieve higher consciousness. A wall, built with emotional and intellectual counter-inspirations, is erected around the injuries, darkening your conscience. It is characteristic of the enemy of human nature to reinforce these emotional and intellectual defenses.

The enemy's purpose is to keep your emotional and intellectual defenses firmly in place, to keep your conscience dark and your true human nature hidden. The enemy's assault is felt as a bolstering and intensification of powerful emotional and intellectual defenses, leading you deeper into self-centered, self-absorbed, self-defended, self-justifying, and narcissistic thoughts, words, and deeds. You become more proud. You are adamantly convinced and hardened in your judgments about the meaning of life, truth, and beauty. These hardened convictions often contradict the Scriptures, received Tradition, the teaching Church and the mystical Christian traditions of West and East.

The defense measures of hardened convictions share the various qualities of desolation's counter-inspiration.[28] The strategic attacks by the enemy of human nature keep you attached to self-oriented, defensive thoughts, words, deeds, and habits, reinforcing rigid reasoning systems and disordered attachments.

The enemy of human nature's chief goal is to permanently camouflage your heart's spiritual, emotional, and psychological wounds. He does this to hide them from an awakened conscience, so you never notice where or why you need healing. Jesus made reference to these forms of defensive structures. They keep people from believing in Him, even if He

425

should rise from the dead (Lk 16:31), and they grieved Jesus because they harden hearts (Mk 3:5).

In our daily press, we can observe evidence of this tactic of the enemy of human nature. In one report, a teenager won a court case forcing a public high school to remove a banner in the school's gym that referred to "Our Heavenly Father." The student, a baptized Roman Catholic, stopped believing in God at ten years of age when her mother fell ill: "I had always been told that if you pray, God will always be there when you need Him," the student said. "And it didn't happen for me, and I doubted it had happened for anybody else. So yeah, I think that was just like the last step, and after that I just really didn't believe any of it."

Much of the media framed the story as a legal and constitutional fight to prevent state-sponsored religion. But another plotline can be detected in this story. The student is opposing religious expression because of deep childhood wounds. The student's mother fell ill and "God did not listen" to a prayer for healing. At the bottom of this story is a deeply wounded heart. On the surface we see a determined and fearless youth standing up to defend constitutional rights against the wrath of classmates and townspeople.

The student is a self-described atheist and revered as a hero by many (including much of the media). This student could be at the beginning of a lifelong crusade. And the enemy of human nature would urge this person on in that fight. The enemy will do anything to keep this person distracted from the interior wound so it cannot be healed. This fight will appear noble to the individual and to others. However, through the lens of discernment, it appears that the person is blind to the emotional and intellectual defense systems that have been constructed. Those defenses of pride, intellectual justification, and defiance conceal the fear and pain of a ten-year-old child's broken heart.

Many people fighting apparently noble causes, are terrified, wounded children running away from their pain. Further, the defense structures erected to protect the wound are hard to penetrate. Pride, rigid determination, anger, and attitudes of "crusader justice" conceal the fearful and wounded heart within. One thinks of St. Paul's attacks on the Church before his conversion. At the opening of the Acts of the Apostles, Saul witnesses the murder of Stephen. Later, he starts a crusade to crush all followers of the Way:

> Now Saul, still breathing murderous threats against the disciples of the Lord, went to the high priest and asked him for letters to the synagogues in Damascus, that, if he should find any men or women who belonged to the Way, he might bring them back to Jerusalem in chains. (Acts 9:1–2)

The enemy of human nature manipulated Saul's anger to legitimize murder. His homicidal rage was cloaked in religious justifications to stomp out all who followed the Lord Jesus. Fear was likely at the root of Saul's rage. It is possible that fear was also a driving force in St. Ignatius's life. Against the advice of the other knights, Ignatius forced the hand of his commander to engage in a futile battle that nearly ended his life.[29]

Much of the violence perpetrated by persons, groups, and countries in our own day is generated by wounded hearts seeking revenge for their suffering. Violence, be it economic, academic, physical, psychological, or verbal, can be self-justified and is often hidden behind nationalism, false religion, laws, cultural norms, and/or mob mentality.

Observe how the enemy of human nature instigates intellectual arguments, fosters a sense of injustice, and promotes defiance against legitimate authority. Ask the Lord, "What motivates my crusade (or crusades)? Where do I hurt? Help me to heal, and forgive me in the same way that I seek to forgive others. Help me spend the energy of my life to produce fruit that endures to eternity."

Cଓ

For he is our God,
we are the people he shepherds,
the sheep in his hands.

Oh, that today you would hear his voice:
Do not harden your hearts as at Meribah,
as on the day of Massah in the desert.
There your ancestors tested me;
they tried me though they had seen my works.
Forty years I loathed that generation;
I said: "This people's heart goes astray;
they do not know my ways."
Therefore I swore in my anger:
"They shall never enter my rest."
(Ps 95:7–11)

ଌ

Dr. Schuchts' Reflection ~ Week Thirty-Seven

Hardness of Heart

Our reflection for Week Thirty-Seven focuses our discernment on how hardness of heart blocks God's grace from being fully effective in our lives.

Fr. Watson emphasizes that "the enemy of our human nature can viciously attack where your wounds have left you vulnerable." This is one of the primary reasons why healing is essential to our spiritual life, leaving no cracks or crevices for the enemy to attack.

All of us are wounded. If we avoid facing and allowing Christ to heal these wounds, we will inevitably develop defensive fortresses around our hearts. This is what Jesus referred to as "hardness of heart."

I encourage you to take the time to study this theme of "hard-heartedness" throughout the Scriptures. Here is a quick overview as it relates to Week Thirty-Seven. The prophet Ezekiel offers the promise that God himself will transform us: "I will give you a new heart and put a new spirit within you. I will remove the heart of stone and give you a heart of flesh." (Ez. 36:26),

This new heart is Jesus' own Sacred Heart. The new spirit is the Holy Spirit. When we yield to the Holy Spirit, he softens our hearts and removes the hardness, replacing it with the tender heart of Jesus.

But we can also resist God's grace, as we see throughout the New Testament. Jesus was grieved with anger at the hardness of heart that he encountered in the Pharisees (Mk. 3:5). Though "God in flesh" stood right in front of them, their hardness made them blind.

429

In the book of Hebrews, we see that hard-heartedness is associated with not listening to God's voice (Heb. 3:7-8) and from the "deceitfulness of sin" (Heb. 3:13). When we become hardened to the inspirations of the Holy Spirit, we become vulnerable to the deceptions of the enemy.

In Ephesians, St. Paul talks about the "hardness of heart" among the Gentiles, who in the darkness of their minds allowed their hearts to become calloused, and then gave themselves over to every kind of impurity, through their deceitful desires (Eph.4:17-23).

Hardness of heart is thus the breeding ground for our false loves and compulsions. When we lose the capacity for the spiritual and emotional pleasure that comes from genuine love, we turn to the cheap substitute of indulging our lusts.

In the same Epistle, St. Paul goes on to describe how the process of hardening comes about. When we give into the temptation of any of the deadly sins (e.g. anger), we grieve the Holy Spirit and give the enemy a foothold in our life. (Eph. 4: 26-27).

Hardness of heart often develops around those areas where our hearts have been broken and our minds darkened by deceptions. When we are wounded, if we don't forgive, we will close our hearts in bitterness, while forming ungodly judgments.

With our hearts closed, we become less able to hear God's voice and more likely to take matters into our own hands, making proud vows about how we are going to save ourselves and others. (See Chapter 8 of Be Healed).

This is how spiritual, emotional, and psychological wounds become fortresses resisting God's grace. These words from the Catechism on hard-heartedness are sobering:
"Now--and this is daunting--this outpouring of mercy cannot penetrate

our hearts as long as we have not forgiven those who have trespassed against us…. In refusing to forgive our brothers and sisters, our hearts are closed and their hardness makes them impervious to the Father's merciful love, but in confessing our sins our hearts are opened to his grace (CCC, 2840).

Forgiving those who wound us, while receiving God's forgiveness for our sins, allows our hearts to remain tender and our spirits docile to the inspirations of the Holy Spirit (Eph. 4: 32).

With an open and tender heart, we are in a much better position to recognize the voice of the Holy Spirit, while abiding in Christ and attending to the movements of our own hearts.

Before anything else, Christ's priestly ministry through you increases as your heart is formed in the image of Jesus' heart. When your heart is soft and docile to the movement of the Spirit, you are able to teach the members of your community to do the same.

As your brother priests note, in their reflections on Week Thirty-Seven all of this requires careful discernment:

✠ *The reminder to reflect upon genuine love was important.*

✠ *All of us have been wounded in a way or another; these wounds constitute the gates where the devil tries to penetrate his victim and strike. Only forgiveness is the means to escape the attack. If not, these wounds become the fortresses for self-reliance which prevents God's grace from changing a heart of stone into a heart of flesh.*

✠ *Healthy anger is a God-given gift of protection for authenticity. But like for all other legitimate and authentic gifts, the evil one knows how to corrupt healthy anger, changing it into bitterness, brawling, resentment, suicidal thoughts. We just need to be awake in order not to let the enemy* of human nature steal and corrupt our God-given gift of healthy anger which helps us to address injustice and immorality around us

✠ These rules take careful reflection as the inspirations and counter inspirations are at work even in the discernment of the rules themselves.

Immaculate Heart of Mary pray for us so that our hearts may be fully aligned with the Sacred Heart of your son Jesus.

෪

NOTES

Week 38

FIRST

I resolve to spend no more and no less than fifteen minutes in each formal prayer period. I will always use my personal name for God.

SECOND

As before, I continue this thirty-eighth week by praying meditations one through five in the Sacred Story prayer, entering my prayer at least once daily, as St. Ignatius suggested. I reaffirm the importance of the simple journal exercises and my monthly practice of sacramental Reconciliation.

THIRD

I will ask God's grace to keep my mind and heart open as I learn the ways of spiritual discernment in my sacred story. This week I am invited to reflect on the second series of discernment rules given by St. Ignatius. This second series of rules details temptations of a more subtle nature. Here the enemy of our human nature manipulates our undetected narcissism to obstruct or disrupt our spiritual growth.

I will awaken to the present moment.
I will awaken to my spiritual nature.
I will not make any decisions based on fear.
I will practice sacramental Reconciliation monthly.
I will ask Jesus for help when I am troubled.

I will thank Jesus daily for life's gifts.

This week, I will say this affirmation aloud once daily:
I will strive daily to pick up the cross, for it leads to my life.
The closer I get to holiness, the more I will
see and feel sin's disorder in my life.

ॐ

Continuing in the School of Discernment:
Guidelines for Integrated Healing and Spiritual Growth

Take some time this week to read and reflect on this eleventh lesson in discernment. Last week we finished a study of St. Ignatius's first set of rules on discernment. The first set of rules is called "Guidelines for Foundational Healing and Spiritual Growth." They are foundational rules because they are directed toward those who can be more easily distracted from their spiritual journey by sensual pleasures and delights from the enemy of human nature.

These rules help build the foundation of one's faith journey. The enemy of human nature seeks his victories at this level by fanning our cowardice and fear in the face of surrendering addictive and sinful thoughts, words, and deeds.

This week we examine St. Ignatius's second set of discernment rules. We call these "Guidelines for Integrated Healing and Spiritual Growth." They apply to those persons whom the enemy of human nature distracts from their spiritual journey with attacks to the reasoning processes. These rules are termed integrated because they facilitate healing of our human nature as a unity of body and spirit. The enemy of human nature seeks his victories at this level by creating illusions and hiding the truth of our thoughts, words, and deeds.

This week we consider five of the seven guidelines for discerning the difference between the Divine Inspirer and the counter-inspirer's tactics at this more subtle, nuanced level of spiritual development.

The Guidelines for Integrated Healing and Spiritual Growth are essential for discerning counter-inspirations of a more subtle nature. They are applicable when a person has matured to the point where vices, sinful habits, addictions, and extravagant appetites are no longer effective temptations to lure one from God.

When a certain level of spiritual, emotional, and psychological maturity has been reached, the enemy of human nature can best deceive with seemingly good, holy thoughts and feelings. He mimics the Divine Inspirer. He is no longer successful in undermining your authenticity and innocence with temptations to false pleasures and obvious discouragements. Direct appeals to narcissistic pride are no longer effective. Instead, the enemy resorts to twisting new and holy inspirations and habits against you, based on the undetected roots of your narcissism.

The enemy of human nature will then disguise counter-inspirations by having them appear as divine inspirations. Ignatius first discovered these new, indirect temptations in the midst of his battle with the crippling guilt of his scruples. The obsessive habit of reconfessing his past sins appeared as a good thing to do. The habit appealed to someone serious about spiritual growth. But the habit appealed especially to Ignatius's desire to be in control of his life and to save himself.

In his former way of living, Ignatius had tried to win fame at the battle of Pamplona by attempting to conquer the French almost single-handedly. Later, in his Christian life, his narcissism appeared under the "holy" guise of winning fame by conquering his sinfulness through his own agency: a different battle but the same concealed narcissism and pride at work.

Ignatius was miserable and experienced the constant reconfessing as damaging. Yet he would not relinquish the obsessive habit even when told to do so by his spiritual director. Ignatius seemed to be held bound by a "pious" and "holy" habit. In fact, he was bound by his narcissism and determination to save himself instead of allowing Christ to be his Savior. The enemy's counter-inspirations that characterized this episode were invisible to Ignatius, most likely because surrendering the habit meant a loss of control and a threat to his pride.

Ignatius was given grace to see the deception by observing the direction it was taking him: away from God. He realized that the inspiration was to "stop" the new life he was living. The enemy of our human nature can inspire desires and choices that are nonharmful or even objectively good. They appear as if they will help us evolve toward more perfect love and life.

Thus in Ignatius's situation, conscientious confession would appear to be a good choice to root out past sins and vices. But to someone susceptible to damaging scrupulosity, it could be the perfect tactic to turn that person from the path of faith and trust in God! And the enemy of human nature will search for any and all vulnerabilities to subvert our journey in faith.

Spiritual and religious persons are especially vulnerable to these more subtle temptations. The narcissism of these persons is concealed in a pious facade. A partial conversion has not sufficiently targeted the narcissistic pride that guides such a person's life. Those not sufficiently purified parade about like just and righteous people. The truth is, they are proud and arrogant. Jesus reserved some of His most serious criticisms for these religious hypocrites. (Lk 18:9–14).

Some things that are good, or appear as good, can gradually lead you away from the good you intend. They lead you away from God toward disintegration, separation, and death. This is exactly what happened to Ignatius. He was so disgusted with the trials and traumas of his obsessive reconfessing of past sins that he was suddenly inspired to be done with the new life he had embraced. As far as Ignatius was concerned, if he could not convert himself, and do it his way, he would not do it at all. This is narcissistic pride, plain and simple.

A habit that appeared noble was silently, slowly, and maliciously eroding his confidence in himself and his confidence in God, and it threatened the new way of life he had chosen. If the enemy of human nature could not lure Ignatius with the obvious vices and sins of his former life, then the enemy would manipulate Ignatius's new and holy inspirations, linking them to his yet undetected narcissistic pride. The enemy turned Ignatius's good habit against him.

It can be difficult to differentiate between divine inspirations and counter-inspirations, especially because a counter-inspiration can appear as a genuine good, or feel authentic. Ignatius offers these guidelines of discernment:

First, the Divine Inspirer works to give you true joy and happiness. This is accomplished by eliminating all sadness and upset caused by the enemy of your human nature. The counter-inspirer works against such joy and happiness. He does this most successfully by using false reasoning, subtleties, and layers of deceptions. The enemy's arguments will be logical yet leave you feeling anxious, discouraged, hopeless, and possibly cynical.

Second, the Divine Inspirer alone can work directly on your heart and soul. The Divine Inspirer can touch your soul at will. What does the Divine Inspirer promote by these spiritual visits?

✠ Increased love of God and love of innocence.

✠ Increased humility, selflessness, and surrendering control of your life to God.

✠ Increased docility of spirit: a spirit capable of listening deeply, accepting and affirming as true the Commandments, the teachings of Christ, and those divinely revealed and definitively proclaimed matters of belief held by the Church.[30]

Inspirations with these signature characteristics can be verified as coming directly from the Divine Inspirer.

Third, both the Divine Inspirer and the counter-inspirer can inspire, but with opposite goals. The Divine Inspirer seeks to promote genuine human freedom, authenticity, and spiritual/psychological growth in harmony with your authentic human nature. The counter-inspirer seeks to erode genuine human freedom and to disintegrate your spiritual and psychological health. The goal is to further damage your authentic human nature.

Fourth, the counter-inspirer can mimic some of the influences of the Divine Inspirer in thoughts, feelings, and desires. However, his purpose in doing so is to gradually lead you in the wrong direction, similar to Ignatius's experience with his damaging habit of reconfessing old sins.

Fifth, distinguishing the difference between Divine and counter-inspirations requires you to develop the habit of examining the overall trajectory of your thoughts and desires. If the beginning, middle, and end are all directed to what is genuine and right, the inspirations are from the Divine Inspirer. If the trajectory of the desires and thoughts:

✠ lead to something contrary to the Commandments or the precepts of Christ,

✠ distract and weaken your aspirations for selflessness, or

✠ in some way diminish the good plans and goals you had previously established, then it is very clear they are a product of the counter-inspirer. The goal of the enemy of human nature is to lead you away from genuine progress, authenticity, innocence, humility, obedience, and peace and to conceal his presence as he does so.

Ignatius was distracted by his re-confession habit, and his aspirations for following the path of conversion were undermined by it. When he realized this, he identified the influence of the counter-inspirer and surrendered the damaging habit. This choice began the process of dismantling his narcissistic pride at its root.[31]

Ignatius once remarked that human beings are no match for the subtle temptations of the enemy of human nature. But God is! God is indeed a match for the enemy's temptations. Never dialogue with the enemy of your human nature. Speak only to Christ, and let Christ deal with the enemy of your human nature. Trust your life, your heart, and your soul to Christ.

LORD, guide me in your justice because of my foes;
make straight your way before me.

For there is no sincerity in their mouth;
their heart is corrupt.
Their throat is an open grave;
on their tongue are subtle lies.
Declare them guilty, God;
make them fall by their own devices.
Drive them out for their many sins;
for they have rebelled against you.

Then all who trust in you will be glad
and forever shout for joy.
You will protect them and those will rejoice in you
who love your name.
For you, Lord, bless the just one;
you surround him with favor like a shield.
(Ps 5:9–13)

SO

Dr. Schuchts' Reflection ~ Week Thirty-Eight

Guidelines for Integrated Healing and Spiritual Growth

Our reflection for Week Thirty-Eight focuses on Ignatius' second set of discernment rules, which serve as guidelines for *Integrated Healing*. As the Catechism so wisely points out, worship is the only truly integrative experience in life:

CCC 2114: Human Life finds its unity in the adoration of the one God. The commandment to worship the Lord alone *integrates* man and saves him an endless *disintegration*.

CCC 2907: "The worship of the one God sets man free from *turning in on himself*, from the slavery of sin, and the idolatry of the world."

Notice the contrast: when we worship God with our thoughts, words, and deeds we become integrated. When we turn in on ourselves and give into sin, we become progressively more and more disintegrated.

These discernment rules alert us to the counter-inspirations of the enemy which lead us out of worshipping God and into self-worship.

The first set of rules (for fundamental healing) addresses our more obvious sins and addictions, i.e. "the slavery of sin and the idolatry of the world".

In contrast, this second set of rules (for integrated healing) addresses the core narcissism which undergirds our tendency to turn away from God and to "turn in" on ourselves.

It may be helpful to review the tree diagram on page 140 to see how these two layers of sin are interconnected. At the top of the tree, the

442

manifest sins and addictions are highlighted. These are what St. Paul refers to as "the works of the flesh" (Ga. I5:19) which are manifested in our thoughts, words and deeds. In Ignatius' life (anger, lust and gambling) would be the sins and addictions at the top of his tree.

At the base of the trunk is the core sin of narcissism. For Ignatius, this was evident in his arrogance, ungodly self-reliance, and scrupulosity.

Our own spiritual lives have a similar structure. Our manifest sins are on the top of our "trees." The core sin of self-centeredness (narcissism) is at the base of the trunk.

Our individual "spiritual trees" are rooted ultimately in the wounds of original sin (the tree of knowledge of good and evil--Gen 2:17).

This core wound is manifested in the seven deadly wounds, playing out through our family and personal history. These wounds fuel our narcissism which in turn gives rise to our addictions and sins, which further increases our self-idolatry.

In this second set of rules, we are addressing the core sin of narcissism. When we are not abiding in Christ, we inevitably "turn in on ourselves". We move from worshipping God to making an idol of ourselves.

Operating from this posture of ungodly self-reliance and self-worship, all of our thoughts, words and deeds originate in self-centeredness.

What makes this so difficult is that our pride and narcissism blind us from seeing the truth. We can't see the motives of our heart's, without the light of the Holy Spirit.

So, the core movement in discernment is to move from self-reliance to a reliance on God. We ask, by the light of the Holy Spirit, to see the movements and trajectory of our thoughts, words and deeds:

- Are my thoughts moving towards God or turning in on myself?
- Are my affections for God growing or diminishing?
- Am I glorifying God by my actions or are they directed to vainglory?
- Am I experiencing peace and joy, or anxiety and hopelessness?
- Am I loving with God's love, or manipulating for my selfish purposes?
- Am I more authentic and free or less real and more guarded?
- Am I surrendered to God, or trying to be in control?

Test all this with 1 Corinthians 13. Go through the passage and insert your name next to all the descriptions: I am.... "patient, kind, not boastful, not rude", etc. As you reflect on this, note where your heart is in peace and where it is not. Can you see how this process of discerning spirits helps to solidify your core identity and your participation in Christ's priestly ministry?

As you continue to grow spiritually, your daily experience of worship integrates your thoughts, words and deeds. You will become more and more rooted in your identity as Beloved Son, in communion with Jesus. From this posture, as you teach and lead your people into true worship, you are helping them heal from all the ways their lives have been disintegrated.

As you personally become more integrated and pure of heart, the family of God you serve will also be led into greater wholeness and holiness. "The Glory of God is man fully alive."

Below are comments from your brother priests for Week Thirty-Eight:

✠ *If somebody is imprisoned in a box, he or she cannot save him- or herself but needs another from outside the box. For this reason, Ignatius' second set of discernment rules, which serve as guidelines for Integrated Healing, discourage any form of self-reliance and promote reliance on the Lord*

Jesus Christ who is the Savior of the world.

✠ *The danger of selfishness and seeking self-pleasure can lead to idolatry of self. I hadn't fully thought of this as clearly before.*

Immaculate Heart of Mary pray for us so that our hearts may be fully aligned with the Sacred Heart of your son Jesus.

ℰ

NOTES

Week 39

FIRST
I resolve to spend no more and no less than fifteen minutes in each formal prayer period. I will always use my personal name for God.

SECOND
I ask God's grace to help me commit to a lifelong habit of praying the five meditations of Sacred Story prayer. With God's grace, I will be able to enter my prayer at least once daily, as St. Ignatius suggested. God's grace will also help me to commit to my simple journal exercises and a monthly practice of sacramental Reconciliation.

THIRD
I am invited to continue reflecting on spiritual discernment by concluding the series of St. Ignatius's rules on integrated healing. This second series of rules takes into account temptations of a more subtle nature. Here the enemy of my human nature manipulates undetected narcissism to interfere with my spiritual growth.

> I will awaken to the present moment.
> I will awaken to my spiritual nature.
> I will not make any decisions based on fear.
> I will practice sacramental Reconciliation monthly.

I will ask Jesus for help when I am troubled.
I will thank Jesus daily for life's gifts.

This week, I will say this affirmation aloud once daily:
The more I experience sin's disorder,
the more tempted I will be to disbelieve my life as sacred story.
The way through the temptation
is to surrender my powerlessness to God.

☙

Continuing in the School of Discernment:
Guidelines for Integrated Healing and Spiritual Growth

Take some time on the weekend or during the week to read and reflect on this twelfth lesson in discernment. Last week our study of St. Ignatius's second set of rules on discernment examined five guidelines to utilize with temptations of a more subtle form. This week we examine the sixth and seventh guidelines. Remember these rules apply to those distracted from the spiritual journey by the enemy of human nature with attacks targeting their reasoning processes with illusions of truth, but not truth itself. We call these integrated rules, because they facilitate healing of our human nature as a unity of body and spirit.

Review the introductory narrative from week 38. These "Guidelines for Integrated Healing and Spiritual Growth" are essential for discerning counter-inspirations of a more subtle nature. They are applicable to those who have matured to the point where vices, sinful habits, addictions, and extravagant appetites are no longer effective in luring one away from God.

Sixth, develop the habit of tracing the trajectory of the thoughts and desires that have led you away from God and away from your authentic self. Do not become discouraged. This discipline takes practice. You will fall for the bait countless times. When you do, examine the initial inspiration, and follow it through the whole course of your deliberations. Notice how you were initially inspired but then gradually, step by step, lost your peace of soul.

Notice how your former holy commitments and resolutions were undermined. From this objective vantage point, reflection will enable you to identify the particular strategy the counter-inspirer uses in your life story. This vigilance will help you develop spiritual radar for these deceptive tactics. You will also learn to identify your personal vulnerabilities that the enemy of your authentic human nature manipulates.

At this level of conversion, the enemy's tactics work on your concealed pride, vanity, and narcissism—the Original Sin of the human family. When you think or feel things like "I do not need God," or "I will control my own life," or "I will set my own rules," or "I will be my own savior," and you feel proud about it, rest assured, the enemy of human nature is at work!

Seventh, when you are progressing towards authenticity, innocence, and genuine human freedom, the effects of the Divine Inspirer are gentle and produce delight. A sense of electrical energy, anxious excitement, or a restless need to make hasty decisions is totally absent. Instead, a calm patience and tranquility abides. When making progress towards authenticity, you can detect the effects of the counter-inspirer by the rush of electrical energy, anxious excitement, or restlessness to make hasty decisions.

But you need to awaken to both the feelings (anxious or calm) and the trajectory (toward or away from authenticity) to accurately interpret what the feelings are signaling. If you are moving toward God, the enemy of your human nature will inspire "black noise," creating anxious thoughts and urgent feelings. The enemy wants to discourage you from turning to God.

If you are moving away from God, God will inspire with alarm bells that you are entering dangerous territory. It can feel like the same anxiety and urgent feelings described above, but this time, it is your awakened conscience that God uses to alert you of an inauthentic trajectory.

Also, if you are moving away from God, the enemy of your human nature will inspire with thoughts that are appeasing, reassuring your complacency and attempting to conceal your movement away from God and from your authentic human nature.

When the inspiration produced in your heart and soul comes directly from the Divine Inspirer, you cannot be deceived or led astray. You will come to know the inspirations of the Divine Inspirer because of the effects on your heart and soul. These inspirations produce an intense sense of devotion and love of God and of innocence. They produce a sense of selflessness and willing surrender of your life to God's control. The inspirations help you understand and trust received Tradition, the Commandments, and the precepts of Christ as proclaimed by the Church.

However, you can be led astray in the afterglow of such inspiration and grace. You can be led astray by your own ideas or by the influence of the counter-inspirer. Be highly attentive during the time following divine inspirations. Be cautious and make no revisions, commitments, or plans during this time, unless you are clear as to the source of the inspiration.

The Divine Inspirer will lead you further along the path of love, innocence, humility, and self-surrender. The counter-inspirer will work toward disintegration and a weakening of your previous commitments and holy resolutions. The counter-inspirer will pull you further down the path of pride and encourage you to justify your angers. The enemy of human nature will inspire you to cling to whatever difficulties you have with gospel values as proposed by the Church.

Conclusion

Understand now how St. Ignatius's divine inspiration to reform his life was corrupted into a damaging habit of confessing old sins. The counter-inspirer accomplished this by manipulating Ignatius's narcissistic nature and long-standing vulnerabilities. If Ignatius had been deceived into walking away from his conversion journey, the Church would have been deprived of the gifts of his spirituality and the many saints who achieved holiness through it.

This was the counter-inspirer's hope for Ignatius. It will be the counter-inspirer's hope for you as well. The counter-inspirer understands the great good that you can accomplish for the Kingdom of Christ and will work to sabotage it at all costs. While we are incapable of matching the subtleties of the enemy of human nature, we can rest in the assurance that God is capable of battling our ancient enemy.

The Divine Inspirer will always offer the graces and insights to lead you home. God's victory is assured for you in Christ's birth, life, death, and resurrection. Have hope in Him. He will help you, just as He helped St. Ignatius. You will achieve the goal of love, the goal of forgiveness, and through your life's sacred story, the goal of service to the Great Work of Reconciliation that Christ has invited you to share with Him.

As you work with God's grace to let your life be transformed into sacred story, never be discouraged by your failings, sins, and weaknesses. The Divine Physician will never tire of forgiving you. Never tire of coming to Him for forgiveness. In this radical, loving trust, you encounter the unfathomable and unbounded mercy of God.

ॐ

Hallelujah!
Praise the Lord, my soul; I will praise the Lord all my life,
sing praise to my God while I live.

Put no trust in princes,
in children of Adam powerless to save.
Who breathing his last, returns to the earth;
that day all his planning comes to nothing.

Blessed the one whose help is the God of Jacob,
whose hope is in the Lord, his God,
The maker of heaven and earth, the seas and all that is in them,
Who keeps faith forever, secures justice for the oppressed,
who gives bread to the hungry.
The Lord sets prisoners free; the Lord gives sight to the blind.
The Lord raises up those who are bowed down;
the Lord loves the righteous.
The Lord protects the resident alien,
comes to the aid of the orphan and the widow,
but thwarts the way of the wicked.
The Lord shall reign forever,
your God, Zion, through all generations!
Hallelujah!
(Ps 146)

ॐ

Dr. Schuchts' Reflection ~ Week Thirty-Nine

Movements Toward Authenticity

During this Thirty-Ninth Week, we are continuing with Ignatius' Second Set of Discernment Rules, attending to the trajectory of our thoughts, feelings and actions as we move toward authenticity. We all desire authenticity, but it is a hard concept to understand, let alone live out in our lives. To be authentic is to be become fully integrated in body, soul and spirit (1 Th. 5:23). When we are authentic, we shine with vitality and exude a freedom that becomes a beacon of Christ's light and love for others.

St. Catherine of Siena expressed it this way: "Become what you ought to be [your true self uniquely made in God's image] and you will set the whole world on fire."

St. John Paul II, as we have noted, speaks of it in terms of our human potential in Christ: "We are not the sum of our weaknesses and failures; we are the sum of the Father's love for us and our real capacity to become the image of His son."

St. Francis De Sales says simply and concisely: "Be who you are and be it well." Isn't that what we all desire: to be free to be ourselves without masks and facades, shedding all the shackles that hinder us from living from our true identity as beloved sons?

And yet we also know the angst and struggle to live as an integrated person with the kind of spontaneity and joy that is the mark of true discipleship. It helps to see all this in light of original sin. These words from Fr. Jacques Phillipe speak directly about the reason for our narcissism and the challenge of authenticity:

"Here it is worth reflecting on the problem of pride. We are all born with a deep wound, experienced as a lack of being. We seek to compensate by constructing a self, different from our real self. This artificial self requires large amounts of energy to maintain it; being fragile, it needs protecting. Woe to anyone who contradicts it, threatens it, or inhibits its expression. When the gospel says we must 'die to ourselves' it means this artificial ego, this constructed self, must die, so that the real "self" given us by God can emerge." (Interior Freedom, 122).

I find it very helpful to think of original sin in this way, as a deep wound that brings about my "lack of being" Think of this "lack of being" as a deficit in capacity to think, feel, and do, all that is good, true and beautiful.

My broken heart and wounds incapacitate me and make me more susceptible to sin, which gives way to addictions. These, in turn, numb the pain of my wounded and broken heart. My shame keeps me hiding in darkness, which further increases my interior sense of disintegration. I want to hide all my sin and deficiencies. I am divided and at war within myself.

So, I construct masks to hide my inadequacies and put a lot of energy into putting on an image, because I have lost the freedom and fullness of being that comes from reflecting His true image.

This is where Ignatius' second set of rules for discerning spirits come into play. They are vitally important for our integration and spiritual healing. Vulnerably opening myself before Jesus, and a few trusted others, I slowly learn that I can be spiritually naked. God's love allows me to risk exposing those areas of ugliness, pain and lack of being, concealed behind my false self.

For me, this process is long and painstaking and requires daily growth in honesty, with a willingness to face the pain of my broken heart. A commitment to authenticity first leads me through the valley of my sins, wounds and deficiencies.

But even when I have the intention of honestly facing these inadequacies of being, I find myself repeatedly covering myself and falling into one of two pitfalls, like two ditches on either side of the road.

On one side, I fall into the ditch of *self-righteousness*. I have a strong compulsion to justify, rationalize, and defend my disintegrated thoughts, feelings, and acts, rather than honestly facing them in light of God's healing balm of compassion and mercy. On the other side, I fall into the ditch of *self-condemnation*. When I can no longer justify myself, I swing to the other side of the road in self-loathing, and fear that God and others are judging me harshly as well. I deny God's mercy entirely.

Through it all, I discover that the road towards authenticity can only be walked in the light of God's truth and mercy. This is true humility and why the saints call us to this virtue above all others.

Humility allows us to see ourselves as God sees us- neither puffed up nor self-hating, but deeply flawed, hurting, and forgiven. The Good Father sees us in our wholeness and pours out his grace as we open our weakness and pain to him (2 Co. 12:8). In His eyes, we are deeply cherished and chosen and on a journey of becoming who we truly are-- beloved sons of the Father. Our healed wounds are becoming a powerful source of grace for others.

As Christ's priest, growing in your identity as beloved son, you also discover how to live authentically as a loving brother, chaste bridegroom, and faithful father. This is the life Christ has called you to as His priest, offering worship for yourself and all God's people.

As you pay attention to the movements of your heart, you will be able to do the same for all who come to you. The more you live in the freedom of your true identity, the more you will inspire the same in those you lead and serve. We all have a long way to go, but the journey itself is fulfilling.

"Be who you are and be it well"! "Set the whole world on Fire." "Become the image of the Son."

This theme of authenticity in Christ seemed to strike a chord with your brother priests. Here are some of their comments from Week 39.

✠ *When St Catherine of Siena says: Become what you ought to be and you will set the whole world on fire, she doesn't give the definition of authenticity, but she invites us to work on our constructed -self until we attain Jesus' stature. Jesus is the Ecce Homo, the true and authentic human nature with whom we are to set the world on fire.*

✠ *It is good to be reminded to simply be who God has created us to be.*

✠ *This is helping to verify my gut feeling about the sneaky pride that can get in the way for myself and those I guide in spite of our good intentions.*

✠ *If I want to discern accurately what is actually taking place within me, I must be patient - in making decisions (where to go, what to do) and in judging the quality of my prayer. I also must be aware of the overall, general direction of my life and how particular inspirations fit within that.*

Immaculate Heart of Mary pray for us so that our hearts may be fully aligned with the Sacred Heart of your son Jesus.

℘

NOTES

Week 40

FIRST

I resolve to spend no more and no less than fifteen minutes in each formal prayer period. I will always use my personal name for God.

SECOND

I ask God's grace to help me commit to a lifelong habit of praying the five meditations of Sacred Story prayer. With God's grace, I will be able to enter my prayer at least once daily, as Ignatius suggested. God's grace will also help me to commit to my simple journal exercises and a monthly practice of sacramental Reconciliation.

THIRD

This week I am invited to conclude my lessons on St. Ignatius's rules for spiritual discernment. This final section offers special discernment advice for those times that my deepening conversion to life as sacred story may prompt life changes of one sort or another.

℘

I will awaken to the present moment.
I will awaken to my spiritual nature.
I will not make any decisions based on fear.
I will practice sacramental Reconciliation monthly.

I will ask Jesus for help when I am troubled.
I will thank Jesus daily for life's gifts.

This week, I will say this affirmation aloud once daily:
It is never too late to open my heart to Christ
and live my life as sacred story.

ↁ

Additional Guidelines on Life Choices

Take some time this week to read and reflect on this thirteenth lesson in discernment. Last week we completed the study of St. Ignatius's second set of rules on discernment. These examined the sixth and seventh guidelines that indicate the presence of temptations of a more subtle form in our lives. This week we conclude the study of discernment by examining the guidelines St. Ignatius offers to those who, open to God's grace, contemplate making life choices.

These rules may not be applicable at this point in your spiritual journey. These guidelines will be helpful whenever you are required to make decisions based on faith in the future. The enemy of human nature is always at work to derail our conversion process, but we are not to be afraid. The Lord is our strength and shield. We must simply learn to be gentle as doves and wise as serpents (Mt 10:16).

As your conversion deepens, grace illumines your mind and heart. What had been in darkness is now revealed. You begin to awaken, to see the true nature of reality, the world, and your authentic human nature. Grace alone facilitates this journey out of spiritual unconsciousness and the darkened conscience of counter-inspiration. As you continue to awaken, you will discover why narcissism and pride are so much more difficult to identify and eliminate than are the sins of the flesh.

The pain of Original Sin, early life trauma, and lost innocence encourages

459

your narcissism. The narcissistic ego is closed to the Spirit. This ego rationalizes and legitimizes whatever it needs to fill its painful void. It is the ancient wound created by the self, displacing God as the heart's center. The defenses that hide your narcissism match the intensity of the hidden pain at the center of your heart. You defend the use of vices and addictions because they protect you from feeling the pain in your heart and keep you from turning to God for help and healing.

Your sacred story begins when you accept the Divine Physician's grace to honestly name your sin and let the heart's healing begin. You need God's grace to both break through and dismantle your defenses. This is the true path to mystical awakening. There are no shortcuts. There is no other way home. You have a unique path to holiness that no one else in all of history can follow. It is God's path for you. It is linked to the unique circumstances of your life. Let the Divine Physician heal you and lead you to wholeness and holiness.

The humility Ignatius discovered in surrendering control of his life—surrendering his pride and narcissism—allowed him to envision a new life, in and for Christ, that he had never known before. This awakened consciousness has its own graces and difficulties, as Ignatius well discovered. These graces abound, regardless of one's state of life and vocation. These graces bring illumination and clarity. They illumine the true portrait of your free and authentic self. They open you to the world, your Catholic faith, and the creator God. They reveal your past and present commitments, and your choices—both well- and ill-conceived. This is where Ignatius found himself after his spiritual and psychological trials at Manresa.

The grace of conversion transforms and heals divided hearts. The values you previously espoused that were contrary to the gospel give way to thoughts, words, and deeds that open you to opportunities never before imagined or thought possible. Purifying graces rush in with new opportunities for your life, filling the void of a heart on the mend. What else would you expect when your heart is touched directly by divine grace? When your heart is flush with the energy, the enthusiasm, and the vitality of God, Ignatius has clear advice.

Ignatius advises that a person in this stage of integrated conversion and healing, who has received these graces of illumination, must consider them very attentively. One needs to cautiously distinguish the initial consolation from the period that follows. In the afterglow of these illuminations and insights, when the consolations themselves have ceased, the soul is still passionate. It has been blessed with graces, and these graces have an afterglow. In the time of the afterglow, the heart and soul often form resolutions and plans that are not directly inspired or granted by God.

These ideas and resolutions can emanate from your own reasoning, creating ideas based on your own judgments. Or these resolutions can be the direct inspiration of the Divine Inspirer or the counter-inspirer. It is critical to distinguish the illuminations themselves and the period of time after the illuminations—the period of afterglow. Carefully, thoughtfully, and cautiously examine your afterglow reflections and plans, before approving them or acting on them.

This advice is especially important if you are transitioning from established habits and lifestyles. Those thoughts, words, and deeds, inauthentic expressions of your human nature, have deep roots and/or a long history. These long-established patterns of sin and dysfunction have created spiritual, mental, and psychological grooves. The grooves are your default narratives for defining "normal" and "success." These false-but-familiar narratives are narcissism's anti-story. They draw strength from your broken heart and wounded innocence.

We experience the spiritual and physical wreckage of the Original Fall in our wounded hearts. Our lost innocence is combined with the evolution of sin in our families, clans and social groups. The energy fueling our narcissistic anti-story shields us from pain and shame, both real and perceived. As you gradually receive the grace and illumination to relinquish the anti-story, you will experience a void.

Surrendering the false definitions of success, and the habits that support these false narratives, creates the void. You will feel a powerful compulsion to fill that void, a compulsion that is easily exploited by the counter-inspirer.

When you relinquish your anti-story, you will also have the desire to make up for lost time and to correct the mistakes of the past. These desires can also fill your heart with urgent and pressing agendas for change. These agendas may feel honorable and right.

This is true especially in light of your past misdeeds and errors. One must exercise caution, however, because these urgent and pressing agendas for change can lead away from the truths, positive resolutions, and commitments recently illumined by divine grace.

If you experience strong inspirations to change your life commitments, test them and the imagined future plans they represent. Do the inspirations of this follow-up period (after the initial consolation) strike the heart gently? Do they create delight and peace? Is there a notable absence of electrical energy or nervous urgency toward immediate action?

Or do the inspirations and ideas of this follow-up period strike the heart violently? Do they disturb the heart with electrical excitement and a compelling urgency to immediately enact the good ideas or plans being pondered? This latter effect is a clear sign that the inspirations and ideas will lead you away from life and love—fruit that endures to eternity—no matter how enlightened these ideas seem.

Be attentive! Be gentle as a dove and wise as a serpent. Honor the process of change. Wait for the signs of peace and humility, and test the decisions being pondered.

Conclusion

Spiritual discernment is an art that takes time to master. Its first phase involves knowing the objective rights and wrongs of thoughts, words, and deeds as taught by the Commandments, Christ, and the teaching Church. Spiritual discernment advances when you consciously attend to your affective/spiritual states and become aware of spiritual movements that are present in your life story. Next, you need to familiarize yourself with the language and signatures of the two different voices: that of the Divine Inspirer and that of the counter-inspirer.

Finally, you need to learn to trust your decision-making based on what you have learned from St. Ignatius's experience and wisdom. This means confronting fears that, in the past, incited cowardice on your part. It also means confronting narcissism's illusions that, in the past, incited self-satisfaction on your part. Confronting both of these will feel difficult, but you must trust Ignatius's wisdom and act rightly. You will make mistakes. But learn from your mistakes, always trusting God's infinite mercy. God has infinite patience for those honestly struggling to live a new life in Christ.

In all of this, God will be your support and guide. Turn your attention and heart to God. God will give you the insight, wisdom, and strength necessary to develop your spiritual self. Do not be fearful or discouraged as you gradually integrate the art of spiritual discernment into your life. The Divine Inspirer will offer all of the graces and insights needed to lead you home. Be not afraid!

Dr. Schuchts' Reflection ~ Week Forty

Additional Guidelines on Life Choices

Congratulations for your dedication to the process of spiritual growth and deeper healing throughout these *Forty Weeks*. More importantly, thank God for his grace, as He has been actively sustaining you throughout this time.

Celebrating this "accomplishment" is also a time of sobriety. Now that the discipline of the Forty Weeks is complete, it is essential that you decide how will you continue to incorporate these rules of discernment into your daily life.

This is a good time to apply Ignatius' "Guidelines on Life Choices". Though these rules are directed towards major life changes, there is no more important decision than how you are going to continue to *abide in Christ*, every day of your life.

I encourage you to spend some time reading and reflecting on Fr. Watson's meditation on John 15: "Abide in Me" at the conclusion of this work. Nothing in your spiritual life is more critical than your dedication to abide in Christ consistently. Every other decision in your day-to-day existence flows from this most essential life choice.

When you pursue this primary relationship of abiding with Christ above all else, you will consistently make good life decisions. When you don't, your life will be marked by emptiness, and you will make many ill-advised decisions.

Many years ago, the Holy Spirit awakened me to this truth, through Jesus' words in John 15: "I am the vine, you are the branches." Though I heard this passage many times, I had missed Jesus' warning: "apart from me you can do *nothing*."

I began to see that I was doing many things apart from Christ that were fruitless, useless, worthless, empty, and vain, because I was acting from narcissism and not actively abiding in Him.

Prior to this awakening, I was in a very dangerous season of my life, without knowing it. I was being blinded by the seductive counter-inspirations of the enemy tempting me to make a major life decision-- to end my marriage and break up my family.

This came in the afterglow of a spiritual high from a retreat, and in the wake of accomplishing many of my life goals--starting our family, getting a degree, establishing a private practice, and purchasing a new home.

But after all the accomplishments, and when the spiritual high waned, my heart still felt empty. I was vainly searching for something to fill the void. I was not aware that the cracks within my broken heart, from my family and childhood wounds, had left me vulnerable to the lies of the enemy. Moreover, my narcissistic self-reliance had shielded my vision: I could not recognize this deeper pain and shame that was embedded in the hidden recesses of my heart.

I was reacting out of fear and pursuing illusions of happiness that had been planted in my mind and heart by the enemy. I will be ever grateful to God that He began the process of healing and deeper conversion through this passage of Scripture, by teaching me how essential it is to *abide in Christ*, and how vain it is to do otherwise.

Now that you have walked through these Forty Weeks, and have greater insight, I encourage you to look back through your life to see what the influence behind your major life choices has been. Your choices to embrace celibacy and to become a priest are most assuredly inspirations from the Holy Spirit. Any voices that tempt you to doubt your vocation or your capacity for chastity are obviously the work of the enemy.
Similarly, the movements of your heart and mind in the direction of faith,

hope, and love are from the Divine Inspirer. Those movements away from trusting and loving God are from the enemy's counter inspirations.

All that we have been discussing throughout these Forty Weeks can be summarized and easily remembered by the acronym "I AM."

Notice Jesus says "I AM the vine." He is referring to his authentic nature, in keeping with God's self-revelation to Moses at the burning bush. This is God's authentic name: "I AM Who AM." (Ex. 3:14).

Along with His name, God revealed his character ("I am kind and merciful, slow to anger and abounding in steadfast love"). He also promises to be present with his people ("I will be with you").

The Catechism explains it this way: "God, who reveals his name as "I AM", reveals himself as the God who is always there, present to his people in order to save them (CCC 207).

Your Sacred Story is written in the Sacred Heart of Christ. You can count on Him always being kind and compassionate with you in order to heal you.

This is a great assurance as we make our Life Choices. God, I AM, is always there to lead us and guide us in the way we should go.

As an acronym, I AM stands for:

I-Inspirations   A-Abiding   M-Movements.

Being led by the *Inspirations* of the Holy Spirit will increase your capacity to *Abide* in Christ. As you abide, you will also learn to attend to the *Movements* of your own heart, the hearts of others, and to the movements of the Holy Spirit within and around you.

As you actively abide in Christ, you will become ever more sensitive to the counter-inspirations of the enemy, and attentive to the things that pull you out of that posture of abiding.

In doing so, you will recognize the movements of your heart leading you away from God and into self-reliance.

If you remember to live these guidelines for spiritual discernment, they will assist you in living your priesthood in Christ as a Sacred Story. You will also have a great impact in the lives of all you serve.

May God be with you and continue to heal you, solidifying your identity as beloved son, and strengthening you to carry out the most important mission on the face of the earth—Christ's priestly ministry which he has chosen to share with you!

These comments from your brother priests summarize their experience of this week and the entire Forty Weeks:

✠ *One thing I learned is that we need to go to the source of our spiritual desolation, to the depths of our spiritual, psychological and physical wounds, in order to grow in wisdom and empower our ministry as confessor, preacher and in pastoral direction. The ministry will thus bear fruit and many people will be transformed through it.*

✠ *I was struck by the reference to doubting one's vocation. It would seem that there are times of wondering if I am doing what I should be or if something else would be better. Yet, these questions are generally because of focus on self.*

✠ *After concluding the Forty Weeks, the desire to get drunk disappeared. Just the grace of God! I have not set out intending to get drunk in that time, praise Jesus. My attachment to alcohol is still very real; but it is not destructive at the moment. I am keeping close eyes on it and turning to Jesus more and more.*

✠ I have enjoyed the company of my brother priests and the leading of Fr. Bill Watson and Dr. Bob Schuchts' on my forty-weeks journey of Sacred Story, which is written in the Sacred Heart of Christ.

✠ Abiding in my Lord and Savior Jesus Christ, I am determined to recognize the movements of my heart leading me away from God and into self-reliance in order to keep living my priesthood as a Sacred Story.

Immaculate Heart of Mary pray for us so that our hearts may be fully aligned with the Sacred Heart of your son Jesus.

☙

છ

The Lord is king, in splendor robed;
robed is the Lord and girt about with strength.
And he has made the world firm,
not to be moved.
Your throne stands firm from of old;
from everlasting you are, O Lord.
Your decrees are worthy of trust indeed;
holiness befits your house,
O Lord, for length of days.
(Ps 93:1–2,5)

જી

NOTES

Week Eternity

Living Your Sacred Story Daily

You have engaged all the spiritual disciplines for Sacred Story. Now is the time to ask God for help to be faithful to the relationship with Him that the prayer invites. Continue praying all the meditations in your fifteen-minute periods. Keep practicing all the other daily disciplines you have learned. You have all the necessary instruction. What follows are all the spiritual disciplines and insights of Sacred Story, arranged for easy reference.

If and when you have difficulties, temptations, stresses, fears, or anxieties associated with the daily consciousness exercise or Sacred Story prayer (when, not if!), read "Sacred Story Affirmations" (available at the beginning and at the end of this book) and the "Guidelines for Healing and Spiritual Growth" ("Foundational" [weeks 30–37] and "Integrated" [weeks 38–39]).

Remember the anxieties that Ignatius suffered as he began his journey. All spiritual and emotional crises soon pass. Christ Jesus will lead you home. Be not afraid!

✠ Prayer Upon Waking—Attune to the day ahead, and invite God's help.

This should take about fifteen to thirty seconds. After you wake up, lie in bed and prevision the day ahead. What does it hold? Are you anxious or energized about the day ahead? What specific issues/persons/events are causing the anxiety and/or energy? Ask God to help you deal constructively with the anxieties or challenges, and give thanks for the events/persons that inspire energy. Ask God to keep you aware as the day progresses. Using the special name you identified, offer the day to God.

If you so desire, on Sunday morning, you can do a brief previsioning of the week in the same way you do for a single day. You might consider looking ahead to any special feast days or saint's anniversaries that week. Ask for their intercession for your sacred story at the beginning of the week and on their feast day.

✠ Exercises During the Day—Awakening to your life
Each one of these should take no more than fifteen seconds. Consciously note the most significant events that inspire aggravation (anger, upset, fear, or temptation) or joy (gratitude, hope, faith). Every day holds many of these events. Consciously attend to the events that seem most notable by the strength of the reaction they incite in you. At the time these notable events transpire, take about ten seconds to 1) turn to God in your heart and using your personal name for God, ask to understand why the event gripped you negatively or positively, and 2) ask for graced insight to understand if the event is linked to something from the past that needs exploration/healing. Then go on with your day.

The more you engage this consciousness exercise in the day, the more readily you will remember these events at the time of your fifteen-minute prayer reflections on Creation, Presence, Memory, Mercy, and Eternity. Every single event that happens in the day is in some way linked to one of these five meditations and your sacred story. But please note: do this exercise for notable events only (two or three times daily at most!). You will know which to attend to, because they will grab you by the gut or the heart.

✠ Sacred Story Prayer at Midday—
Creation, Presence, Memory, Mercy, Eternity

✠ Exercises During the Day—Awakening to your life

✠ Sacred Story Prayer at Evening—
Creation, Presence, Memory, Mercy, Eternity

✠ Sacred Story Daily Journal—Note two significant events of the day. This should take no more than one minute. Before going to bed, jot down the two most notable events of the day—one negative (depleting hope) and one positive (increasing hope). All you need is to note two events. Write a short phrase to remember both what the event was and your reaction to it. Here are some examples:

Examples: Depleting Faith, Hope, and Love
office meeting—very dispirited about things working out in the future
letter from Joyce—very hurt that she excluded us from the event
my moral indiscretion on Saturday—How come I never seem to improve?

Examples: Increasing Faith, Hope, and Love
the incredible sunset Tuesday—Thank you God for your creation!
Saturday's confession—cried because of the priest's hopeful words
Bob's medical news—Thank you God for hearing our prayers!

✠ Prayer upon Retiring—
 Attune to your heart; invite God into your dreams.

✠ Week's-end Journal—Listen for trends, patterns, and links. This should take about ten minutes. Read your journal comments from the week. Notice any patterns or trends. Did any persons appear more than once? Can you discern patterns in the events depleting hope or increasing hope? Does a certain type of failure occur at "predictable times"? Jot down any patterns you discover. Then write the two most significant "depleting hope" and "increasing hope" events from the week.

Examples: Patterns Discovered, with Suggested Insights/Actions

Fear of being criticized always precedes my gossiping about others. Perhaps I need to ask God's help on why I fear being criticized and examine what in particular I fear. I will also pray to hold my tongue, to see what I can learn from this discipline.

Every time I meet Carol or someone who reminds me of Carol, I get angry. I need to ask God to help me to forgive Carol.

I have constant anxiety around regular confession, because I am afraid that the priest will think I am not a good person. I need to learn not to let fear control my decisions.

Three times my boss appeared in my journal. Do I need to make a decision?

I seem more negative than positive about God's love for me. (I need to challenge this feeling and affirm God's love by focusing on gratitude.)

Example of Strongest "Depleting Hope" from Daily Journal

My moral indiscretion on Saturday—how come I never seem to improve?

Example of Strongest "Increasing Hope" from Daily Journal

Saturday's confession—cried because of the priest's hopeful words

Example of Note to Myself

My two examples above seem to be connected. I fear that I never seem to improve, yet I also felt great hope when I went to confession. I will trust the feelings of hope and not the feelings based on fear.

✠ Month's-end Journal—Listen for trends, patterns, and links.
This should take no more than fifteen minutes. Read over your weekly summaries, and do the same winnowing process with them as you did for the individual days.

✠ Renew with Monthly Reconciliation—You will be powerfully graced.
This should take one hour total, between preparation and confession. Spend thirty minutes reading over your journal summaries and writing a one-page letter to Jesus. Use the same pattern as your whole-life confession. Do not write more than one page! Discipline yourself to tell the Lord the most essential things for which you need His help and forgiveness, and no more. Take your letter to Reconciliation, and make your confession. Keep your letters, and use them for prayer. You will see your growth and begin to understand much better the outlines of your own sacred story and the Sacred Story of Jesus as well.

✠ Consult the Affirmations Frequently—
   They are your thumbnail discernment aids.

✠ Consult the Guidelines for Healing and Spiritual Growth—
You need them.
Guidelines for Foundational Healing and Spiritual Growth: weeks 30–37
Guidelines for Integrated Healing and Spiritual Growth: weeks 38–39

✠ Live Your Faith—
 Engage its spiritual disciplines, serving God and neighbor.

Sacred Story Affirmations

My sacred story takes a lifetime to write.

Be not afraid! Fear comes from the enemy of my human nature.

The pathway to God's peace and healing runs
through my heart's brokenness, sin, fear, anger, and grief.

God resolves all my problems with time and patience.

℘

I will have difficulties in this life.

There are just two ways to cope with my difficulties.
One leads to life; one to death. I will choose life.

℘

"Impossible" is not a word in God's vocabulary.

Sacred Story practice leads to my freedom and authenticity,
but does not always make me feel happy.

℘

My life's greatest tragedies can be transformed
into my life's major blessings.

Times of peace and hope always give way
to times of difficulty and stress.

Times of difficulty and stress always give way
to times of peace and hope.

ဢ

I will not tire of asking God for help,
since God delights in my asking.

The urge to stop Sacred Story practice
always comes before my greatest breakthroughs.

ဢ

God gives me insights, not because I am better than others,
but because I am loved.

The insights and graces I need to move forward in life's journey
unfold at the right time.

ဢ

My personal engagement with Sacred Story prayer accomplishes,
through Christ, a work of eternal significance.

Inspirations can have a divine or a demonic source.
I pray for the grace to remember how to discern one from the other.

ဢ

Christ, who has walked before me, shares my every burden.

Christ, who has walked before me, will help me resolve every crisis.

Christ, who has walked before me, knows my every hope.

Christ, who has walked before me, knows everything I suffer.

Christ, who walks before me, will always lead me home to safety.

I will strive to curb temptations to react to people and events.

I will ask myself what causes my anger and irritation
at people and events.
I will seek to identify the source of my anger and irritation.

I will give thanks for what angers and upsets me,
for identifying their source will help to set me free.

I will strive to listen, watch, and pray. Listen, watch, and pray.
I will listen, watch, and pray!

Everyone has been mortally wounded spiritually, psychologically, and
physically by Original Sin and the loss of paradise.

Journeying with Christ to the roots of my sins and addictions
will help break their grip.

I will not waste time worrying about my sins and failures.
I will use my time wisely and ask God to help me
understand the source of my sins and failings.

I will trust that Christ came to heal all my wounds.

✵

I alone control Christ's ability to transform my life into a sacred story.
The process begins when I ask for the grace to
honestly name my sins and addictions.

The process continues when I invite Christ to illuminate my narcissism.

Only God's grace and mercy can write my sacred story.

I will strive daily to pick up the cross, for it leads to my life.

The closer I get to holiness, the more I will see and feel
sin's disorder in my life.

The more I experience sin's disorder, the more tempted I will be
to disbelieve my life as sacred story. The way through the temptation
is to surrender my powerlessness to God.

It is never too late to open my heart to Christ
and live my life as sacred story.

Christ, who is close to the brokenhearted, restores my lost innocence.

The path to my sacred story is
Creation, Presence, Memory, Mercy, and Eternity.

Two Benchmark Guidelines for Spiritual Discernment

To help your awakening and initiation into spiritual discernment, two benchmark guidelines will be beneficial in many life situations. It is important to understand that divine inspiration, or consolation, does not always feel good. Equally important is to realize that an unholy inspiration, or spiritual desolation, does not always feel bad. We will explore this seeming paradox in a later lesson. For now, it is sufficient to absorb the two benchmark guidelines and to understand that each is intended to influence the direction of our life in every thought, word, and deed either toward or away from God.

Benchmark One

Authentic Divine Inspirations, called Consolations, will:

1. Increase the heart's love for God and others,

2. Increase the virtues of docility, humility, and self-generosity, and

3. Not oppose the truths and teachings of Scripture, the Tradition, and the teaching Church.[32]

Consolation can be the consequence of the Divine Physician's Spirit working in you. This form of consolation helps strengthen your heart and soul, encouraging you to turn to God. Consolation helps you to choose thoughts, words, and deeds that express your authentic human nature made in the divine image.

Consolation can also be the consequence of the body/spirit aspect of your divinely shaped human nature. God created your human nature as a gift in the divine image and likeness. In spite of Original Sin's impact, cooperating with God's grace activates embedded life forces of your divinely shaped human nature, helping to heal biochemical, physiological, and emotional imbalances; energizing you; and enabling thoughts, words, and deeds that express your authentic human nature.

Benchmark Two

Authentic Counter-inspirations, called Desolations, will:

1. Increase narcissism, displacing God and others,

2. Decrease docility and humility and increase pride and self-satisfaction,

3. And arouse hungers and desires that, although they feel good, will typically contradict the truths and teachings proposed by the Scripture, Tradition, and the teaching Church. This is because the author of counter-inspirations is opposed to Christ and will lead you away from life and truth.

Counter-inspirations will produce desires that feel authentic because they are linked to fallen human nature's physical lusts and spiritual pride. They are the familiar default drives of a broken heart and a broken human nature.

Desolation can be the consequence of the enemy of human nature working in you. This form of desolation helps weaken your heart and soul, encouraging you to turn from God. Desolation helps you choose thoughts, words, and deeds that are opposed to your divinely shaped human nature.

Desolation can also be the consequence of your own fallen human nature. God created your human nature as a gift in the divine image and likeness. Yet because of Original Sin's impact, not cooperating with God's grace erodes the embedded life forces of your divinely shaped human nature, helping to destroy biochemical, physiological, and emotional balance; de-energizing you; and increasing thoughts, words, and deeds that are in opposition to your authentic human nature

When struggling with these issues, the "Guidelines for Integrated Healing and Spiritual Growth" will be of help (see weeks 38–39).

ATTENDING TO MY REACTION RESPONSES
OF ANGER, FEAR, AND GRIEF
General Awareness Exercises During the Day

When you experience your manifest sins and addictions

Using your own words, speak personally to Christ:

✠ Declare the specific sin, addiction, narcissistic habit, or destructive compulsion as a false lover.

✠ Describe the specific sin, addiction, narcissistic habit, or destructive compulsion as coming from the enemy of your human nature.

✠ Descend with Christ into your memory, to see and feel your first experience of this specific sin, addiction, narcissistic habit, or destructive compulsion, asking Him to compassionately reveal the stress fractures, loneliness, and wounds in your heart that it promised to satisfy.

✠ Denounce the specific sin, addiction, narcissistic habit, or destructive compulsion for its ruinous effect in your life.

✠ Decide for Christ to heal this wound, defuse the stress, anxiety, and fear feeding it, and transform its damaging effects on your life into sacred story.

When you are struggling with these issues, the "Guidelines for Foundational Healing and Spiritual Growth" (weeks 30–37) will be very helpful.

ɔ3

ATTENDING TO MY REACTION RESPONSES
OF ANGER, FEAR, AND GRIEF

Particular Awareness Exercises During the Day

When you have identified your particular sin of narcissism
and react with anger, anxiety, fear, or grief

Determine if Original Sin's principal manifestation in your life story is in the form of aggressive or passive narcissism. Take notice of the sudden anger, anxiety, fear, or grief that creeps up during your day. Pay particular attention to how these emotions might be touching your narcissism, manifesting as sin and contributing to addictive tendencies. For those one or two standout events in a day that capture your attention, do this short exercise below.

Speak to Christ from your heart:

✠ Ask to be conscious of what you are reacting to rather than reacting impulsively, without thinking.

✠ Ask to feel the heart's fear, temptation, anxiety, anger, and grief present in the reaction.

✠ Ask for knowledge—for graced insight—to begin dismantling this immature, damaging, and self-glorifying process, which for a passive narcissist is particularly depressing and for an aggressive narcissist is particularly electrifying.

✠ Ask who or what initiated this particular pattern of reaction—of overpowering or of blaming others—and why?

✠ Ask for courage to face the negative story of being a passive victim, because facing it can cause panic when you are used to being its slave. But confronting it can bring you peace and freedom.

☙

ORIGINAL SIN'S NARCISSISM IN MY LIFE STORY

The *Passive Narcissist*	The *Aggressive Narcissist*
SELF-IDENTIFIES AS A VICTIM.	SELF-IDENTIFIES AS A WINNER.
IS DETERMINED TO HAVE OTHERS NOTICE HOW SPECIAL ONE IS BY POINTING TO HIS UNFAIR SUFFERING.	IS DETERMINED TO HAVE OTHERS NOTICE HOW SPECIAL ONE IS BY DEFEATING ALL OPPONENTS.
IS CYNICAL AND EXCUSES BAD BEHAVIOR BY INSISTING IT IS JUSTIFIED BECAUSE OF HOW MUCH THEY HAVE SUFFERED.	IS CYNICAL AND EXCUSES BAD BEHAVIOR BY INSISTING IT IS JUSTIFIED BECAUSE THEY HAVE EARNED IT.
WALLOWS IN SELF-PITY WHEN HURT, WHETHER THE HURT IS REAL OR IMAGINED.	IS VINDICTIVE WHEN HURT, WHETHER THE HURT IS REAL OR IMAGINED.
BLAMES ANYONE WHO CRITICIZES OR OPPOSES THEM.	THREATENS ANYONE WHO CRITICIZES OR OPPOSES THEM.
PROTECTS HERSELF FROM BEING HURT AGAIN BY KEEPING WOUNDS AS FRESH AS POSSIBLE. IF ANYTHING IS TOO DIFFICULT OR PAINFUL, THEY WILL RETREAT INTO THOSE PAINFUL MEMORIES AND TURN INWARD, AWAY FROM OTHERS.	PROTECTS HERSELF FROM BEING HURT AGAIN BY ERADICATING VULNERABILITIES. IF ANYTHING IS TOO DIFFICULT OR PAINFUL, THEY WILL ACT IN A CONQUEROR ROLE AND DOMINATE OTHERS.
WINS BY EMOTIONAL MANIPULATION.	WINS BY DIRECT CONFRONTATION.
IS SECRETLY ATTACHED TO THEIR OWN WOUNDEDNESS.	IS SECRETLY ATTACHED TO THEIR POWER OF DEFEATING OTHERS.
IS TERRIFIED OF TAKING CONTROL AND PERSONAL RESPONSIBILITY AND HAS DIFFICULTY ADMITTING THIS TO ONESELF.	IS TERRIFIED OF SURRENDERING CONTROL AND BEING VULNERABLE AND HAS DIFFICULTY ADMITTING THIS TO ONESELF.

SACRED STORY INTEGRATION AND AWARENESS TEMPLATE

The Sacred Story practices awaken you to patterns of sin and dysfunction, grace and healing. The Divine Physician helps you identify and unmask the diseases caused by Original Sin, so that you can continue integrated healing and grow in interior freedom. In this wholeness, you are able to serve the Great Work of Reconciliation.

No thought, word, or deed is ever neutral. Everything one thinks, says, or does contributes to the work of the Divine Inspirer or the counter-inspirer. This is not a reason to become obsessed about everything you think, say, and do. It is a reminder to be attentive to the spiritual reality of life, and to labor with God's grace, to choose Christ.

As you listen to your life each day, keep the Sacred Story template in mind. You are seeking a comprehensive view of the enemy of human nature's work to keep you asleep, and a comprehensive view of the Divine Physician's work to awaken you. Watch your life with compassionate, patient, and merciful attention. That is the way of the Divine Physician, who is working for your redemption and complete, integrated healing. As your memory awakens and you become conscious of your life's issues, you will become sensitive and discerning of movements in both directions as shown by the arrows in the template following:

Manifest Sins

The Fruit or Ornamentation

Manifest fear, anger, and grief, and moral weaknesses, vices, addictions, and sinful habits that are the most visible to you.

Core Sins

The Trunk or Superstructure

Disobedience and narcissism, along with its fear, anger, and grief, that forms the trunk or superstructure of your daily life, feeding on originating sins and events.

Original Sins

The Roots or Foundation

Ancient, originating events that rooted the patterns of disobedience and narcissism along with their fear, anger and grief.

THE FOUR STAGES OF IGNATIUS'S CONVERSION

STAGE ONE

AWAKENING

Ignatius's Awakening Experience Mirrors →	*His Examen Prayer*
A GRACED EXPERIENCE OF GOD'S LOVE OPENED IGNATIUS TO... ↓	GIVE THANKS FOR FAVORS RECEIVED ↓
A DISSATISFACTION WITH VAIN FANTASIES, WHICH LED TO SURRENDERING TO HOLY DAYDREAMS, CHARACTERIZED BY CONSOLATION, WHICH IN TURN... ↓	PRAY FOR GRACE TO SEE CLEARLY ↓
CAUSED HIM TO REVIEW HIS LIFE AND ACTIONS, LEADING TO... ↓	GIVE A DETAILED ACCOUNT OF CONSCIENCE: GENERAL AND PARTICULAR ↓
GRIEF WITH YEARNING FOR PENANCE AND REPENTANCE FOR HIS PAST SINS, CULMINATING IN... ↓	ASK PARDON FOR ONE'S FAULTS ↓
IGNATIUS'S PASSION TO AMEND HIS LIFE AND A DESIRE TO LOVE GOD WHOLEHEARTEDLY.	RESOLVE AND AMEND TO SERVE GOD

STAGE TWO

FIRST CRISIS—SPEAKING TRUTH TO POWER

Ignatius's Experiences ➜	Discernment Principles Revealed
AN ENEMY VOICE EVOKED IGNATIUS'S FEAR OF A LIFELONG STRUGGLE WITH HIS SINFUL HABITS. ↓	THERE IS CONSCIOUS FEAR AND ANXIETY OVER SURRENDERING SINFUL AND ADDICTIVE HABITS. ↓
IGNATIUS REJECTED THE "ENEMY OF HUMAN NATURE" AND CONFRONTED THIS ENEMY'S FALSE PROMISES. ↓	ONE CONFRONTS THE THREATENING "VOICE" OF SIN AND ADDICTION WITH THE TRUTH THAT THEY BRING DEATH, NOT LIFE. ↓
PEACE WAS RESTORED AFTER IGNATIUS TRUTHFULLY NAMED SIN AND ADDICTION AS DEATH DEALING.	FINALLY, PEACE RETURNS AND ANXIETY DISSOLVES.

STAGE THREE

SECOND CRISIS—SURRENDERING CONTROL
AND ADMITTING POWERLESSNESS TO SAVE ONESELF

Ignatius's Experiences ➜	Discernment Principles Revealed
IGNATIUS'S STRUGGLE WITH SCRUPLES HID HIS VAINGLORY. ↓	THE INITIAL CONFRONTATION WITH ONE'S ROOT SIN ↓
IGNATIUS CONSTANTLY RECONFESSED TO SEEK SALVATION BY WILLPOWER ALONE. ↓	THE EFFORT TO CONTROL ONE'S ROOT SIN ONLY BY PERSONAL EFFORT OR FORCE OF WILL ↓
IGNATIUS EXPERIENCED SUICIDAL IMPULSES, DISGUST, AND THE DESIRE TO WALK AWAY FROM HIS NEWFOUND FAITH. ↓	DESPAIR AND DESIRE TO GIVE UP FAITH WHEN HUMAN EFFORT ALONE FAILS ↓
IGNATIUS TRACED THE SPIRIT OF DISGUST TO A DEMONIC SOURCE. ↓	INSIGHT THAT DESIRE TO REJECT THE SPIRITUAL JOURNEY IS A TEMPTATION ↓
IGNATIUS ABANDONED HIS COMPULSIVE CONFESSING OF PAST SINS.	THE ADMITTING OF POWERLESSNESS TO SAVE ONESELF AND THE SURRENDERING OF PRIDEFUL ACTIONS

STAGE FOUR

LIFE-LONG PATIENCE WHILE GOD WRITES OUR SACRED STORY

Ignatius's Experience	Universal Principle	Mystical Path
IGNATIUS, JUSTIFYING HIMSELF, ANXIOUSLY RECOILED AND FOCUSED ON HIS SINFULNESS. ↓	PANIC OVER ONE'S SALVATION DUE TO WEAKNESS AND SINFULNESS →	PURGATION ↓
IGNATIUS, NO LONGER FEARFUL, REGRETTED NOT HAVING RESPONDED SOONER TO GOD'S GRACES. ↓	SADNESS AT SLOWNESS OF ONE'S RESPONSE TO GOD'S LOVE AND INVITATION TO INTIMACY →	ILLUMINATION ↓
IGNATIUS FELT INTENSE JOY AT THE THOUGHT OF DYING AND BEING WITH GOD. →	AN ARDENT, ALL-EMBRACING LOVE OF GOD AND DESIRE FOR COMPLETE UNION WITH THE TRINITY →	UNION

SACRED STORY PRAYER MEDITATIONS

Pray the whole fifteen-minute Sacred Story prayer once or twice daily, and consciously repeat to Christ Jesus the five-word litany whenever you are in the grip of fear, anxiety, or grief or dealing with sins, addictions, and destructive compulsions.

CREATION
I believe God created everything in love and for love; I ask for heart-felt knowledge of God's love for me, and for
gratitude for the general and particular graces of this day.

PRESENCE
I believe God is present in each moment and event of my life, and I ask for the grace to awaken, see and feel where and how,
especially in this present moment.

MEMORY
I believe every violation of love committed by me and against me is in my memory, and I ask God to reveal them to me, especially those that have manifested themselves today, so I can be healed.

MERCY
I believe that forgiveness is the only path to healing and illumination. I beg for the grace of forgiveness, and the grace to forgive, especially for the general and particular failures of this day, and from my past.

ETERNITY
I believe the grace of forgiveness opens my heart, making my every thought, word, and deed bear fruit that endures to eternity. I ask that everything in my life serve Christ's Great Work of Reconciliation.

❀

Our Father

Our Father, who art in heaven,

hallowed be Thy name.

Thy Kingdom come, thy will be done,

on earth, as it is in heaven.

Give us this day our daily bread,

And

forgive us our trespasses,

as we forgive those who trespass against us.

Lead us not into temptation,

but deliver us from evil.

Amen.

(This is the prayer favored by Ignatius for this discipline.)

Suscipe

Take Lord, receive,

my liberty, my memory, my understanding, my entire will.

Whatsoever I have or hold,

You have given to me.

I surrender it all back to you

to be governed by your will.

Give me only Your love and grace.

This is enough for me,

and I ask for nothing more.

Amen.

(This is the prayer of St. Ignatius that concludes his Spiritual Exercises)

‪CZ‬

Your ways, O Lord, make known to me;
teach me your paths. Guide me in your truth and teach me,
for you are God my savior, and for you I wait all the day.
Good and upright is the Lord; thus he shows sinners the way.
He guides the humble to justice, and teaches the humble his way.
All the paths of the Lord are kindness and constancy
toward those who keep his covenant and his decrees.
The friendship of the Lord is with those who fear him,
and his covenant, for their instruction.
(Ps 25:4–5,8–9,10,14)

‪8‬

NOTES

Abide in Me

A Daily Relationship with Christ as Savior,
Divine Physician, and Lord of All

I invite you to pray with the first few verses of chapter fifteen from the Gospel of St. John. Take as many minutes, hours, or days as you wish to pray with St. John. There is no hurry.

> I am the true vine, and my Father is the vinedresser. Every branch of mine that bears no fruit, he takes away, and every branch that does bear fruit he prunes, that it may bear more fruit. You are already made clean by the word which I have spoken to you. Abide in me, and I in you. As the branch cannot bear fruit by itself, unless it abides in the vine, neither can you, unless you abide in me.
>
> I am the vine, you are the branches. He who abides in me, and I in him, he it is that bears much fruit, for apart from me you can do nothing. If a man does not abide in me, he is cast forth as a branch and withers; and the branches are gathered, thrown into the fire and burned. If you abide in me, and my words abide in you, ask whatever you will, and it shall be done for you. By this my Father is glorified, that you bear much fruit, and so prove to be my disciples.

As the Father has loved me, so have I loved you; abide in my love. If you keep my commandments, you will abide in my love, just as I have kept my Father's commandments and abide in his love. These things I have spoken to you, that my joy may be in you, and that your joy may be full. (Jn 15:1–11)

The Ignatian Examen that inspires Sacred Story prayer became an active part of my Jesuit life in 1994. Having entered the Society of Jesus in 1973, I had already lived for twenty years as a Jesuit—eight of those years as a priest. My practice of this prayer was inconstant for many years. By most measures, one could say that I had a Christian vocation. I mean this in much the same way that one looking at a Catholic married couple with children or a single person doing service work would agree that each of these persons has a Christian vocation.

A life of prayer and daily Mass, a yearly eight-day retreat, and a fair amount of theological living (faith-oriented reading plus lots of God/Church conversations) made me feel I had a real religious life. And I did. The question for me had become instead: was I fully living a Christian vocation? The answer to that is much more complex. For simplicity's sake, let me say that I have learned more clearly that a Christian vocation is not equivalent to simply belonging to a religious order. To use an analogy, a Christian marriage is different from being Catholic and married with children.

My Christian vocation requires that I daily open myself to Jesus and allow my actions, emotions, desires, loves, hurts, fears, and plans (especially my precious plans) to be shared with and shaped by Jesus's influence. Sharing means that I submit myself to Jesus and let Him have a say in what I am doing and whom I am daily becoming, what I hold on to and what I relinquish. Acting in a Christian way means that I no longer belong to myself. Rather, I belong to Christ.

Some good friends of mine who have been married for several years recently shared with me one of the biggest adjustments they have had to make as a result of being married. They can no longer make plans in blissful isolation but have to consult with each other about practically every aspect of their lives. This consultative sharing can be both a joy and an annoyance.

Each one is called out of the prison of their own ego and invited to love, sacrifice, and make adjustments so that the other can grow and flourish. We really grow when we are called out of ourselves. But there is joy in sharing intimately in the life of the Beloved. We are created for the joy of sharing intimately in the life of the other. We are made in the image and likeness of God who is relationship.

A Christian vocation requires an intimate relationship with Christ. It requires making this relationship a priority on a daily basis. Sacred Story prayer, more than any other spiritual discipline I have encountered in my forty years in religious life, brings me face-to-face with Christ in a relationship that calls me out of myself. It is the most effective path that has enabled me to be true to the man and priest that God desires me to be.

It is not always easy, and I do not want to minimize the challenge it has been in terms of my honesty and openness. It is a joy and an annoyance for exactly the same reasons as with any serious relational commitment. I have had moments of aggravation and difficulty in praying Sacred Story. I have also experienced times when I did not want to pray because I knew I would be confronted with things I would prefer to ignore.

Here is a typical example. Some time ago, I was struggling internally with someone who, I judged, had wronged me. I was hurt, frustrated, and upset from what I perceived to be an injustice against myself. I discovered I was not at all upset when this person experienced misfortunes, for I felt this person deserved it. In prayer, I was not speaking with Jesus about this person. Instead I found myself rehearsing conversations in my head about how I had been wronged. My focus was on myself.

One day I was awakened to my lack of Christian charity. Instinctively I understood that I needed to bring my feelings about this person to Jesus, and yet, I resisted. A part of my heart wanted to simply rehearse my justified hurts. It took several Sacred Story prayer periods for me to begin to speak from my heart to Christ about what I was feeling. The insight that I needed to reach out and forgive this person came in a split second. I was also able to accept some of the fault lines in my own personality, which may have contributed to the initial difficulties. It is amazing how that clarity comes with honesty. This was a graced experience!

However, upon leaving the time of Sacred Story prayer, a new inspiration took hold. Perhaps it is unwise to forgive? I could lose ground. The re-emerging frustration and darkened spirit—the counter-inspiration—accompanying this new inspiration was in marked contrast to the peacefulness I had experienced previously in the time of Sacred Story prayer. In testing the spiritual inspirations, it was clear which inspiration was from the Divine Inspirer and which inspiration was from the counter-inspirer.

Honestly, I was strongly tempted to ignore the truth of my spiritual discernment and go with the refusal to forgive. But I was being invited by God to disarm. I was invited to be vulnerable. It was an invitation to greater spiritual freedom, the freedom that Ignatius calls detachment. Freedom sounds good, but it is not something we always really want.

This event was a wake-up call, because it clearly presented the difficult choice of forgiveness. It may sound odd, but it gave me the conviction that Jesus is interested in everything I am doing. Every thought, word, and deed I have is important to Christ. He wants to be part of everything I experience. Sacred Story, prayed faithfully, has made me aware of what being in relationship with Jesus means. I feel the effects of the surrender that is necessary for a real relationship with Jesus, and I feel it in a particularly powerful way twice a day. I have chosen to make spiritual surrender the center of my Jesuit life. And praying Sacred Story prayer has revealed how many areas of my daily life I keep off-limits from Christ.

A strong intellectual tradition is a characteristic of the Society of Jesus; it is a good in and of itself. But there is something that Ignatius wanted Jesuits to value above learning: virtue, the spiritual life, and the surrender of our will and our hearts to Christ. The human gifts we cultivate only reach their fruitfulness in light of a well-grounded spiritual life. In section 10 of the Jesuit Constitutions, entitled "How the Whole Body of the Society is to be Preserved and Increased in its Well-being," Ignatius says the following:

> Thus it appears that care should be taken in general that all the members of the Society devote themselves to the solid and perfect virtues and to spiritual pursuits, and attach greater importance to them than to learning and other natural and human gifts. For these interior gifts are necessary to make those exterior means efficacious for the end which is being sought. (part X [813] 2)

This advice is written for Jesuits, and for the care and growth of the Society of Jesus. Yet it offers good pragmatic Ignatian wisdom that is applicable to any vocation or situation in the Church. Human gifts and qualities reach their perfection and the height of their potency when the bearer of those gifts and/or qualities is grafted to the vine of Christ— when they surrender to Christ.

This holds true for the talents of the athlete, the intellectual acumen of the college student, the artistic skills of the singer or architect, the healing gifts of the doctor or nurse, the ministry of religious and priests, the leadership skills of the politician and the professional business person, and the love of husband and wife for each other and for their children.

The personal decision I face daily—twice daily—is how much of my life will I allow to be grafted onto the vine of Christ? How much will I allow myself to abide in His Love? Jesus must have been looking at grapevines when He spoke this passage from John's Gospel. The vine or stalk is the source of all nutrients. Only shoots which grow directly from it, or have been grafted onto it, bear fruit. As I look back over my life, I can see that I have produced all sorts of fruit by my own effort.

What has become a much more important question at this point is, how much of what I produce is the fruit of my relationship with Jesus? In other words, have I allowed myself to become a "daily disciple" of Jesus by being in relationship with Him? Am I grafted onto the vine of Christ?

The bottom line of my experience of Sacred Story is that I am being challenged to open all of my heart and my life to God's grace. While the commitment to the Jesuits and the priesthood always felt full-time and lifelong, the relationship with Jesus seemed to have an on-again, off-again feel to it. Quite frankly, I was more in control than Christ. Now I feel that I have truly begun to commit to Jesus. Twice daily I need to come to Him with my ups and downs, my joys and angers, my loves and victories, my failures and grief, and my constant need.

My constant need: what does that mean? It means that Sacred Story prayer makes me more aware of my weaknesses, my failures, and my need for redemption. I have been graced with the eyes to see the reason for Christ's redeeming sacrifice, more clearly than ever before. It is a sacrifice and grace I cannot live without. Perhaps it is the same discovery of the alcoholic or drug addict. One day, the addict finally wakes up and realizes that the life they thought they controlled is actually out of control.

The only way to salvation is to surrender to love's sobriety and embrace. The alcoholic genuinely in touch with the truth of his life knows he is always recovering and is never fully recovered. He must live constantly with the knowledge of his vulnerability and turn to God for help and aid. It is a life of submission, humility, and holy dependence.

Is the invitation to submission, humility, and holy dependence the best way for me to convince you to stay committed to Sacred Story prayer? Is this good marketing? Perhaps not, but I am convinced that while your issues may be different from mine, your experience will pull you into the same position of humility, submission, and dependency on God when confronted with the truth of your weakness and need.

What could possibly be attractive about living this way? Praying and living Sacred Story enables a person to be vulnerable, humbly submissive, and dependent on God. I can rely on Jesus, who has promised to give me what I need: "If you remain in me and my words remain in you, ask for whatever you want and it will be done for you" (Jn 15:7). These words utterly change a person and her worldview. Jesus offers this relationship so that her joy "may be full."

How so? Because I experience that even in the weakest and most vulnerable condition of my life, Love does not walk away from me. Love has irrevocably committed Himself to me. He sacrificed for me so that I could be whole, and He wants the knowledge of this great love to be known by me on the most intimate level. He has also promised that this life of discipleship gives great glory to the Father in heaven. Allowing myself to abide in His love will bear fruit that will give glory to the Father of Jesus Christ. What an awesome reality!

At the beginning of a retreat or in my daily Sacred Story prayer, I try to commit to this relationship. The renewal of my vocational commitment to Christ in the daily engagement with Sacred Story prayer is a means to deepen the knowledge of my radical dependence on God. It fosters the joy of a personal relationship with Christ Jesus that grounds me and opens me up to the deepest yearnings of my heart.

The more I open my heart to a serious relationship with Christ, the more I come to understand the joy for which I have been created. You also have been created for this joy. That is why I am confident you will remain in the embrace of Sacred Story and the Lord Jesus, who loves you beyond all reckoning. The Love that grounds the universe holds you in His Heart.

Ↄℬ

Glorious Lord Christ,
You who are the first and the last,
The living and the dead and the risen again;
You who gather into your exuberant unity
Every beauty, every affinity, every energy,
Every mode of existence;
It is you to whom my being cried out with a desire
As vast as the universe,
"In truth you are my Lord and my God."[33]

ℰↄ

NOTES

NOTES

NOTES

NOTES

NOTES

NOTES

NOTES

About the Author

Fr. William Watson, S.J., D.Min., has spent over thirty years developing Ignatian programs and retreats. He has collaborated extensively with Fr. Robert Spitzer in the last fifteen years on Ignatian retreats for corporate CEOs. In the spring of 2011, he launched a nonprofit institute to bring Ignatian spirituality to Catholics of all ages and walks of life. The Sacred Story Institute is promoting third-millennium evangelization for the Society of Jesus and the Church by using the time-tested Examination of Conscience of St. Ignatius.

Fr. Watson has served as director of retreat programs at Georgetown University, vice president for mission at Gonzaga University, and provincial assistant for international ministries for the Oregon Province of the Society of Jesus. He holds master's degrees in divinity and in pastoral studies 1986, from Weston Jesuit School of Theology: Cambridge, Mass.). He received his Doctor of Ministry degree in 2009 from The Catholic University of America in Washington, DC.

Sacred Story Press
Seattle, USA
sacredstorypress.com

Sacred Story Press explores dynamic new dimensions of classic Ignatian spirituality, based on St. Ignatius's Conscience Examen in the Sacred Story prayer method, pioneered by Fr. Bill Watson, S.J. We are creating a new class of spiritual resources. Our publications are research-based, authentic to the Catholic Tradition, and designed to help individuals achieve integrated spiritual growth and holiness of life.

We Request Your Feedback

The Sacred Story Institute welcomes feedback on Forty Weeks. Contact us via email or letter (see below). Give us ideas, suggestions, and inspirations for how to make this a better resource for Catholics and Christians of all ages and walks of life. Please also contact us for bulk orders and group discounts.

admin-team@sacredstory.net
Sacred Story Institute & Sacred Story Press
1401 E. Jefferson, Suite 405
Seattle, Washington 98122

JOHN PAUL II Healing Center
Transformation in the Heart of the Church

Dr. Bob Schuchts' Program for Healing the Whole Person

Experience Jesus in His mission of healing! Physical, spiritual and emotional healing, central to the Church's life and 2,000 year tradition, come to life today. The uniquely engaging format will help you see and experience God's healing love through teaching, prayer, personal reflection, adoration and the Sacraments.

Visit: https://jpiihealingcenter.org/healing/

RECLAIM SEXUAL HEALTH
GOD'S PLAN FOR YOUR LIFE!

RECLAiM Sexual Health is a private anonymous, online recovery program for those struggling with compulsive pornography use and other unhealthy sexual behaviors. Combining The Brain Science of Behavior Change, insights from Theology of the Body, and the full support of our faith, RECLAiM is a powerful tool for reclaiming sexual health and holiness. While rooted in Catholic teaching and understanding, this program is open to people of all faiths who desire to reclaim sexual health. Want to get started?

Visit www.reclaimsexualhealth.com

GHISLAINE HOWARD

The art in this book is by Ghislaine Howard who was named as Woman of The Year in 2008 for her contributions to art and society. She is a painter of powerful and expressive means. She first came to public attention with her ground-breaking exhibition concerning pregnancy and birth, the first of its kind, at Manchester City Art Gallery. The exhibition, *A Shared Experience*, attracted much critical acclaim.

Her art is present in many public and private collections, including the Royal Collection. A major monograph, *The Human Touch*, dedicated to her work, was published in October of 2016.

http://ghislainehoward.com

METHODIST MODERN ART COLLECTION

The art for this book was approved for use by the Methodist Modern Art Collection. It exists because Methodist people in the 1960s collected works of art in order to open up faith conversations, and then gave their collection to the British Methodist Church. The works have been bought or commissioned with money given specifically for the purpose; their acquisition has not been a charge on general Methodist Church funds.

www.methodist.org.uk/artcollection"

ENDNOTES

1   Paul Doncoeur, SJ, The Heart of Ignatius, (Baltimore: Helicon, 1959), 34.

2   The Soul of Sponsorship explores the relationship of Bill Wilson, co-founder of Alcoholics Anonymous, and his Jesuit spiritual adviser and friend, Father Ed Dowling, SJ, whom he met in 1940. Among the issues Bill Wilson still dealt with as a sober alcoholic were depression, unhealthy dependencies and knowing God's will and plan. Fr. Dowling taught Bill Wilson about discernment, as handed down by Ignatius of Loyola through the Jesuits. Bill learned to listen to his desires, be aware of his inner dynamics, and tune into the action of God within. AA's Twelve Steps and Twelve Traditions, published in 1952, , reflects much that Bill learned from his friend.

3. There is no need to read the Scripture passages during your fifteen-minute prayer periods. If your heart leads you to read these Scripture passages apart from the fifteen-minute prayer periods, you are encouraged to follow your heart!

4. A suggestion: Use this name to address God every time you naturally think of God throughout the day. For example, you may say in your heart before a meeting: "Lord Jesus, be with me now." Say it, and then just move on with your meeting. Do not make this a tedious exercise, but one that feels natural and relaxed. You do not have to think long and hard about God. The purpose of this spontaneous prayer is just a short, friendly reminder of God's presence. Use this name if you find yourself conversing with God during the day.

5. Ignatius is very specific that spiritual exercises should be kept to the exact time allotted for them. The only exception he makes is that an exercise may be extended by one minute if one is having difficulty, or is experiencing some upset or turmoil. Ignatius believed that this brief extension of an exercise in times of difficulty works positively to help us confront and not be cowed by spirits of darkness and the psychological and emotional anxieties they manipulate.

6   "Likewise, he behaves like a military leader setting about the conquest and seizure of the object of his desire. For the commander of an army, after setting up his camp and inspecting the fortifications and defenses of the castle, attacks it at its weakest point; and in the same way the enemy of our human nature makes his rounds to inspect all our virtues, theological, cardinal and moral, and where he finds us weakest and in greatest need as regards eternal salvation, there it is that he attacks and tries to take us." Saint Ignatius of Loyola: Personal Writings. Joseph Munitiz & Philip Endean, Penguin Books, London. 1996, p. 351.

7. If you feel called, you can reflect on the entire Decalogue as enumerated in the Catechism of the Catholic Church (CCC, 561–672). You can either purchase an inexpensive paperback, or you can access the text online: http://www.vatican.va/archive/ccc_css/archive/catechism/p3s2c1a1.htm

8. "Compulsion, impaired control, persistence, irritability, relapse, and craving—these are all the hallmarks of addiction—any addiction." Gabor Maté, In the Realm of Hungry Ghosts: Close Encounters with Addiction (Berkeley: North Atlantic Books, 2010), 136-9.

9. See the material on the previous page from RECLAiM Sexual Health.

10. "The Life Model: Living from the Heart Jesus Gave You", James Friesen et al., Shepherds House Inc., 2000

11. Catechism of the Catholic Church (CCC) 1469--John Paul II, RP 31, 5.

12. Our studies have shown that those who committed to two times a day for prayer were more faithful in cultivating a sustainable daily practice. Also, research revealed that those who practiced a simple logbook or journal exercise were also more faithful to the prayer disciplines.

13. See endnote 13.

14. From the Catechism of the Catholic Church [CCC #1854-64] on THE GRAVITY OF SIN: MORTAL AND VENIAL SIN:

    Sins are rightly evaluated according to their gravity. The distinction between mortal and venial sin, already evident in Scripture, became part of the tradition of the Church. It is corroborated by human experience.

    Mortal sin destroys charity in the heart of man by a grave violation of God's law; it turns man away from God, who is his ultimate end and his beatitude, by preferring an inferior good to him. Venial sin allows charity to subsist, even though it offends and wounds it.

    Mortal sin, by attacking the vital principle within us - that is, charity - necessitates a new initiative of God's mercy and a conversion of heart which is normally accomplished within the setting of the sacrament of reconciliation: When the will sets itself upon something that is of its nature incompatible with the charity that orients man toward his ultimate end, then the sin is mortal by its very object, whether it contradicts the love of God, such as blasphemy or perjury, or the love of neighbor, such as homicide or adultery. But when the sinner's will is set upon something that of its nature involves a disorder, but is not opposed to the love of God and neighbor, such as thoughtless chatter or immoderate laughter and the like, such sins are venial.

    For a sin to be mortal, three conditions must together be met: "Mortal sin is sin whose object is grave matter and which is also committed with full knowledge and deliberate consent."

    Grave matter is specified by the Ten Commandments, corresponding to the answer of Jesus to the rich young man: "Do not kill, Do not commit adultery, Do not steal, Do not bear false witness, Do not defraud, Honor your father and your mother." The gravity of sins is more or less great: murder is graver than theft. One must also take into account who is wronged: violence against parents is in itself graver than violence against a stranger.

Mortal sin requires full knowledge and complete consent. It presupposes knowledge of the sinful character of the act, of its opposition to God's law. It also implies a consent sufficiently deliberate to be a personal choice. Feigned ignorance and hardness of heart do not diminish, but rather increase, the voluntary character of a sin.

Unintentional ignorance can diminish or even remove the imputability of a grave offense. But no one is deemed to be ignorant of the principles of the moral law, which are written in the conscience of every man. The promptings of feelings and passions can also diminish the voluntary and free character of the offense, as can external pressures or pathological disorders. Sin committed through malice, by deliberate choice of evil, is the gravest.

Mortal sin is a radical possibility of human freedom, as is love itself. It results in the loss of charity and the privation of sanctifying grace, that is, of the state of grace. If it is not redeemed by repentance and God's forgiveness, it causes exclusion from Christ's kingdom and the eternal death of hell, for our freedom has the power to make choices for ever, with no turning back. However, although we can judge that an act is in itself a grave offense, we must entrust judgment of persons to the justice and mercy of God.

One commits venial sin when, in a less serious matter, he does not observe the standard prescribed by the moral law, or when he disobeys the moral law in a grave matter, but without full knowledge or without complete consent.

Venial sin weakens charity; it manifests a disordered affection for created goods; it impedes the soul's progress in the exercise of the virtues and the practice of the moral good; it merits temporal punishment. Deliberate and unrepented venial sin disposes us little by little to commit mortal sin. However venial sin does not break the covenant with God. With God's grace it is humanly reparable. "Venial sin does not deprive the sinner of sanctifying grace, friendship with God, charity, and consequently eternal happiness."

While he is in the flesh, man cannot help but have at least some light sins. But do not despise these sins which we call "light": if you take them for light when you weigh them, tremble when you count them. A number of light objects makes a great mass; a number of drops fills a river; a number of grains makes a heap. What then is our hope? Above all, confession.

"Therefore I tell you, every sin and blasphemy will be forgiven men, but the blasphemy against the Spirit will not be forgiven." There are no limits to the mercy of God, but anyone who deliberately refuses to accept his mercy by repenting, rejects the forgiveness of his sins and the salvation offered by the Holy Spirit. Such hardness of heart can lead to final impenitence and eternal loss.

---

[15]   The Preamble [104] "On the Incarnation" Spiritual Exercises of St. Ignatius.
[16]. GOD WILLED HUMAN NATURE [CCC #362-8]:

The human person, created in the image of God, is a being at once corporeal and spiritual. The biblical account expresses this reality in symbolic language when it affirms that "then the LORD God formed man of dust from the ground, and breathed into his nostrils the breath of life; and man became a living being." [Gen 2:7.] Man, whole and entire, is therefore willed by God (emphasis supplied). In Sacred Scripture the term "soul" often refers to human life or the entire human person. [Cf. Mt 16:25-26; Jn 15:13; Acts 2:41.] But "soul" also refers to the innermost aspect of man, that which is of greatest value in him, [Cf. Mt 10:28; 26:38; Jn 12:27; 2 Macc 6:30.] that by which he is most especially in God's image: "soul" signifies the spiritual principle in man.

The human body shares in the dignity of "the image of God": it is a human body precisely because it is animated by a spiritual soul, and it is the whole human person that is intended to become, in the body of Christ, a temple of the Spirit: [Cf. 1 Cor 6:19-20; 15:44-45.]

Man, though made of body and soul, is a unity. Through his very bodily condition he sums up in himself the elements of the material world. Through him they are thus brought to their highest perfection and can raise their voice in praise freely given to the Creator. For this reason man may not despise his bodily life. Rather he is obliged to regard his body as good and to hold it in honor since God has created it and will raise it up on the last day. [GS 14 § 1; cf. Dan 3:57-80.]

The unity of soul and body is so profound that one has to consider the soul to be the "form" of the body: [Cf. Council of Vienne (1312): DS 902.] i.e., it is because of its spiritual soul that the body made of matter becomes a living, human body; spirit and matter, in man, are not two natures united, but rather their union forms a single nature.

The Church teaches that every spiritual soul is created immediately by God - it is not "produced" by the parents—and also that it is immortal: it does not perish when it separates from the body at death, and it will be reunited with the body at the final Resurrection. [Cf. Pius XII, Humani Generis: DS 3896; Paul VI, CPG § 8; Lateran Council V (1513): DS 1440.]

Sometimes the soul is distinguished from the spirit: St. Paul for instance prays that God may sanctify his people "wholly", with "spirit and soul and body" kept sound and blameless at the Lord's coming. [1 Thess 5:23.] The Church teaches that this distinction does not introduce a duality into the soul. [Cf. Council of Constantinople IV (870): DS 657.] "Spirit" signifies that from creation man is ordered to a supernatural end and that his soul can gratuitously be raised beyond all it deserves to communion with God. [Cf. Vatican Council I, Dei Filius: DS 3005; GS 22 § 5; Humani Generis: DS 3891.]

The spiritual tradition of the Church also emphasizes the heart, in the biblical sense of the depths of one's being, where the person decides for or against God. [Cf. Jer 31:33; Deut 6:5; 29:3; Isa 29:13; Ezek 36:26; Mt 6:21; Lk 8:15; Rom.5:5.]

17. MAN IN PARADISE [CCC #374-9]:

The first man was not only created good, but was also established in friendship with his Creator and in harmony with himself and with the creation around him, in a state that would be surpassed only by the glory of the new creation in Christ.

The Church, interpreting the symbolism of biblical language in an authentic way, in the light of the New Testament and Tradition, teaches that our first parents, Adam and Eve, were constituted in an original "state of holiness and justice". [Cf. Council of Trent (1546): DS 1511.] This grace of original holiness was "to share in divine life". [Cf. LG 2.]

By the radiance of this grace all dimensions of man's life were confirmed. As long as he remained in the divine intimacy, man would not have to suffer or die. [Cf. Gen 2:17; 3:16,19.] The inner harmony of the human person, the harmony between man and woman, [Cf. Gen 2:25.] and finally the harmony between the first couple and all creation, comprised the state called "original justice."

The "mastery" over the world that God offered man from the beginning was realized above all within man himself: mastery of self. The first man was unimpaired and ordered in his whole being because he was free from the triple concupiscence [Cf. 1 Jn 2:16.] that subjugates him to the pleasures of the senses, covetousness for earthly goods, and self-assertion, contrary to the dictates of reason.

The sign of man's familiarity with God is that God places him in the garden. [Cf. Gen 2:8.] There he lives "to till it and keep it." Work is not yet a burden [Gen 2:15; cf. 3:17-19] but rather the collaboration of man and woman with God in perfecting the visible creation. This entire harmony of original justice, foreseen for man in God's plan, will be lost by the sin of our first parents.

[18]. For Augustine, the problem was the will, not the body. He came to define Original Sin as narcissism, the turning of the will "to live according to oneself" (secundum se vivere). Here is his classic account from On the City of God, Book 14: (13) Moreover, our first parents fell openly into the sin of disobedience only because, secretly, they had begun to be guilty. Actually, their bad deed of their bad will was nothing else than pride. For "pride is the beginning of all sin" (Sir 10:13). And what is pride but an appetite for inordinate exaltation? Now exaltation is inordinate when the souls cuts itself off from the very Source to which it should keep close and somehow makes itself—and thus becomes—an end in itself. This takes place when the soul becomes inordinately pleased with itself, and such self-pleasing occurs when the soul falls away from the unchangeable Good which ought to please itself. Now this falling away is the soul's own doing, for if the will had merely remained firm in the love of that higher immutable Good which lighted its mind into knowledge and warmed its will into love, it would not have turned away in search of satisfaction in itself and, by so doing, have lost that light and warmth. And thus Eve would not have believed that the serpent's lie was true, nor would Adam have preferred the will of his wife to the will of God or have supposed this transgression of God's command was venial when he refused to abandon the partner of his life even if it meant a partnership of sin.

Our first parents, then, must have already fallen before they could do the evil deed, before they could commit the sin of eating the forbidden fruit. For such bad fruit could come only from a bad tree. That the tree became bad was contrary to its nature, because such a condition could come about only because of a defect of the will—and a defect is

518

whatever goes against nature. Notice, however, that such worsening by reason of a defect is possible only in a nature that had been created out of nothing. In a word, a nature is a nature because it is something made by God, but a nature falls away from That Which Is because the nature was made out of nothing." William Harmless, SJ, Augustine In His Own Words (Washington, DC: The Catholic University of America Press, 2010),351-2.

[19]. Ignatius was a great admirer of St. Francis of Assisi and it was the Franciscans who managed the holy sites in Jerusalem. There he could be near the sons of St. Francis and walk in the footsteps of Jesus.

[20]. "Brothers and sisters: The Spirit scrutinizes everything, even the depths of God. Among men, who knows what pertains to the man except his spirit that is within? Similarly, no one knows what pertains to God except the Spirit of God. We have not received the spirit of the world but the Spirit who is from God, so that we may understand the things freely given us by God. And we speak about them not with words taught by human wisdom, but with words taught by the Spirit, describing spiritual realities in spiritual terms. Now the natural man does not accept what pertains to the Spirit of God, for to him it is foolishness, and he cannot understand it, because it is judged spiritually. The one who is spiritual, however, can judge everything but is not subject to judgment by anyone. For "who has known the mind of the Lord, so as to counsel him?" But we have the mind of Christ." (I Corinthians 2: 10b–16)

A sermon by Pope St Leo the Great: I SHALL PUT MY LAWS WITHIN THEM:

Dearly beloved, when our Lord Jesus Christ was preaching the Gospel of the kingdom and healing various illnesses throughout the whole of Galilee, the fame of his mighty works spread into all of Syria, and great crowds from all parts of Judea flocked to the heavenly physician.

Because human ignorance is slow to believe what it does not see, and equally slow to hope for what it does not know, those who were to be instructed in the divine teaching had first to be aroused by bodily benefits and visible miracles so that, once they had experienced his gracious power, they would no longer doubt the wholesome effect of his doctrine. In order, therefore, to transform outward healings into inward remedies, and to cure men's souls now that he had healed their bodies, our Lord separated himself from the surrounding crowds, climbed to the solitude of a neighboring mountain, and called the apostles to himself.

From the height of this mystical site he then instructed them in the most lofty doctrines, suggesting both by the very nature of the place and by what he was doing that it was he who long ago had honored Moses by speaking to him. At that time, his words showed a terrifying justice, but now they reveal a sacred compassion, in order to fulfill what was promised in the words of the prophet Jeremiah: Behold the days are coming, says the Lord, when I shall establish a new covenant with the house of Israel and with the house of Judah. After those days, says the Lord, I shall put my laws within them and write them on their hearts.

And so it was that he who had spoken to Moses spoke also to the apostles. Writing in the hearts of his disciples, the swift hand of the Word composed the ordinances of the new covenant. And this was not done as formerly, in the midst of dense clouds, amid terrifying sounds and lightning, so that the people were frightened away from approaching the mountain. Instead, there was a tranquil discourse which clearly reached the ears of all who stood nearby so that the harshness of the law might be softened by the gentleness of grace, and the spirit of adoption might dispel the terror of slavery.

Concerning the content of Christ's teaching, his own sacred words bear witness; thus whoever longs to attain eternal blessedness can now recognize the steps that lead to that high happiness. Blessed, he says, are the poor in spirit, for theirs is the kingdom of heaven. It might have been unclear to which poor he was referring, if after the words Blessed are the poor, he had not added anything about the kind of poor he had in mind. For then the poverty that many suffer because of grave and harsh necessity might seem sufficient to merit the kingdom of heaven.

But when he says: Blessed are the poor in spirit, he shows that the kingdom of heaven is to be given to those who are distinguished by their humility of soul rather than by their lack of worldly goods. (Taken from Roman Catholic Office of Readings, book III, weeks of the year 6–34).

21. People today often form judgments about human nature based on the experience of human nature in its fallen state. We forget that at one point human nature, as a unity of body and spirit, was undivided: Our hearts were undivided. With the Fall, our hearts are divided and we can no longer easily determine right and wrong: "Ignorance of the fact that man has a wounded nature, inclined to the evil, gives rise to serious errors in the areas of education, politics, social action and morals." [CCC #407].

22. THE PRIMACY OF THE SPIRITUAL OVER THE MATERIAL:

Every year science grounded in a materialist-only view of the universe confronts inexplicable phenomena, indicating the primacy of the spiritual realm as the main animator of the physical world. Mario Beauregard's The Spiritual Brain is a work on this topic and the source of some of the ideas below. See also the classic work, The Healing Light by Agnes Sanford. Sanford's Christian healing ministry helped launch the Catholic Charismatic Renewal movement.

✠ Why does the placebo effect work, in which the mind creates curative processes reducing or eliminating ill and diseased states in the human organism?

✠ Why do repeated studies show that some persons are able to mentally affect physical objects outside themselves when the odds of this being mere chance are a trillion to one?

✠ Why are the neurological brain maps of individuals in deep prayer states (feeling connected to a reality outside themselves) identical to individuals actually in direct contact to other persons— with both maps displaying the radically complex neural brain states of real experiences involving human emotion, body representation, visual, motor imagery and spiritual perception?

✠ Why do deep spiritual experiences rewire the neural networks of the brain and lead to deep, long-lasting, attitudinal and behavioral changes such as growth in compassion, love for others, willingness to forgive and awareness of the unity of creation?

✠ Why, when persons are revived after clinical death (zero heart or brainwave activity), do they frequently possess vivid recall of all the events that took place while they were "dead"?

✠ Why, since the discovery of quantum theory, do some physicists affirm that the universe is more mental than physical in the way it behaves? (Richard Conn Henry "The Mental Universe," Nature 436, no. 29, July 7, 2005).

✠ Why can people with certain mental disorders be trained to rewire their neural networks using attentive consciousness (demonstrating that the mind creates the brain and not the other way around)?

23. From a sermon by St Bernard of Clairvaux, "On the Stages of Contemplation:"

Let us take our stand on the tower, leaning with all our strength on Christ, the most solid rock, as it is written: He has set my feet on a rock, he has guided my steps. Thus firmly established, let us begin to contemplate, to see what he is saying to us and what reply we ought to make to him. The first stage of contemplation, my dear brothers, is to consider constantly what God wants, what is pleasing to him, and what is acceptable in his eyes. We all offend in many things; our strength cannot match the rightness of God's will and cannot be joined to it or made to fit with it. So let us humble ourselves under the powerful hand of the most high God and make an effort to show ourselves unworthy before his merciful gaze, saying, "Heal me, Lord, and I shall be healed; save me and I shall be saved." And again, "Lord, have mercy on me; heal my soul because I have sinned against you."

Once the eye of the soul has been purified by such considerations, we no longer abide within our spirit in a sense of sorrow, but abide rather in the Spirit of God with great delight. No longer do we consider what is the will of God for us, but rather what it is in itself.

For our life is in his will. Thus we are convinced that what is according to his will is in every way better for us, and more fitting. And so, if we are concerned to preserve the life of our soul, we must be equally concerned to deviate as little as possible from his will.

Thus having made some progress in our spiritual exercise under the guidance of the Spirit who gazes into the deep things of God, let us reflect how gracious the Lord is and how good he is in himself. Let us join the Prophet in praying that we may see the Lord's will and frequent not our own hearts but the Lord's temple; and let us also say, My soul is humbled within me, therefore I shall be mindful of you.

These two stages sum up the whole of the spiritual life: when we contemplate ourselves we are troubled, and our sadness saves us and brings us to contemplate God; that contemplation in turn gives us the consolation of the joy of the Holy Spirit. Contemplating ourselves brings fear and humility; contemplating God brings us hope and love. (Sermo 5 de diversis, 4-5:: Opera omnia, Edit. Cisterc. 6, 1 [1970], 103-4)

Used in the Roman Catholic Office of Readings for Wednesday of the 23rd week in Ordinary Time with the accompanying biblical reading taken from Habakkuk 2:5-20).

From Gaudium et Spes

Although he was made by God in a state of holiness, from the very onset of his history man abused his liberty, at the urging of the Evil One. Man set himself against God and sought to attain his goal apart from God. Therefore man is split within himself. As a result, all of human life, whether individual or collective, shows itself to be a dramatic struggle between good and evil, between light and darkness. Indeed, man finds that by himself he is incapable of battling the assaults of evil successfully, so that everyone feels as though he is bound by chains. But the Lord Himself came to free and strengthen man, renewing him inwardly and casting out that "prince of this world" (John 12:31) who held him in the bondage of sin. For sin has diminished man, blocking his path to fulfillment.

The call to grandeur and the depths of misery, both of which are a part of human experience, find their ultimate and simultaneous explanation in the light of this revelation.

Though made of body and soul, man is one. Through his bodily composition he gathers to himself the elements of the material world; thus they reach their crown through him, and through him raise their voice in free praise of the Creator. For this reason man is not allowed to despise his bodily life, rather he is obliged to regard his body as good and honorable since God has created it and will raise it up on the last day. Nevertheless, wounded by sin, man experiences rebellious stirrings in his body. But the very dignity of man postulates that man glorify God in his body and forbid it to serve the evil inclinations of his heart.

Now, man is not wrong when he regards himself as superior to bodily concerns, and as more than a speck of nature or a nameless constituent of the city of man. For by his interior qualities he outstrips the whole sum of mere things. He plunges into the depths of reality whenever he enters into his own heart; God, Who probes the heart, awaits him there; there he discerns his proper destiny beneath the eyes of God. Thus, when he recognizes in himself a spiritual and immortal soul, he is not being mocked by a fantasy born only of physical or social influences, but is rather laying hold of the proper truth of the matter.

Man judges rightly that by his intellect he surpasses the material universe, for he shares in the light of the divine mind. By relentlessly employing his talents through the ages he has indeed made progress in the practical sciences and in technology and the liberal arts. In our times he has won superlative victories, especially in his probing of the material world and in subjecting it to himself. Still he has always searched for more penetrating truths, and finds them. For his intelligence is not confined to observable data alone, but can with genuine certitude attain to reality itself as knowable, though in consequence of sin that certitude is partly obscured and weakened.

The intellectual nature of the human person is perfected by wisdom and needs to be, for wisdom gently attracts the mind of man to a quest and a love for what is true and good. Steeped in wisdom, man passes through visible realities to those which are unseen.

Our era needs such wisdom more than bygone ages if the discoveries made by man are to be further humanized. For the future of the world stands in peril unless wiser men are forthcoming. It should also be pointed out that many nations, poorer in economic goods, are quite rich in wisdom and can offer noteworthy advantages to others.

It is, finally, through the gift of the Holy Spirit that man comes by faith to the contemplation and appreciation of the divine plan. (Vatican II—Gaudium et Spes: The Dignity of the Human Person (13-15).

24. The following section from the Church's Code of Canon Law describes the types of beliefs that are non-negotiable for faithful Catholics. This is not intended as a list of all those things one must adhere to in order to be considered a "faithful Catholic." The most important aspect is the docility of spirit granted by God that enables one to approach the teachings and the authority of the Church with trust, instead of a spirit of obstinacy. The spirit of docility, trust, humility and obedience characterize God's presence in one's soul.

A person must believe with divine and Catholic faith all those things contained in the word of God, written or handed on, that is, in the one deposit of faith entrusted to the Church, and at the same time proposed as divinely revealed either by the solemn magisterium of the Church or by its ordinary and universal magisterium which is manifested by the common adherence of the Christian faithful under the leadership of the sacred magisterium; therefore all are bound to avoid any doctrines whatsoever contrary to them. Each and every thing which is proposed definitively by the magisterium of the Church concerning the doctrine of faith and morals, that is, each and every thing which is required to safeguard reverently and to expound faithfully the same deposit of faith, is also to be firmly embraced and retained; therefore, one who rejects those propositions which are to be held definitively is opposed to the doctrine of the Catholic Church. [Can. 750 §1, §2].

25. Ignatius provides wise counsel for those tempted by evil thoughts and feelings and helps us know how to conduct ourselves during such times. He writes this advice to Sister Theresa Rejadell:

"I insist that you think of God as loving you, as I have no doubt He does, and that you correspond with this love and pay no attention whatever to the evil thoughts, even if they are obscene or sensual (when they are not deliberate), nor of your cowardice or tepidity. For even St. Peter and St. Paul did not succeed in escaping all or some of these thoughts. Even when we do not succeed fully, we gain much by paying no attention to them. I am not going to save myself by the good works of the good angels, and I am not going to be condemned because of the evil thoughts and weaknesses which bad angels, the flesh, and the world bring before my mind. God asks only one thing of me, that my soul seek to be conformed with His Divine Majesty. And the soul so conformed makes the body conformed, whether it wish it or not, to the divine will. In this is our greatest battle, and here the good pleasure of the eternal and sovereign Goodness. May our Lord by His infinite kindness and grace hold us always in His hand." Ignatius of Loyola: Letters and Instructions (St. Louis: The Institute of Jesuit Sources, 2006), 25.

26. Such panic attacks and terrors are similar to aspects of what psychologists refer to as "catastrophic thinking," often suffered by those with serious anxiety disorders. The

"racing thoughts" of catastrophic thinking may lead to ideas of self-wounding or other types of bodily harm, similar to what Ignatius experienced at Manresa when, in the grip of severe scruples, he had an urge to throw himself off a cliff.

[27]. Those suffering from biochemical addictions would be wise to seek professional guidance on extracting oneself from their grip. It is notable however that because of our mind-body connection, people who are withdrawing from spiritual darkness and spiritual addictions often "feel" a dread that is similar to the feelings experienced during biochemical withdrawals. It is obvious that eliminating physical addictions will be a tremendous benefit to one's overall health, but despite this knowledge, the biochemical addict still "feels" afraid of letting go of the addiction. It is clear that the fear and dread we experience when withdrawing from sinful addictions is very similar. Despite the painful emotions, we know that withdrawal from spiritual and physical addiction only leads to life.

[28]. Review the definition of counter-inspirations; see week 3.

[29]. See week 37 "E&W" at www.sacredstory.net.

[30]. See endnote 16.

[31]. For a modern example of these types of temptations, see week 38 "E&W" at www.sacredstory.net.

[32]. The following section from the Church's Code of Canon Law describes the types of beliefs that are non-negotiable for faithful Catholics. This is not intended as a list of all those things one must adhere to in order to be considered a "faithful Catholic." The most important aspect is the docility of spirit granted by God that enables one to approach the teachings and the authority of the Church with trust, instead of a spirit of obstinacy. The spirit of docility, trust, humility and obedience characterize God's presence in one's soul.

A person must believe with divine and Catholic faith all those things contained in the word of God, written or handed on, that is, in the one deposit of faith entrusted to the Church, and at the same time proposed as divinely revealed either by the solemn magisterium of the Church or by its ordinary and universal magisterium which is manifested by the common adherence of the Christian faithful under the leadership of the sacred magisterium; therefore all are bound to avoid any doctrines whatsoever contrary to them. Each and every thing which is proposed definitively by the magisterium of the Church concerning the doctrine of faith and morals, that is, each and every thing which is required to safeguard reverently and to expound faithfully the same deposit of faith, is also to be firmly embraced and retained; therefore, one who rejects those propositions which are to be held definitively is opposed to the doctrine of the Catholic Church. [Can. 750 §1, §2].

[33]. Thomas M. King, SJ, Teilhard's Mass: Approaches to The Mass on the World (Mahwah: Paulist Press, 2005) 120.

FORTY WEEKS

A Journey of Healing and Transformation

FOR PRIESTS

Made in the USA
Middletown, DE
27 May 2022